God and Psychology

God and Psychology

How the Early Religious Development of Famous Psychologists Influenced their Work

Stephen E. Parker

LEXINGTON BOOKS
Lanham • Boulder • New York • London

Published by Lexington Books
An imprint of The Rowman & Littlefield Publishing Group, Inc.
4501 Forbes Boulevard, Suite 200, Lanham, Maryland 20706
www.rowman.com

86-90 Paul Street, London EC2A 4NE

Copyright © 2023 by The Rowman & Littlefield Publishing Group, Inc.

All rights reserved. No part of this book may be reproduced in any form or by any electronic or mechanical means, including information storage and retrieval systems, without written permission from the publisher, except by a reviewer who may quote passages in a review.

British Library Cataloguing in Publication Information Available

Library of Congress Cataloging-in-Publication Data
Names: Parker, Stephen E. (Stephen Eugene), author.
Title: God and psychology : how the early religious development of famous psychologists influenced their work / Stephen Parker.
Description: Lanham : Lexington Books, [2023] | Includes bibliographical references and index.
Identifiers: LCCN 2022041046 (print) | LCCN 2022041047 (ebook) | ISBN 9781666919158 (cloth) | 9781666919172 (paper | ISBN 9781666919165 (ebook)
Subjects: LCSH: Psychology and religion. | Psychologists.
Classification: LCC BF51 .P45 2023 (print) | LCC BF51 (ebook) | DDC 150.1—dc23/eng/20220919
LC record available at https://lccn.loc.gov/2022041046
LC ebook record available at https://lccn.loc.gov/2022041047

Contents

	Acknowledgements	vii
	Introduction	ix
Chapter 1	Sigmund Freud	1
Chapter 2	Carl Jung	41
Chapter 3	Erik Erikson	73
Chapter 4	B. F. Skinner	107
Chapter 5	Carl Rogers	135
	Conclusion	171
	References	185
	Index	201
	About the Author	217

Acknowledgments

I want to express my thanks to several people who have played a part in the completion of this book. It had its beginnings during a sabbatical made possible by the former dean of the School of Psychology and Counseling, William Hathaway, and the board of trustees of Regent University. I also want to thank my colleagues at Regent who were supportive of the book and provided an atmosphere where such pursuits were nurtured. I especially valued conversations about the book with a former colleague, Mark Newmeyer, whom I never went away from without jotting something down that enhanced the expression of my ideas. Several graduate assistants also saved me countless hours by compiling notes and quotations from numerous publications; my thanks to Jason Cotton, Meredith Johnson, Laura Lamirand, Carrie Minnis, Alyssa Narvell, Deborah Nazareth, Melanie Patino, and Laura Sprinkle. Most of these were my students and it is my students that provided much of the inspiration for this book by way of their interests in and questions about the lives of the psychologists covered here.

I also wish to thank an anonymous reviewer whose comments allowed me to improve the manuscript in several places, especially the Freud and Jung chapters. The staff at Rowman and Littlefield Publishers with whom I worked, Linda Kessler, Judith Lakamper, Mark Lopez, and Jasper Mislak, have been especially helpful throughout this process. Finally, I wish to express my appreciation to my wife Regina and my son Sean who keep me anchored in what is important.

Introduction

This book tells the stories of how the early religious background of several famous psychologists influenced their life and work. These are fascinating stories often overlooked in the biography of these thinkers, especially in the brief summaries that serve to introduce their work. These are stories worth knowing.

People like to understand something about the life and background of those whose ideas they study, especially how various biographical events influenced a person's thinking. Knowing something of the various psychologists' development helps humanize them and makes their ideas less strange. For instance, knowing that a younger Freud after overhearing his teacher Charcot remark that in cases of "hysteria" (an early name for certain kinds of psychological problems) "it always comes down to sex" wondered "if he knows that, why does he never say so," helps one hear Freud's (1914a, p. 14) own comments about the centrality of sexuality in a different light. However, few current texts about these people and their ideas give more than cursory attention to their biography and even more rarely mention their religious background. But, if as Carl Jung (1958a) has argued, the religious impulse is as powerful, if not more so than the sexual one, then this book fills a gap regarding a neglected dimension of these psychologists' background and how it influenced their work.

The Primary Audience for This Book

At the broadest level, I have written for anyone who may have heard of the psychologists in this book and who would wish to know something of the psychologists' religious background and especially how this religious background may have influenced their life and work. Such people can be found in many places, but I have most often encountered them in college classrooms. Majors in psychology, human services, social work, and education are required to take courses in which these psychologists are prominent figures of study. This book has such students in mind. These students gain significant exposure to the psychologists covered here in courses such as counseling or personality theories, human development, and psychology of religion. I envision this book as a supplemental text for such courses (one can see the influence of my teaching such courses in the choice of psychologists considered for this text). However, I based the final selection on those psychologists of widest interest and have tried to write in such a way that those encountering these psychologists for the first time can follow the main ideas. Thus, I try to avoid technical language where I can and try briefly to explain when such language occurs, and also other technical terms not part of the larger exposition. In their exposure to these psychologists, students often become aware that they make pronouncements about the influence of religion (sometimes complimentary, sometimes critically) and often wonder what lies behind such pronouncements. This book has in mind those who want to know more about how these psychologists' own religious background influenced their ideas, not only about religion but in general.

This book also will be of interest to those who are interested in the intersection between psychology and religion/spirituality. The explosion of texts in this area testifies to the recognition that the religious/spiritual dimension has a powerful formative influence on humans. Oddly enough, a neglected dimension in this intersection is an exploration of the religious background of the psychologists whose work informs our perspectives on religion. By summarizing what is known about the religious background of these people and how this background influenced their work, this text offers a different window on the intersection between psychology and religion/spirituality.

Questions That Informed This Study

The major question that drove this research was an interest in how the early religious background of these psychologists influenced their later work; are there remnants of their early religious backgrounds that remain implicit (if not explicit) in their psychological theories, including their ideas and attitudes toward religion? I argue that there are and try to show the various ways these remnants linger.

This is the main question that drove this study. However, I note two other questions that arose during my research that, though less central, generated enough interest to mention in this introduction and to return to them in the conclusion. The first of these questions arose in reading the afore mentioned comment of Jung (1958a) that the religious impulse was as strong as, if not stronger than the sexual one. Jung's comment caused me to ask what becomes of such interests in those who report a loss of interest or even antipathy to religion later in life (as happened to some of those studied here). Each chapter will comment briefly on this question as a prelude to some summary thoughts in the concluding chapter. The second less central question arose from observations that several early psychologists had relational issues with their fathers and were drawn to psychology because of this (Cohen, 1977; Homans, 1982). Are such observations true? If so, did these relational issues have anything to do with their families' religious backgrounds? Each chapter also comments on what is known of the psychologists' relationship with their family (especially their fathers) before returning to this question in the conclusion.

Who Is Covered and Why?

At this point I need to comment on the choice of psychologists for this book. Those covered are Sigmund Freud, Erik Erikson, Carl Jung, B.F. Skinner, and Carl Rogers. The psychologists included in this book were selected based on three criteria: (1) how well known they are (both inside and outside their field), (2) how influential their work is (both inside and outside their field), and (3) did their religious background influence their work in discernible ways. The psychologists named above are the most well-known, not only in the field of psychology but outside it as well. They are the psychologists whose names are most likely to be familiar even to those who know little about psychology and will make the book of more general interest. Furthermore, these psychologists are those whose work remains influential not only in psychology and related fields such as counseling, education, and social work but in the larger culture as well. Their legacy endures far beyond their original field. Finally, these psychologists were chosen because the story about their religious background and its influence on their life and thought is both obvious and worth telling.

These criteria developed in reverse order during the work on this book. Originally conceived as a supplemental text for a personality or counseling theories course it began with a list of 10–12 people who had developed somewhat comprehensive theories of human functioning. I began with a couple of these that I knew had stories of religious influence worth telling but after producing the initial drafts it became obvious that trying to write on this many people was too ambitious a goal for me given the time it was taking to do the research and writing. In deciding who to delete, I of course chose those whom preliminary research indicated there was not a sufficient story to tell in terms of religious influence on their work. Alfred Adler and Melanie Klein fell into this group (see Grosskurth, 1986; Hoffman, 1994). Next, I decided to eliminate those whose work was no longer widely known or influential despite their being an interesting story to tell about the influence of their religious background upon their work. Karen Horney and Gordon Allport fell into this group (see Allport, 1978; Horney, 1980; note that Hoffman [2011] has given a brief account of Horney's religious background and its influence on her work). Having pared the list to such an extent, I decided I should focus on those psychologists whose influence extended beyond their contribution of a counseling or personality theory. The five who remain are not only those apt to be encountered in other psychology and counseling courses, but they are also those who have left the widest influence in Western culture and are thus of more general interest.[1]

The Methodology

The methodology of this study is primarily biographical. It gathers what is known of these psychologists' religious development and background along with an exploration of how their religious development influenced and lingered on in their theory and personal lives. Because the major focus of this book is on the religious development of these psychologists, I need to say a few words about my use of sources.

Information on the religious development of these psychologists is often scattered across dozens of sometimes obscure sources. I make no claim to have uncovered them all although I have tried to attend to all the significant ones I found. Also, because one encounters a significant repetition of what is known about a person's religious background among those who cover this material (e.g., biographers), I have not tried to cite every source if this material is readily available in another source. This is especially true for Freud and Jung for whom there are dozens of general and specialty biographies. For these two, I have tended to limit citations to the two or three biographies that I found most helpful and which I think those interested in further study will find useful. Similarly, because of my particular focus I did not cite several well-known biographical studies on Freud (e.g., Crews, 1998; Masson, 1984) because such biographies do very little with his religious background; similar choices are relevant to Jung as well. In addition, since my focus was on religious development, I have given limited attention to other developmental issues (one can usually find attention to these in a good biography).

Another aspect of the methodology is that this book is primarily descriptive rather than prescriptive. Although one cannot avoid evaluative comments altogether (e.g., inquiring about the reliability of sources, noting inconsistencies in a person's thought), in taking a descriptive approach I do not make evaluating the "orthodoxy" of the various psychologists' pronouncements about religion in particular or human nature in general a main focus of this book. I take this route because of two reasons. The first reason is because there is no generic Jewish or Christian theology, no single vision by which all aspects of a theory or theorist can be judged. Rather, there are specific theologies (e.g., in the Christian tradition theologies might be Wesleyan, Catholic, Reformed, etc.) that have differing anthropologies and visions regarding things like how much choice humans have, the nature of "sin," and human flourishing (Olson, 2002; Wright, Jones, & Strawn, 2014). Thus, different readers can (and will) make their own evaluations if I have done a sufficient job in the descriptive task. Second, I take this route in fairness to the psychologists themselves. That is, none of these psychologists present themselves as a theologian and none of them talk in terms of God's saving activity (except Jung and on this see that chapter). Thus, all are deficient as "theologies." However, in articulating a vision of the good life each of these theories make mention of goals toward which humans ought to move and which often compare favorably with Jewish or Christian ideas of what is good because these men developed their theories out of cultural and personal contexts deeply influenced by these religious traditions (Browning, 1987; Homans, 1982; Kirschner, 1996). Thus, some comparison and evaluation between these secular visions and the religious traditions that inform or contrast with them are inevitable though that is not the chief purpose of this text. On these occasions, I attempt an irenic tone.

The Plan of the Book

Each of the next five chapters has three major sections. The first section summarizes what is known of the religious background of each of the psychologists covered. It seeks to expand upon the brief statements often made in introductory textbooks that Freud was Jewish or that Rogers or Skinner grew up in conservative Christian homes. This section on their religious background describes aspects of the psychologists' relationships within their family of origin as these are relevant to the questions of their religious development. All these psychologists had religious parents; thus, one must inquire not only about how particular religious experiences of each were formative, but how all these psychologists experienced the religiousness of their parents. One notes in this regard that as different as Freud (1905) and Skinner (1948/2005, 1953) might be in their developmental theory, both concede that there is something powerfully formative in these early exposures (even if in different ways and for different reasons). This section of each chapter also will trace the role of religion in the adult life of these psychologists. For some, this role was minimal (e.g., Skinner, Rogers); for others it remained considerable (e.g., Jung and Erikson). This section will comment on how one might account for these differences.

The second section of each chapter serves as a prelude to the third section that looks at the impact of the religious background on the later life and work of these psychologists. This second section summarizes several key ideas of each of these psychologists. This section does not attempt to cover every important idea from these thinkers but will focus on those ideas helpful in following the trajectories of influence that are traced in the section that follows. Thus, the reader should not anticipate a comprehensive survey of a given psychologist's ideas but will find a sufficient introduction to each psychologist's key ideas to make the focus of this book intelligible. Such brief introductory sections will of necessity have to simplify if not oversimplify some ideas while omitting others altogether. My defense for any weaknesses of these sections is that the audience envisioned for them is not the person who knows these theories well but the student or person being introduced to the work of these psychologists. I assume that where this is a supplemental text, students will have other texts with fuller surveys of their ideas.

The third section of each chapter explores how the psychologists' religious background influenced their later life and work. Since this section lies at the heart of this book, I offer some extended comments below. A concluding chapter will return to the three questions that were of interest to this study and offer some answers. It also will draw together some lessons learned from the study of all five psychologists taken together.

Preliminary Thoughts on the Influence of these Psychologists' Religious Background

In the first part of the section on the influence of the religious background on the life and work of these psychologists in the chapters that follow I look at some of the indirect ways that this happens simply because of their cultural heritage. Such influences are not always consciously present because they are so deeply embedded in the context in which one lives. As someone once quipped, "we do not know who discovered water, but we can be almost certain it wasn't a fish." All cultures immerse us in a set of beliefs from birth (if not *in utero*), and in the culture of the West these beliefs have been deeply shaped by Jewish and Christian influences for millennia (Glover, 1984; Groothuis, 2000; Hauerwas, 1997; Homans, 1982). These preliminary thoughts focus particularly on two ways these cultural religious influences are present in the life and work of the psychologists explored: (1) a certain way of structuring human experience and (2) certain ideas about the way life ought to be lived.

Susan Kirschner (1996) has argued that one of the things the Jewish and Christian traditions have bequeathed to our way of structuring experience is the idea of "development": that is, the concept that human life and history unfold toward some end. This is sometimes noted in the idea that in the West history is seen as linear rather than circular. Kirschner is especially interested in showing the influence of this idea in the field of psychology (e.g., there is an entire field devoted to developmental psychology). She sees this view of history evolving particularly from the Christian construction of the Biblical narrative as telling a three-fold story of "creation, fall and redemption." (Kirschner calls this the "Judeo-Christian tradition" in that the Hebrew Bible is also considered scripture for Christians; however, such a designation is not without problems [cf. Loeffler, 2020]; therefore, in this book I will speak of the traditions individually though much of my focus is on commonalities in these traditions). Briefly stated, the biblical narrative that Kirschner outlines is one in which the world and humans were created by God, that there was then an estrangement from God, but that this relationship is then restored through Christ. This reading sees God's plan in creation moving toward an end (i.e., "salvation") but that such understanding of this movement occurred in stages, the most obvious illustration of which is the Christian division of their Scriptures into an "Old Testament" witness followed by a "New" one. However, the idea that history moves linearly in a progressive revelation is not absent from Judaism (e.g., see the covenant with Abraham that is reaffirmed to Moses to see additions and developments; cf.

Gen. 17:5–8 with Ex. 6:2–8; 20:1–20). This notion of development is so ubiquitous in psychology (e.g., Freud's and Erikson's developmental stages) and we are so accustomed to construing experience this way that we hardly notice its presence, much less appreciate its origins. One of the ways that the psychologists studied here are influenced by their religious traditions is that they are all heirs of and participate in this way of structuring experience; this is noted as appropriate in the chapters that follow.

In addition to Kirschner's (1996) observations, another way that the Christian tradition in particular has influenced cultural notions of development is through the deep influence that the Christian theologian Augustine has had on the way we think about salvation as the restoration of something that has been lost (i.e., the early chapters of Genesis tell of humans created perfect but who lost this through disobedience [the "fall"] and now need to be restored to their former state). Augustine's interpretation of salvation has so dominated Western thought that alternatives to his view sound strange to most people in the West. For instance, Irenaeus (a Christian theologian who lived a couple of centuries before Augustine) argued that the story in Genesis concerns the creation of immature humans who were to develop in their spirituality (their love of God); redemption is then the completion of something already there in nascent form rather than the restoration of something lost as for Augustine. One sees the dominance of the Augustinian way of viewing the purpose of salvation in clinical thinking where therapy and counseling is more often thought of as working to correct or repair something that is broken (whether that be irrational thoughts, failed relationships, or impaired emotions, to name a few things considered broken) than as developing something already there toward maturity (see Hathaway & Yarhouse 2021). This religious influence is also commented upon in the chapters that follow as appropriate.

Beyond these thoughts regarding the structuring of experience as developmental, a second way the Jewish and Christian traditions have influenced Western culture is through a set of beliefs about the way life ought to be lived (i.e., a moral or ethical legacy). This moral framework includes certain ideas about right and wrong, good and bad, how to interact with others, things one is obligated to do, and qualities that enhance or hinder the good life (such as a more just world; Browning, 1987). A prime illustration would be the Ten Commandments (cf. Ex. 20:1–17). These commandments enshrine values such as respect for life, property, truth-telling, and fidelity in relationships among others (values most people in the West still affirm). Another illustration of these ethical beliefs would be Jesus' echo of the Torah that one should "love the Lord your God with all your heart, soul and mind" and "love your neighbor as yourself" (cf. Mt. 22:37–39; Dt. 6:5; Lv. 19:18). This ethic of love is also deeply embedded in Western culture (though there is not always agreement on how to apply it). These illustrations by no means exhaust the ethical legacy of these traditions but indicate where the strong commitment to the pursuit of truth and justice in the West draws much of its strength (Bennett, 2008; Perkins, 2008; Schwarzschild, 2007; Scott, 2009). Although these values are not unique to these traditions in the West (cf. Plato and Aristotle), it is these religious traditions that have most informed our ideas regarding them (Neher, 2007). One also should note that such ideas about how to live and interact with others are further bound up with questions of meaning and purpose (that is, if life develops toward some purpose, what is the nature of that end and what kind of actions bring one closer to that goal) as well as questions of autonomy and its restrictions.

In noting some of the values shared by Jewish and Christian ethical traditions I do not mean to imply that these ethical traditions are identical. Some differences can be significant, and though my focus is often on the commonality it is helpful to remember this non-identity especially when reflecting on the influence of Freud's Jewish ethical tradition in comparison to the influence of the Christian ethical traditions that influenced the other psychologists covered here. For instance, one might note the different emphases regarding justice in the two traditions. At the risk of oversimplification given the differences between Jewish and Christian approaches to ethics, and even among perspectives within these traditions, one might characterize the Jewish concern with justice as primarily focused on the present world while a Christian concern tends to understand justice to be something that also might be settled in the world to come. Thus, as a result of this difference a Jewish concern regarding Christian ethics sometimes identifies the latter as tending to offer forgiveness too easily following an offense without adequately addressing the wrong committed (cf. Wallwork, 1991). This seemed to be part of Freud's issue with the Christian interpretation of loving one's neighbor as oneself (see Freud chapter). Jewish and Christian ethical traditions also tend to differ in their approach to Torah (or "Law") with Christians sometimes emphasizing such a contrast between "law vs. grace" that to Jewish eyes it may seem that the law has been suspended altogether. Again, these are overgeneralizations that would not be true in every articulation of either Jewish or Christian ethics. Nevertheless, such examples highlight the fact that though Jews and Christians share many ethical concerns (e.g., for justice) they can differ on particulars regarding implementation of these values. Although I have tried to be careful where I talk about the influence of the Jewish and Christian ethical traditions on the various psychologists,

I write as one influenced primarily by the Christian traditions of the West and no doubt have missed some of the nuances of Jewish thought that would be obvious to one from that tradition. The reader should bear this in mind especially when reading the Freud chapter.

Sometimes the psychologists studied here were aware of these various ethical legacies and even endorsed aspects of them; at other times they consciously fought against aspects of them. The section on these cultural religious influences in the subsequent chapters will also comment upon these conscious adaptations and rejections where appropriate. But in identifying the indirect influence of this ethical legacy, I am especially interested to explore ways that this influence remained despite their repudiations. Of course, one way its influence remained is that all the psychologists studied think life is and should be lived toward certain goals (often referred to as a vision of the "good life"). Thus, the ethical legacy of these traditions gives direction to the developmental trajectory of human life, conveying meaning and purpose. Although these goals sometimes differ significantly from the ones offered by their religious traditions, the retention of ideas about meaning and purpose are indebted to such traditions. Browning (1987) goes as far as to argue that all the therapeutic psychologies have embedded within them systems of moral obligation. That is, those psychologies that undergird therapeutic practice not only have visions of a better life, but they also assume that failure to move toward such a goal constitutes a deficit in mental health and maturity (certainly a moral assumption). This section will comment on the varying ideas about meaning and purpose in each psychologist and how they reflect some of the psychologist's religious tradition.

Another way the ethical legacy of these two traditions is present on all the psychologists studied is in their adoption of what is sometimes called the "Protestant work ethic" though its origins go back much further than the Protestant movement in Christianity. This ethic is concerned with meaning, purpose, and ways they are pursued and finds a first expression in the opening chapter of Genesis where the humans God created are given charge to tend the garden in which they are placed. There one encounters the idea that work is for something other than survival. The popularization of this idea in its Christian form owes much to Max Weber's (1904/1958) elaborations. Weber connected certain ideas of John Calvin's theology (Calvin was one of the early founders of Protestantism) with the generation of capital, not simply for survival but in hopes that it might give insight into one's status before God. By the nineteenth century the defining emphasis in Calvinistic theology was that of predestination (i.e., one's status as part of God's elect or not—a status one could not know with certainty; see Gonzalez, 1975).

Weber's articulation of this association between Calvin's theology and the generation of capital pointed out that if one cannot know whether one is part of the elect until after death this created a certain anxiety about one's status. To reduce this anxiety, one looked for signs that would give some indication of whether one might be among the elect. Thus, in this way of thinking, prosperity came to be considered a likely sign of God's favor. According to Weber in the new emerging industrial culture of the West hard work tended to produce prosperity and thereby created a new Protestant work ethic; one did not work simply to survive but toward another purpose. In America, Protestantism came to think that "it was through action that God was served and a state of grace assured; idleness was the worst of sins" (Demorest, 2005, p. 95). Even though in more contemporary times the religious origins of this concept are often muted, and work is often seen as having its own intrinsic value, remnants of the religious influence that work is toward a purpose remain. One continues to see the influence of this work ethic in the very idea of therapy and counseling as means of helping people become more "functional," meaning more able to participate in relationships and *work* (American Psychiatric Association, 2013), ideas that began with and remained part of the thinking of these founding psychologists. Where this ethic is significant in its influence on the psychologists studied here this is noted as appropriate.

There is yet one other way that the ethical legacy of their religious traditions shows up in the work of these psychologists despite their repudiations of such traditions and that is through what some have called "borrowed moral capital" from these traditions (e.g., Groothuis, 2000; Hauerwas, 1997; Homans, 1982). That is, values from these traditions still influence one's activities even if their origin has been forgotten, or just as likely, go unacknowledged because they are so much a part of culture that one does not recognize their religious nature. A contemporary illustration of this lingering influence of the Jewish and Christian ethical traditions can be found in certain values enshrined in the ethical codes of the clinical professions, often without understanding this contribution, so common are these values in Western culture (Fitzgerald, 2019; Hathaway & Yarhouse, 2021). For instance, these ethical codes hold clinicians to actions characterized by justice, non-maleficence (doing no harm), beneficence (doing good), and integrity among others, all values influenced by their promulgation by the Jewish and Christian religions. Each of the psychologists studied here also show these kinds of lingering influences and I will identify them as appropriate. In anticipation of things to come I might note Hoffman's (2011) comment that Freud's pursuit of the truth regardless of the cost was indebted to the prophetic tradition of his Jewish heritage and Browning's (1987) argument that the utopian vision of Skinner's (1948/2005) novel, *Walden Two* draws heavily from Christian visions of justice and beneficence. Skinner himself acknowledged something of the borrowed moral capital from this tradition when he observed that Carl Rogers could only suspend judgment in the kind of therapy he did because such therapy presupposed this moral framework in the background (see Evans, 1981).

In summary then, the first part of the section on how their religious backgrounds influenced these psychologists identifies how these two indirect ways of influence are present—that is, how is the developmental perspective present in their work, especially in terms of their visions regarding the purpose of life (what one works toward), and where are the lingering influences of the Jewish and Christian ethical traditions present. However, I also argue that the influence of the respective religious backgrounds of the psychologists studied here extends beyond these two indirect ways of influence.

In the chapters on the individual psychologists the second part of the section that explores how their religious background influenced their life and work looks at more direct ways this happened. Again, I do this in two parts. First, I look at how their religious background might have influenced specific ideas in their thought. For instance, several scholars have noted how similar Rogers' notions of unconditional positive regard seem to Christian notions of grace and agape love (e.g., Feltham, 2010; Oden, 1978; Watts, 1998; cf. Roberts, 1993 for a more critical comparison). Is Rogers' psychological idea one encountered in his religious past but now given a secular explanation? Each chapter will explore these kinds of connections. In tracing such connections, it is important to note that one can rarely make a one-to-one correspondence between ideas from a person's early life and their later thought because documentary evidence for such connections is lacking. People rarely keep childhood or adolescent writings. At best, one might have an adult recollection of earlier influences that shaped their later ideas but even then, one must recognize that adult memories of childhood are often reshaped to fit one's current understandings of these events and are not necessarily the way things were seen at the time (Phillips, 2014). For example, in the example mentioned, it is impossible to trace a straight line from Rogers' notion of unconditional positive regard to ideas present in his early religious background (for the reasons noted), but the question of whether there might be lingering influences is a reasonable one worth exploring. In trying to answer such questions the information one most often has is simply suggestive of connections or points to broad contours of similarity in ideas. Thus, there will always be a tentativeness to these connections that one must contend with.

The other way I note direct influences of their religious backgrounds is in the various ways they approach their work and its content (including their comments about religion). For some of these men, these latter comments are part of their overall psychological theory and can be quite extensive (constituting a theory of religion), while for others the comments are more cursory. This section of the individual chapters will note these various influences of their religious traditions.

Note

1. This leaves the list of psychologists chosen absent any women. This is regrettable because I fear it may further the idea that the story of psychology is only the story of "great men." This is not true of course (note Klein and Horney above), but for the reasons given this book did not seem the place for their stories (although the problem of women in psychology lacking the kind of early recognition and influence accorded to men is its own story to tell, e.g., see Scarborough & Rutherford [2018] on the neglect of women's contributions in the early days of the American Psychological Association and Kristeva's [2001] introduction on the neglect of the contributions of women in early psychoanalytic circles); this is worth remembering when considering criteria such as recognition and influence).

A further word on the absence of Klein is in order, since she is more well-known, and her work has remained influential (and even grown in influence) at least in that part of psychology devoted to psychoanalytic thought and would have been a good addition here. The decision on omitting Klein came down to the question of whether there was a pattern of religious influence upon her work. Unlike the other psychologists in this book for whom there are often multiple stories regarding the influence of their religious backgrounds on their work, no one has attempted this for Klein, raising the question as to whether there is such a story. The little that is known about Klein's religious background suggests it had little influence upon her. Drawing upon some unpublished autobiographical notes, her chief biographer reports few incidents or memories from Klein's childhood that have to do with religion (Grosskurth, 1986; when Klein's religious background is repeated by others it is essentially a repetition of what is found in Klein's unpublished notes, e.g., Kristeva, 2001). Although Klein was reared in a Jewish home, she herself indicated later in life that her parents were "assimilated Jews" who had not been especially religious. She remembered they observed Passover and the Day of Atonement but characterized these as more indicative of family traditions than religious piety. She further noted with some pride that she herself was not religious. A few hints from her main biographer indicate that there might be more to her story than meets the eye. For instance, although Grosskurth notes that Klein never disavowed her Jewish roots, she also notes that

Klein had some short-lived preoccupations with Catholicism as a young girl and later converted to Christianity as an adult (joining and having her children baptized in the Unitarian Church). The motives behind this conversion are not altogether clear; it may have been expedient given the tone of anti-Semitism where she lived and perhaps made for less economic and social problems, but it may also have involved family influences from in-laws that had converted as well, and not simply for expediency. In the end, the conversion does not seem to have had a lasting effect once the Klein family moved. However, these tantalizing hints remain only that. There seems to be little documentary evidence that might allow one to move beyond some general speculations regarding the influence of Klein's early religious background upon her work (i.e., the kind of indirect influence one might see in anyone who grew up in the West). For instance, in her published work Klein hardly mentions religion and then only to affirm the Freudian view of its pathology (Grosskurth; cf. Klein, 1975); even some who have tried to show how one can connect her thought with biblical material would have surely known that Klein herself never made these attempts (e.g., Hunt, 2018; Peri, 2010) Thus, in the end I concluded that there was not a discernable religious journey that influenced Klein's work in the specific ways it did for the others included in the book.

CHAPTER ONE

Sigmund Freud

In *Totem and Taboo*, Freud (1913) considers the psychological origins of God, writing that one's "personal relation to God depends on his relation to his father in the flesh and oscillates and changes along with that relation, and that at bottom God is nothing other than an exalted father" (p. 147). Such a comment leaves one wondering what Freud's relationship with his own father might have been like and what qualities of his father he might have projected onto God. This chapter seeks to answer these questions along with several others. It traces the trajectory of Freud's religious journey from his early years as a child growing up in a moderately liberal Jewish household to his atheism as an adult, giving attention to what role his father played in this journey.

Of the psychologists covered in this book, Sigmund Freud's name is likely the one most familiar. Even those who know little of psychology and even less of Freud have still heard his name and experienced his influence, so pervasive is his presence in contemporary culture (Rieff, 1979; e.g., few think developmental history irrelevant when trying to understand a person's behavior, so ubiquitous are Freud's ideas about the importance of early childhood). The literature on Sigmund Freud is now so large it is impossible to do justice to it; even the literature that explores the relationship between Freud and religion fills several shelves. Thus, this chapter cannot be exhaustive even with such a circumscribed topic and risks oversimplifying complex associations. Nevertheless, it seeks to tell an important part of Freud's story, one often neglected in the texts that introduce him: how Freud's religious background impacted his work.

What Is Known of Freud's Religious Journey?

This section looks at what is known of Freud's religious journey. It draws from Freud's own comments about this as well as other biographical material. It tells the story of Freud's life-long ambivalence toward his religious background, an ambivalence rooted in his relationship with his father. Although the adult Freud embraces an ethnic and ethical identification with his Jewishness, he firmly eschews any kind of religious identification. In addition to exploring Freud's relationship to Judaism, we also will discover some interesting turns in his relationship with Christianity.

Religion in Freud's Early Childhood Home

In his brief autobiographical statement Freud (1925) noted tersely that his "parents were Jews" and that, unlike many Jews of his generation, he had never disavowed his Jewish identity (p. 7). One is left to wonder what is not disclosed by this contracted description. What is known of Freud's parents and their religious practices? What kind of religious environment might they have provided the young Freud?

Freud's father, Jacob, is described by various sources as being an easygoing, overly optimistic person, who loved his children and grandchildren. Jacob was about 40 when he married Freud's mother, a woman about 20 years his junior. It was his second (or third) marriage, and little is known of these previous wives. Jacob had two sons by his first wife, neither of whom lived at home when Freud was born. Jacob seems to have struggled financially for most of his life, being supported in part by his older children during Freud's childhood years (Gay, 1988; Krull, 1979/1986).

Although a conservative Hassidic Jew during his adolescence, as an adult Jacob Freud practiced a more moderate Reform Judaism (Freud, 1960; Phillips, 2014). Such changes were often part of an attempt to assimilate to the larger culture by the Jews of Jacob's era (Ellenberger, 1970). In this assimilation, some Jewish practices and modes of dress were given up and Jewish beliefs were reframed in ethical terms to maintain something of the spirit of Judaism while appearing less different from one's neighbors. Jacob's religious practices before marriage to Freud's mother are not known though his two older sons remained Orthodox Jews throughout their lives (Rizzuto, 1998). However, during Freud's first three years, Jacob and his family lived in a town (Frieburg, now Příbor in the Czech Republic) without a Jewish synagogue and Jacob seems not to have observed the Sabbath regularly though Passover and Purim were observed on a regular basis (Gay, 1988; Vitz, 1988).

But after moving his family to Vienna (when Freud was three) there also are indications that Jacob remained active, even conservative in his faith (Krull, 1979/1986). For instance, he spent time reading the Bible with his young son (Rainey, 1975) and often studied both the Bible and the Talmud in Hebrew (Bernays-Heller, 1956). This Bible reading occurred very early in Freud's life since he once disclosed that he had been fascinated with the Bible from the time he could read (Freud, 1925). The Bible Jacob and his son studied was the Philippson Bible, a bi-lingual German-Hebrew Bible with annotations and over 600 pictures, including pictures of Egyptian gods and other ancient artifacts (and an indicator of his more liberal religiosity; Pfrimmer, 1982; Rizzuto, 1998).

After the move to Vienna Jacob worked less regularly and became more dependent on his adult sons (Gay, 1988; Krull, 1979/1986). This arrangement probably gave Jacob more time for his studies and perhaps with his son (e.g., the Bible reading together), but information on how Jacob related to his young son is sparse. Freud only reported two specific memories of interactions with his father that give insight into how he related with him during these early years. In the first memory Freud (1900) reported that when he was about seven, he urinated in his parents' bedroom in their presence. This led his father to say that the boy would never amount to anything. This is a complicated memory connected to Freud's analysis of his dreams of ambition and what he will later call the Oedipus complex. He interprets his response to his father's remark as impelling him to prove that eventually he did amount to something. Although the adult interpretation of such childhood memories is fraught with problems by Freud's own admissions, at the least the memory suggests some sense of struggle in their relationship.

The second memory comes from a time when Freud was around 10 or 12. He reported that about this time his father used to take him on walks about the city and on one occasion he was trying to illustrate to his son how things had improved in the way people treated Jews by recounting an incident from Jacob's earlier days. Jacob was dressed for a nice walk in a new hat when he was accosted by a Christian youth who knocked it into the gutter, shouting "Jew! Get off the pavement." The young Freud asked with great interest, "What did you do?" to which his father replied, "I stepped into the road and picked up my cap" (Freud, 1900, p. 197). Freud reported his great disappointment in his father's lack of "heroism." Again, while one must not over-interpret single incidents, this story, like the first, points to some ambivalence in Freud's relationship with his father. This ambivalent relationship between Freud and his father has implications for Freud's religious development that is discussed below.

Freud said less about his mother, Amalie, than one might anticipate from the founder of a theory that touts the importance of early relationships (Phillips, 2014). What is known of her personality comes partly from Freud's memories and partly from other sources. According to Gay (1988), Freud's biographers differ on particulars about her (including how to spell her name) but tend to agree on three major things: her beauty, her domineering style, and her devotion to her oldest son whom she thought would be great someday (Breger, 2000; Ellenberger, 1970; Rizzuto, 1998). Regarding her dominance, a granddaughter who stayed with Jacob and Amalie after Freud was grown and away from home described her shrill and temperamental volatility (Bernays-Heller, 1956; cf. M. Freud, 1967). Even as an adult Freud found it hard to resist her dominance and would arrange his Sundays to accommodate her wishes (Rizzuto, 1998). Regarding her favoring her oldest son, at one point his sister had to stop her piano lessons because the young Freud found her practice disturbing to his studies. However, Gay (1988) sees her devotion as narcissistic; that is, her devotion had as much to do with what she might get from him as he might get from her. In this regard, it is interesting that the only relationship Freud seems to have idealized is that between a mother and her son; given his own theory one might ask why he exempted this particular relationship from the kind of scrutiny with which he viewed all others. Breger (2000) suggests it was because this relationship in Freud's own life could not bear such scrutiny.

In writing of his relationship with his mother, it is interesting that Freud's references to his love for his mother always appear indirectly as in those occasions when he speaks of his love for her in the context of his oedipal desires (e.g., Freud, 1900). Similarly, the one occasion he identified her as his "beloved mother" was when analyzing a childhood dream about her death (Freud, 1900; Rizzuto, 1998). Although one must be careful not to overinterpret events, from a psychoanalytic perspective, one cannot help but wonder about the quality of the relationship between mother and son where her one identification as "beloved" is in the context of her death (cf. Jonte-Pace [2001] on the "entanglement of mothers and death" in Freud [1900, p. 58]). It also is of interest to understanding Freud's religious journey to note that Freud identified the imagery in the dream of his mother's death as coming from drawings in the Philippson Bible (Anzieu, 1986; Freud, 1900).

Amalie, like Jacob, came from a family with a religious background. She was the granddaughter of the chief Rabbi of Hamburg. Although her father was a merchant, her family was observant in their practice of the Orthodox faith (Breger, 2000; Gay, 1988). However, following her marriage to Jacob she seems to have shown less interest in these practices. It is perhaps telling that after Jacob's death, she no longer observed the few Jewish holidays that he had observed (Rizzuto, 1998). The only indication of Amalie's involvement with Freud in a religious way comes from a story he told concerning an encounter with her when he was about six. He had objected to her teaching him that the Bible said that humans come from dust and so to prove it she rubbed her hands together and showed him the dark, sloughed off epidermis which both amazed and convinced him at the time (Freud, 1900)!

There is one other aspect of Freud's earliest years that impacted his religious development. During the first three years of Freud's life (before the move to Vienna), his mother was pregnant for 18 of those months. First, with Freud's younger brother who subsequently died when six months old, and then with his younger sister. These circumstances mean at least some limited emotional availability of the mother to her son (Breger, 2000; Vitz, 1988). To assist with his care, the Freuds employed a nanny to whom the young Freud became deeply attached (Krull, 1979/1986). For instance, in an analysis of a dream about the nanny, Freud (1900) reported that "it is reasonable to suppose that the child (i.e., Freud) loved the old woman" (p. 248) and on another occasion credited her as "provid[ing] me at such an early age with the means of living and surviving" (Bonaparte, Freud & Kris, 1954, p. 220). Thus, one concludes that the nanny became a mother-figure for the young Freud, not surprising given his mother's preoccupation with her pregnancies and mourning of her dead infant.

This nanny was a devout Catholic who often took the young Freud to church with her (an allowance that also indicates the liberalness of Jacob and Amalie's own religious commitments; Breger, 2000; Vitz, 1988). Freud said of his times together with the nanny that she taught him "about God and hell" (Bonaparte, et al., 1954, p. 219). Freud's mother added that when he returned home from attending church with the nanny, he would preach to his parents telling them about how "'the loving God' conducted his affairs" (Bonaparte et al., 1954, p. 222). However, when Freud was about three this nanny disappears quite suddenly and completely from his life. Accused of theft she appears to have been sent to prison. A poor explanation for her absence coupled with the limited ability of a three-year-old to understand such circumstances, caused the young Freud to suffer severe anxiety at her absence (Breger, 2000; Gay, 1988; Masson, 1985).

Of relevance to our concern is to note that these interactions with the nanny and her religion would have been rich sources of Freud's earliest ideas about God and things religious (Krull, 1979/1986; Vitz, 1988). On the one hand, God seems to be a being about which the young child feels positive excitement (he preaches about this "loving" God to his parents; there is something about this God worth passing on). On the other hand, the nanny and her God are associated with being abandoned and powerful sexual feelings. These connections are further explored later.

In trying to characterize Freud's religiousness at this age one must take account of these various primary relationships and their multiple layers. They impact both Freud's understanding of what it means to be Jewish as well as his exposure to and understanding of Christianity as a young child (especially in its Catholic form via his nanny; the general tenor of Catholicism in nineteenth-century Austria is also a factor, see Cooper-White, 2018). Freud's relationship with his father seems to have its greatest impact on Freud's reactions to his religious background (Gay, 1988; Krull, 1979/1986). The Bible reading with his father leaves him with images that excite his imagination and dreams (Freud, 1900), but Freud also experiences some grave disappointments toward his father. For example, the story of his father and the incident with his hat leaves the young boy feeling not only ashamed of what he perceives as a weak father but struggling with whether God also might be a weak actor (cf. Freud, 1910; Rizzuto, 1998). It is even possible that the Bible reading times left Freud with some ambivalence. For instance, when Jacob later gave the Philippson Bible to his 35-year-old son, it was prefaced by a handwritten dedication filled with biblical allusions that made it plain that Jacob saw his son's career in the light of an overarching plan of God for him. Given the strange absence in Freud's writing of any comment regarding his reaction to this gift, one is left to wonder what associations remained toward it (Rizzuto, 1998). At the least, Freud's relationship with his father left him with some ambivalence toward the religion of his roots.

The impact of Freud's mother on his religious sensibilities during this period appears mostly anxiety provoking (Breger, 2000; Rizzuto, 1998; Vitz, 1988). The incident with the sloughed off epidermis left him amazed and cowed; the dream of her death he himself connects to a cosmos that requires such deaths (Freud, 1900). On the other hand, she (as well as Jacob) appears a receptive audience for the young Freud's preaching (Bonaparte, et al., 1954). The other person from this period, his nanny, gives Freud his first exposure to Christianity, conveying in the process powerful feelings and images associated with God, images that excite in both positive and negative ways (e.g., he learns of both the "loving God" and "hell"; she herself both loves and abandons him) (Rizzuto, 1998; Vitz, 1988). From these three relationships, the young Freud takes away images of God in which God is alternately exciting and loving as well as abandoning, frightening, weak and disappointing.

In summary, the young Freud (up to about eight or ten) would have taken away from this earliest period, both some fascination with things religious (especially early on) but some emerging ambivalence as this period comes to an end. Most children of this age have not yet developed abstract reasoning abilities (Piaget, 1970) and tend to accept without question the religion of the parents and significant others to which they are attached (Fowler, 1981). Given the curiosity of three-year-olds, it is likely that the young Freud who learned about heaven and hell asked either his nanny or his parents, perhaps both, what had happened to his little brother who had died (Vitz, 1988). Because there are no reports of such conversations there is no way to know the impact of such common questions. What is known is that Freud's relationships from this period provided him resources for images of and feelings about God that included both positive and negative ones (Rizzuto, 1998).

Religion in Freud's Adolescent Years

This section looks at Freud's religious development from about the time of his tenth year up until his graduation from the *Gymnasium* (i.e., equivalent to completing high school and perhaps the first year or two of college). As an adult Freud wrote little about his religious development during these years. What is known about this period is drawn from two collections of letters Freud wrote to friends during this time as well as an important documentary study of the curriculum of the school Freud attended.

Early Adolescence

During the years Freud would have attended school in Vienna religious education was compulsory for all students. Jewish students were allowed several options to satisfy this requirement and so for his elementary school years Freud attended a private Jewish school for about two years before moving on to the community Gymnasium in a Jewish district of Vienna. Rainey's (1975) review of the curriculum from this period showed it to have been based upon the Hebrew Bible with a heavy focus on the first five books (the Books of Moses or *Torah*). The instruction included Hebrew grammar as well as Jewish history and liturgy.

During his time at the Gymnasium Freud received religious instruction from Samuel Hammerschlag, who had a very positive effect upon the young Freud (Rainey, 1975). Freud often visited in his home and found his presence balm for a weary student. Freud would later write of him "he has been touchingly fond of me for years; there is such a secret sympathy between us that we can talk intimately together. He always regards me as his son" (cited in Jones, 1953, p. 179). At Hammerschlag's death Freud (1904) wrote "a spark from the same fire that animated the spirit of the great Jewish seers and prophets burned in him" (p. 255); Freud goes on to credit Hammerschlag with helping develop in his students a love for the humanities and an enthusiasm for Jewish history that went beyond nationalism and dogma. Hammerschlag's teaching emphasized a "free autonomous personality" and "innate human rights" as two of the central ethical tenets of Judaism (Rainey, 1975, p. 43). Freud's own appreciation for the deep ethical strains in Judaism mirror these emphases of Hammerschlag.

The first letters that provide insight into Freud's religious development during this period are to his childhood friend, Emil Fluss, a friend who lived in the village where Freud spent his first three years and whom Freud visited and corresponded with in his early teens (Rizzuto, 1998). In his letters to Fluss Freud wrote of typical teen topics: girls, school, home, and family. These letters offer insight regarding Freud's religious development when he is about 16. In one letter Freud wrote of his encounter with some pious, provincial Jews on the train. Freud (1969) made it clear that he held these people in disdain, voicing some of the common prejudices that one would have heard from many Austrians of the time (Gay, 1988). It is obvious that growing up in Vienna had given Freud a sense of his separateness from these poorer, pious Jews from the provinces. The Fluss letters also reveal that the adolescent Freud believed in divine providence though he was not entirely sure of the goodness of God's providence (Freud, 1969).

Later Adolescence

One gains some similar insights into Freud's emerging adolescent views of religion in a second series of letters written to another friend, Edward Silberstein (Boehlich, 1990). This correspondence covers a ten-year period from Freud's fifteenth year until his graduation from medical school at 25. Spanning such a lengthy period the letters speak of many things: issues of identity, relationships with girls including his relationship with Martha whom he later marries, relationships with family and home, career ambitions, and religious beliefs. Regarding the latter, Rizzuto (1998) noted that in a two-year period from Freud's seventeenth to nineteenth years, Freud spoke of religion over 50 times and made over a dozen references to the Bible in these letters.

Freud's early letters to Silberstein confirm Rainey's (1975) point that the curriculum at the Gymnasium was based on the Hebrew Bible for they are full of references from the Five Books of Moses and later to the book of Job which served as a focus of Freud's last year at the Gymnasium (Boehlich, 1990). One notes several things about Freud's religious development in adolescence in these letters. One is a playfulness in Freud's comments about religion. For instance, Freud appealed to a story in Genesis when chiding Silberstein about his need to find a girlfriend from among his father's people (Boehlich, 1990; cf. Genesis 24 and the story of Abraham's servant who is sent to find a bride for Isaac). Similarly, he quoted from Proverbs (25:22) saying he has "heap[ed] coals of fire upon [his sister's] head[s]" trying to get them to write to Silberstein (p. 76). In other places he poked fun as well as raised questions about Jewish rituals of eating on holy days.

The letters to Silberstein also show Freud wrestling with the question of God's providence (Boehlich, 1990). Some letters affirm the goodness of God's providence; others suggest that providence may be more malevolent toward him. In this last letter Freud was inconsolable regarding the loss of a previous letter that contained a biblical study of which Freud was particularly proud. Several letters in which Freud referred to the book of Job are especially revealing of Freud's adolescent religious sensibilities. For instance, Freud made several identifications with the book of Job. Like Job, he bemoaned his experience of loss at the hands of Providence; yet in a more playful and irreverent twist, he also compared himself to God. In another allusion to Job Freud told about his decision to cease production of a journal he had started, writing that the journal had "passed peacefully into the keeping of the Lord. It was I who delivered the death blow; it had been ailing for a long time and I took pity on its suffering. I gave it life, and I have taken its life away, so blessed be my name, for ever and ever. Amen" (p. 86; cf. Job 1:21). These incidents from Freud's adolescent years are revealing in several ways. First, they show a young Freud steeped in the text of the Bible, no doubt due in large measure to the nature of his religious training in his years in the Gymnasium. They also show a young Freud coming to grips with his sense of self-direction and identity. Part of this identity is of a young man who is beginning to question the relevance and the power of God. In this ironic allusion, Freud placed himself in the role of God, a rather telling revelation in the light of Freud's later ideas concerning religion (Rizzuto, 1998).

How might one characterize Freud's religious development during these years? From his religious instructors at the Gymnasium he took an appreciation for the Jewish emphasis on ethical behavior and concern for the rights of all (Rainey, 1975). On the other hand, we see that Freud questions, if not disparages, other qualities in Judaism, showing a particular distaste for various Jewish rituals. Although Freud can show a playfulness toward religion, he also questions the goodness of Providence and whether there even is a need for God (Freud, 1969; Gay, 1988). Regarding these latter points it is important to note that the kinds of questions Freud raises are ones that are common to adolescence and young adulthood (Fowler, 1981). However, Freud's answers to these questions clearly show him leaning toward atheism.

Religion in Freud's Young Adult Years

This period takes in Freud's years in medical school following graduation from the Gymnasium up until his marriage to Martha Bernays at the age of 30. Freud's letters to Silberstein also provide insight into his religious development as a young adult (Boehlich, 1990). During Freud's first year or so in medical school, in addition to his medical classes, Freud signed up for a series of philosophy courses taught by the Christian philosopher, Franz Bretano (Gay, 1988; Rizzuto, 1998). These courses are the only non-medical ones that he took (Vitz, 1988). Bretano was a former priest who remained a committed believer. He was a well-known and respected philosopher at the University of Vienna who taught courses on Aristotle, empirical psychology, and proofs for the existence of God (based largely on Aquinas) (Ellenberger, 1970; Gay, 1988). By this time, Freud was referring to himself as a "godless medical man and empiricist" (Boehlich, 1990, p. 70), thus, it is interesting to read Freud's letter to Silberstein regarding his enrollment in this latter course; to his surprise he had found Bretano to be "an ideal human being" who had invited Freud to his home following a letter expressing objections to some of Bretano's ideas (p. 95). He also wrote that Bretano's ideas about and support for the "airy existence of God" provided him with great intellectual challenge.

> I have not escaped from his influence—I am not capable of refuting a simple theistic argument that constitutes the crown of his deliberations.... He demonstrates the existence of God with as little bias and as much precision as another may argue the advantage of the wave over the emission theory.
>
> Needless to say I am only a theist by necessity, and am honest enough to confess my helplessness in the face of his argument; however, I have no intention of surrendering so quickly or completely. Over the next few semesters, I intend to make a thorough study of his philosophy, and meanwhile reserve judgment and the choice between theism and materialism. For the time being, I have ceased to be a materialist and am not yet a theist. (Boehlich, 1990, pp. 104–105)

This letter is remarkable in several ways. First, it shows the 19-year-old Freud seriously considering arguments for the existence of God that place severe reservations on his materialistic and atheistic perspective. Furthermore, though these are philosophical arguments for the existence of God, they are drawn primarily from the Christian tradition. Thus, both in his arguments and in his person Bretano provided the young Freud with some positive exposure to the Christian tradition. However, in the end, Freud is not persuaded to join the ranks of believers. It is interesting in the light of Freud's later theory of religion, to note that Freud's answers are not responses to Bretano's arguments about the existence of God, but rather take a different route by exploring the origins of religion. In fact, Freud (1927) stated in his most acerbic attack on religion that he cared little for the God of the philosophers. To what extent his inability to answer Bretano's arguments play into this aversion, one can only surmise.

Another source of information about Freud's religious development during this period are his letters to his fiancé, Martha Bernays. Freud began writing to her when he was 26 and courted her through a series of more than 900 letters written over the next four years (Breger, 2000; Gay, 1988). What Freud (1960) revealed in his letters to Martha was both a deep appreciation for the "essence" of Judaism (though he found it hard to define exactly what that was), and a deep conviction that their home was to be devoid of religious observances (Gay, 1988). A measure of Freud's commitment to this latter conviction was his refusal on the first Friday after their wedding to let Martha light the Sabbath candles, an observance she had participated in all her life as the daughter of a rabbi (Breger, 2000), and one she reinstated after Freud died (Rizzuto, 1998). (It is interesting that Freud's aversion to Jewish ceremonies led to one of the small ironies of his life in that he briefly considered converting to Christianity to avoid having to endure a Jewish wedding to make his marriage to Martha legal in Austria. However, he took his friend and colleague Joseph Breuer's advice against this solution; see Rainey, 1975.)

Despite his atheism and aversion to religious beliefs and practices Freud (1960) nevertheless conceded a deep appreciation for what he termed the "life-affirming" essence of Judaism even if its "form" (i.e., its beliefs and practices) "no longer offers us any shelter" (p.22). He defined this life-affirming essence differently over the years, always struggling to find words for what he called in one place its "many dark emotional powers, all the mightier the less they let themselves be grasped in words" (Freud, 1960, p. 367), a wording that suggests Freud himself is still deeply moved by it in his less intellectual moments (see his comment to Jones below). One gains another insight into Freud's religious development in his letters to Martha and this comes in comments he made regarding his visits to the museums in Paris when he was there to study with Charcot. Freud wrote of being deeply moved by several pieces of Christian art (e.g., Holbein's and Raphael's portraits of the Madonna and a portrait of Christ by Titian). Of Titian's portrait of Christ, he wrote how his presentation of such a "noble human countenance" left his heart full (Freud, 1960, pp. 82–83).

Given Freud's commitment to his atheism during this period one should acknowledge that there were some counter forces that shaped the intellectual and religious ideas of the young Freud while at university. For instance, Darwin's theory and Enlightenment rationalism would have been influential at the time. In addition, as a medical student at the University of Vienna during the last quarter of the nineteenth century, Freud studied with Ernst Brucke, one of the founders of the so-called Helmholtz School. Helmholtz and Brucke sought to explain human beings in terms of biophysical components. A convinced positivist, Brucke's naturalist and rationalistic approach to the study of human beings had no room for "mysterious innate powers" to say nothing of supernatural explanations. Freud would serve as Brucke's lab assistant for several years (Breger, 2000; Gay, 1988; Phillips, 2014). Other philosophical forces that influenced Freud include Ludwig Feuerbach who proposed that ideas about God were reflections of human qualities, an idea that finds correspondence in Freud's own theories of religion (Freud, 1913).

One final aspect of university life that had an impact on Freud's religious identity was the anti-Semitism that was prevalent there (Gay, 1987, 1988; although Gay notes this, he generally does not think anti-Semitism was a significant factor in Freud's life but see Cooper-White [2018]). Freud energetically rejected the expectation that he should feel inferior because he was Jewish and one sees early on that Freud's most vigorous identifications with his Jewish roots come during his responses to manifestations of anti-Semitism (Ellenberger, 1970; Gay, 1987). In a story that is telling for its contrast to the story about his father and his hat, a 27-year-old Freud (1960) wrote to his fiancé about his response to some anti-Semitic remarks and threats made to him on a train; he yelled at the more vocal ones, inviting them to put up or shut up (cited in Gay, 1988, pp. 84–85).

So, how might one summarize Freud's religious development during this period? Regarding his attitude toward his religious background there are several things to note. On the one hand, Freud continued to admire the ethical dimensions of Judaism and its life-affirming qualities but on the other hand considered its religious beliefs and practices superstitions and avoided them. Thus, one notes that Freud's relationship to his Jewish background is one of ambivalence; he is glad to be a Jew ethically and ethnically but is not comfortable with the overtly religious aspects of being Jewish. To some extent this can be traced back to his ambivalence in his relationship with his father (Rizzuto, 1998). One knows from Freud's (1910) own remarks that part of his questioning of God's existence was the result of his diminished respect for his father's authority. Thus, Freud's movement toward atheism involved both developmental factors as well as these more personal, psychological dimensions. To what extent his brief consideration for Bretano's arguments may also have involved a need to differentiate himself from his father and his father's religion is unclear, though it would have been understandable in the light of normal adolescent development (Erikson, 1968a; Fowler, 1981). However, it also is important to note that at the same time Freud pulled away from all the visible signs of religiousness, he maintained some deep, unexplainable tie to what he considered the essence of Judaism. This tie is especially visible in the face of anti-Semitism (Cooper-White, 2018; Ellenberger, 1970).

Regarding Freud's relationship to Christianity during this time, there also are several points to note. He clearly is attracted to Christian art, especially images of the holy family. He expresses appreciation for the humanity of Jesus and is uplifted by Titian's portrait of Christ (Freud, 1960; Vitz, 1988). From his exposure to Bretano Freud contemplates Christian arguments for theism and the existence of God, finding himself almost persuaded but not quite (Boehlich, 1990; Rizzuto, 1998). In the end, he retreats to the materialistic philosophy of his medical studies (Gay, 1988).

Religion during Freud's Adult Years

Freud's adult life continued to show a great ambivalence toward religion. On the one hand, one of the most obvious aspects of his adult life was his militant atheism, evidenced both by his own profession of atheism and his increasingly strident critiques of religion in others. On the other hand, Freud exhibited a deep fascination with religion and various other "spiritual" phenomena as well as a deep interest in understanding why others persisted in believing in God (Phillips, 2014; Rainey, 1975; Rizzuto, 1998; Vitz, 1988).

Convinced Atheist

As already noted, during his young adult years Freud became a confirmed atheist, both at an intellectual as well as personal level (Gay, 1988). The more personal dimensions of his atheism were connected to his relationship with his father and continued to influence his adult commitment to atheism (Rizzuto, 1998). This atheism manifested itself in the prohibition of any religious rituals connected to being Jewish and in his attempts to convert Martha away from such "superstitions" (Gay, 1988).

Freud's atheism also manifested itself in the way he handled various losses in his life. Freud (1927) wrote of religion that one of its tasks was to provide a buffer against significant losses, such as the death of loved ones. Yet Freud

(1927) not only wrote that he found no solace in God, he stated that he did not need this from God. Rather he would face his losses alone. This point is poignantly made in remarks regarding the death of his daughter Sophie at age 20. To her in-laws he wrote that there is no one to blame, that "one must bow one's head under the blow, as a helpless, poor human being with whom higher powers are playing" (cited in Gay, 1988, p. 392). He wrote similarly to a colleague on this occasion: "since I am the deepest of unbelievers, I have no one to accuse and know that there is no place where one can lodge an accusation" (cited in Gay, 1988, p. 393).

In a similar vein Freud claimed that he had never experienced religious "feelings" within himself. A friend of Freud (Romain Rolland), who sympathized with Freud's ideas that the essence of religion was not to be found in its dogmas, argued nonetheless that religion found its origins in deep feelings of unity or harmony with the universe, what he called an "oceanic feeling." In response Freud (1930) acknowledged that others may have had such experiences, but such feelings were totally foreign to him.

Nevertheless, Freud expended much time and energy trying to understand the nature of religion and its hold upon people. He devoted no less than three books to the topic (Freud, 1913, 1927, 1939), as well as commented on religion in several other essays and books (e.g., Freud, 1901, 1907b, 1910, 1918, 1930). It seems religion is never far from his mind. A central argument was that religion originated in infantile needs and wishes and their satisfaction (Freud, 1910, 1927). Having made this argument, Freud could not fathom why an adult would persist in believing, nor could he conceive of such a thing as a mature religious expression (Rizzuto, 1998).

Militant Critic of Religion

It was this later point that took Freud from a personal atheism to a militant stance toward others who might persist in religious beliefs. He wanted to convince others that religion is not simply an immature manifestation for the adult, but pathological as well (Freud, 1927). Freud's theories of religion are investigated in detail later; for now, it is sufficient to note that each of his forays into the topic of religion became more critical than the previous one so that his later engagements of religion concluded that its basis lay in infantile wishes for a powerful father who could save one from the grief and anxieties of life and should be given up as one matured enough to face the harsh realities of life without such "illusions" (much as he had done at the death of Sophie) (Freud, 1927).

Yet Deeply Interested in Religion

Given the amount of time and effort Freud expended on explaining religion, one concludes that despite his atheism Freud remained deeply interested in religion throughout his life. This interest manifested itself in several ways other than his writings. For instance, Freud demonstrated a multifaceted identification with the figure of Moses. Freud (1939), like Moses, saw himself as the founder of a new movement (with a new "law" regarding our deepest longings). Freud also identified with Moses as one who was rejected by the very people he tried to lead, an identification that fit Freud's personal myth of himself as one who often fought alone against great opposition (Breger, 2000; Gay, 1988). And like his projections onto Michelangelo's statue of Moses, Freud (1914b) saw himself as one who could hold his strong emotion in check (Gay, 1988).

Another way Freud's interest in religion manifested itself was in his life-long friendship with the pastor-analyst Oskar Pfister, a Swiss Reformed pastor who became acquainted with Freud and his entire family after reading Freud's *Interpretation of Dreams* (Breger, 2000; Gay, 1988). A life-long disciple and friend to Freud (Vitz, 1988), Pfister remained a pastor, telling Freud that being a psychoanalyst made him better at his job because he could understand so much better the needs and motivations of his parishioners (Freud and Pfister, 1963). Freud, for his part, shared a deep affection for Pfister. Pfister provided Freud with an example of someone who exhibited a positive expression of religion (Bretano was a previous example), a stark contrast to the pathological religion of his clients (such as the religion of the obsessive "Wolfman"; Freud, 1918). As a Swiss Reformed pastor Pfister espoused a more liberal type of Christianity that was focused on religion's ethical influence toward social good and less wedded to restrictive dogmas (Freud & Pfister, 1963). Thus, Pfister both saw and argued for religious expressions that were capable of mature psychological processes. Through his friendship with Pfister Freud conceded that religion and psychoanalysis need not be opposed (at least in theory), though Freud's own prejudices against religion did not subside and were mirrored in most other analysts from his circle (Gay, 1988).

We have already noted how Freud's interest in the essence of Judaism was an ongoing concern. In trying to identify this essence he once credited his Jewish heritage as saving him from the common prejudices of the masses (i.e., being the recipient of anti-Semitism, Freud knew how easy it was to hold to unexamined prejudices toward others) and enabling him to stand alone against opposition (i.e., he was accustomed to being an outsider) (Cooper-White, 2018; Freud, 1960). In this same place he also identified this essence as the Jewish concern for ethics. In yet another place he pointed to the Jewish ability to "preserve our unity through ideas" as what had allowed Jews to survive (Jones, 1957, p. 254; Cf. Freud, 1939). Although he was never satisfied with his ability to state this essence, that he often tried testifies to his enduring interest in certain dimensions of religion.

"Spiritual Substitutes"

There is one further way that Freud's enduring interest in religion manifested itself and it is worth its own sub-section. One cannot look at the life and work of the adult Freud without recognizing that he engaged in several types of behavior that point toward a preoccupation with a variety of "spiritual" phenomena despite his open claims to atheism (Rainey, 1975; Vitz, 1988). Some of these phenomena seem to function in ways similar to religious phenomena and give the impression of being substitute ways to keep a spiritual dimension alive in Freud even though he eschewed any recognition of formal religion (Rizzuto, 1998).

The first thing one might note is Freud's preoccupation with various superstitious behavior throughout his adult life (Rainey, 1975; Vitz, 1988). For instance, Freud was known to be disturbed by certain numbers which he associated with his death. Gay (1988) notes that for years he was plagued by the thought that he would die at 51; then later that he would die at 61 or 62 (he even thought the telephone number he was assigned confirmed this. The number contained the number 43 which was his age when he published the *Interpretation of Dreams* followed by the number 62 which he thought to be the terminal point of his life). Other superstitions that concerned Freud were those regarding the doppelganger (Jones, 1955) and thoughts that sometimes the dead came back to life (Freud, 1907a; Rainey, 1975). He even characterized his breaking of valuables on several occasions as "sacrifices" to ward off misfortune (Freud, 1901, pp. 169–70). This superstitious nature in Freud stands in sharp contrast to his espoused materialism (and atheism). To his credit, Freud recognized these inconsistencies in himself for he tried to analyze his superstitions to get beyond them though he was never able to rid himself of them (Freud, 1901; Jones, 1957).

Freud was also intrigued with phenomena such as telepathy, clairvoyance, and thought transfer (and to a lesser degree occult phenomena) (Rainey, 1975). Regarding the former, Freud reported on various telepathic communications he thought Martha had sent during their courtship (Freud, 1901; 1960, Jones, 1953). Later in life he wrote papers on his openness to telepathy (Freud, 1921b, 1922). As with his superstitions Freud considered such phenomena subjects for scientific investigation (i.e., analysis). Regarding his interest in occult phenomena Freud was more ambivalent. He did not write such phenomena off a priori but was clearly reticent about Jung's and Ferenczi's (two early colleagues) enthusiasm and involvement with occult phenomena (Rainey, 1975). Of particular interest in this regard is a discussion of "occultism and kindred topics" that Ernest Jones (another early disciple and Freud's authorized biographer) had with Freud. Noting that Freud liked to regale him, often till late in the night, with stories of strange and uncanny experiences with patients, Jones on one occasion found himself reproving Freud when the stories tested Jones' credulity. Jones pointed out that if one could believe in "mental processes floating in the air" one might as well believe in angels. Jones reports that at this comment,

> He [Freud] closed the discussion at this point (about three in the morning!) with the remark: "Quite so, even der liebe Gott [the loving God]." This was said in a jocular tone as if agreeing with my reduction ad absurdum and with a quizzical look as if he were pleased at shocking me. But there was something searching also in the glance, and I went away not entirely happy lest there be some more serious undertone as well. (Jones, 1957, p. 408)

We noted above how such remarks pointed to Freud's continued fascination with the powerful, emotional elements of religion despite his attempts to distance himself from such.

In noting Freud's fascination with the occult, one might note his similar fascination with the underworld; that is, with ideas of the devil, hell, eternal punishment and such (Bakan, 1958; Vitz, 1988). Although the devil is not entirely absent from Jewish tradition, Freud's imagination seems especially taken with Christian versions of these ideas such as Signorelli's frescos of the last judgment (Freud, 1901) and his fascination with the story of Faust (who sold his soul to the devil only to trick him later) (Bonaparte, et al., 1954). Jones (1953) also reports that one of Freud's earliest memories had to do with leaving Frieberg (when he was three) and thinking the gas lamps were like the souls burning in hell. It is quite possible that this association derives from stories remembered during the outings with the nanny who first taught him about "hell" and the underworld (Bonaparte, et al., 1954).

Another "spiritual" substitute to note in the adult Freud is his well-known interest in collecting antiquities (small figurines of gods and goddesses). Jones (1955) notes he would often bring his latest purchase to the dinner table for examination and reflection. Rizzuto (1998) connects the beginnings of this collection to the crisis Freud underwent following his father's death. This death set off a series of questions and anxieties in Freud that eventually led to his self-analysis (conducted in large measure through analysis of his dreams and his correspondence with his close friend Wilhelm Fleiss) and the discovery of the principles of psychoanalysis. Rizzuto argues that Freud's collecting of antiquities was a means of keeping his father present in symbolic form. Her argument regarding Freud's connection of the antiquities to the memory of his father is strengthened by her demonstration that many of these antiquities were purchased because they resembled and thus reminded Freud of illustrations from the Philippson Bible. That some of these are "gods" is also telling. That these objects perform something of a religious function is seen in the fact that none of the objects illustrate the ubiquitous sexuality for which Freud is known (Rizzuto, 1998). Rizzuto further proposes that Freud's antiquities functioned as an adult-appropriate transitional object that in many ways performed the comfort function that believers often find in religion. (Winnicott [1971] describes a transitional object as something that helps the child tolerate the anxiety of the mother's absence, e.g., a teddy bear; in adults, things that help one manage anxiety appropriately can take many forms.)

Finally, one might note that in this last regard several authors have pointed out that psychoanalysis seemed to perform for Freud (and his followers) several of the functions that religion has traditionally served for believers (Breger, 2000; Clifford, 2008; Rieff, 1979; Rizzuto, 1998; Wallace, 1983a, b). For one, psychoanalysis provided a means of making sense of the world and one's experience in the face of the collapse of religion as an explanatory system. Second, psychoanalysis gave the early analysts a sense of purpose and vocation. Similarly, others have observed that the feelings experienced in the early psychoanalytic meetings were similar to religious ones in that one felt among a company of like-minded believers (e.g., Graf, 1942; cf. Clifford, 2008). In this same vein others have pointed out how often religious metaphors were used to describe the work and the organization of the psychoanalytic movement. Followers were "disciples," analysts were likened to secular "priests" for their "care of the soul" (Freud & Pfister, 1963; Gay, 1988; Jones, 1959; Stekel, 1950). Freud occasionally spoke of psychoanalysis in what sounded like quasi-religious tones. For instance, he noted on one occasion that "psychoanalysis either possesses [the analyst] entirely or not at all" (Freud, 1932a, p. 153). On another occasion he wrote "we possess the truth. I am as sure of it as fifteen years ago" (quoted in Jones, 1955, p. 158), an affirmation of certainty that could rival any religious profession.

How then might one characterize Freud's religious development during his adult years? Regarding his Jewish identity, Freud continued to affirm this, never wavering in this regard though it is always clear that this identification was more an ethnic or cultural one, never a religious one (Gay, 1988; note that Freud once described himself to Pfister as a "godless Jew"; i.e., not religious but still Jewish; Freud & Pfister, 1963, p. 63). Phillips (2014) describes him as a Jew "psychologically." As in earlier years, Freud's identification with his Jewish heritage strengthens in the face of anti-Semitism (Ellenberger, 1970). The stronger the anti-Semitism, as it was under Hitler, the stronger Freud's affirmation that he was Jewish. Yet despite a growing identification with his Jewish heritage in the face of anti-Semitism, Freud's adult years are an occasion for his strongest attacks against religion (Freud, 1927, 1939). Late in life when asked about the threat of the Nazis, Freud responded that what he really needed help against was his "true enemy" which he identified as "religion" (quoted in Ruitenbeek, 1973, p. 344).

Using Freud's own theory, one concludes that there is something more at work here than his intellect. There are deep, emotional reasons going back to his earliest childhood that prevent Freud from believing; feelings that might even create a need for him not to believe. We will return to this question in the conclusion but for now we turn to the question of how Freud's religious background may have influenced his work. To aid the reading of that section we look briefly at some key ideas in Freud.

Some Key Ideas in Freud's Thought

It is impossible to adequately summarize Freud's key ideas in the space allotted to this topic. There is no attempt to review every key idea, nor can justice be done to those that are reviewed. Scholars will find this section severely wanting (if not appalling!) given the complexity and shifting nature of Freud's thought over the 50 years he wrote (e.g., he proposed two models of the mind, two theories of the instincts, two theories of repression, two theories of anxiety, little of which is covered here). My chief defense is that the audience in view for this oversimplified summary is the student or person perhaps encountering Freud's thought for the first time, and even here I am assuming that such a reader has access to the kind of summary that can be found in an introductory text on psychological theories (e.g., Monte, 1999). Thus, in covering only those ideas for which some connection to Freud's religious background can be made, the goal here is simply to make the next section more understandable.

The Unconscious

Although not a concept original to Freud (Ellenberger, 1970), Freud's articulation of the unconscious takes in several other key ideas, including his thoughts about dreams and the defense mechanisms. In trying to understand Freud's ideas about the unconscious it is important to clarify that Freud spoke of the unconscious in at least two ways (Freud, 1912; cf. Kahn, 2002; Monte, 1999). Sometimes it is a noun referring to a region of psychic function, a kind of repository of embarrassing, frightening, and unsavory wishes and animalistic desires that one "represses" or buries. At other times it is an adjective that speaks to the nature of various motivational drives (i.e., those which lie outside of awareness). These two ways of speaking of the unconscious are connected to two models of the mind that Freud proposed. The first model envisions the mind as having various regions (called the topographical model because it tries to chart these regions—that is, their topography). Some regions lie in awareness (or near awareness) called the "conscious" and the "preconscious." An illustration of things in the conscious might be your awareness of reading this sentence. An illustration of the preconscious might be your ability to recall your mother's birthdate now that you have been prompted to do so. A third region of the mind in this model is the "unconscious," a region where one buries things "known but unthought" (to borrow from Christopher Bollas [1987]). This region, with its unknown activity, nevertheless deeply influences human thought and action (Anzieu, 1986).

Freud's second model of the mind envisions certain psychological "structures" within the mind (hence called the structural model), generally termed the "id," "ego," and "superego." The id points to mental processes connected to one's deepest instincts for biological survival and motivates behavior accordingly. Primarily these deep instincts function at an unconscious level and are what Freud is most interested in. According to Freud humans are motivated by two powerful, largely unconscious instincts (often and perhaps more properly called "drives" because of this motivational dimension). Freud envisioned a tension between these two biologically rooted drives that keep humans in a state of conflict or tension. Sometimes the drives are in tension with one another, sometimes the tension involves conflict between the drives and social/environmental restraints; other times the conflict is between the drives and internalized prohibitions (Freud, 1932a). In his early work Freud (1916) described these as the drives for species preservation (libidinal drives) and self-preservation (ego drives). In later work he described the drives toward preservation as a singular life drive (Eros) directed toward two objects (i.e., the species or the self), and saw this life drive in tension with a drive toward death and destruction (e.g., Thanatos) (Freud, 1920). Rooted as they are in our biological survival, they are not easily controlled and arouse within us powerful, sometimes frightening ideas of aggression and sexuality (in its most primary sense of species and self-preservation as well as its aspects of desire). Such strong, sometimes threatening motives cause us tension or anxiety (both known and unknown) which we try to manage. One way we do so is through various "ego" functions (see below); the other way we try to manage the anxiety of these drives is to adhere to personal and social prohibitions regarding their expression, the so-called "superego" functions of the mind (e.g., Freud, 1930). Such internalized prohibitions can be either too loose or two stringent and their use in managing one's drives is one of the issues explored in psychoanalysis.

Freud devoted considerable attention to the various ego processes for managing the anxiety generated by these powerful drives. He called these management strategies "defenses" (i.e., against the anxiety) (Freud, 1932a). These strategies, commonly called the "defense mechanisms," might less technically be thought of as coping strategies. The strategies can be more mature and conscious in their use or less mature and more unconscious in their employ. For instance, on the more helpful side, one might engage the intellect (an ego function) to "understand" such powerful, instinctual motives; alternately, one might find reasonable or acceptable means for their expression (e.g., hitting a punching bag instead of a person; an example of *displacement*). An alternative to physical expression of sexual desire might be to *sublimate* it through creative work since Freud (1905) saw such work as a mature expression of the libidinal or life drives. Less helpful strategies for coping with this anxiety might be *denial* or *projection* (attributing one's own struggles to someone else). Sometimes there is awareness of one's defenses (e.g., realizing that procrastinating for an exam is because it is easier to think of oneself as a waster of time than as not up to the intellectual challenge—a *rationalization*) but most often these defenses work outside conscious awareness so that one of the key things that is "analyzed" in psycho*analysis* is one's defenses.

Because they mostly operate outside of awareness, these strong instinctual drives leave humans in danger of being overwhelmed by the tension they generate; Freud (1900, 1932a) found himself rather pessimistic about a person's ability to manage them in mature ways without help (e.g., psychoanalysis). Thus, humans are rather weak in Freud's eyes; they are not heroic creatures and even those who are thought heroic can be understood as motivated by unflattering and infantile ideas (Freud, 1900, 1921a, 1927, 1932a). Freud took a dim view of human potential to be good and to do good toward others (Freud, 1930). Drives for preservation cause humans to place consideration of themselves before consideration of others and drives toward destruction wreak havoc on both self and others (Freud, 1920). For Freud (1927, 1930) humans are rarely as bad as they could be (because of various restraints in civilization and in the mature personality) but also never quite as good as they imagine themselves to be.

Our final comments on the unconscious concern its access. For Freud this might be achieved in several ways (e.g., paying attention to slips of the tongue, the so-called "Freudian slip") but the chief access to the unconscious is through our dreams (Freud, 1900). Through interpreting his own dreams Freud saw that dreams gave expression to various embarrassing, frightening, unsavory wishes, and animalistic desires but in disguised form. To understand the wish or desire expressed in this disguised manner one must attend not to the manifest content of the dream (what the dream is actually about, its characters and actions), but to what the dream symbolizes, what Freud (1900) called its latent content. Thus, there are deeper layers of meaning in the dream than first appear. The chief process for accessing this deeper or latent content is through "free association" to the manifest content. Free association involves a chain of connections to a given dream element or character without censoring what thoughts come to mind. For instance, if one dreamt of one's pet, one might be asked, what else comes to mind when you think of this pet? And what else? And what else? Until there is a pause! Pausing (i.e., a censoring moment) before speaking the thought that had come to mind is an indication that one has tapped something of the unconscious wishes or desires (i.e., the deeper, disguised meaning of the dream).

Developmental Stages

Another key idea that Freud (1905) proposed was that one's biological drives expressed themselves in a developmental pattern which he labeled psychosexual stages. Freud (1905) identified four stages of development (or five depending on how "latency" is counted) that extended from infancy to puberty. At each stage aspects of one's psychological development are localized in interaction with aspects of one's biological development to produce various personality correlates. Disruptions and fixations can occur anywhere along the course of development and will impact one's intrapsychic and interpersonal development.

Without elaboration of the details and in very oversimplified terms one might think of the first stage in Freud's theory as concerned with not only the biological function of taking food in through the mouth (the "oral" stage) but as involved with what to take in (or not take in) psychologically. There are possibilities for problems by either taking in too much or too little (cf. a person who is "gullible"—that is, takes in everything without discrimination—with a person who takes in very little of the outside world—i.e., paranoid tendencies). The second stage is concerned not only with a shift of biological focus (the "anal" stage with its attention to new-found biological control over elimination processes) but also with a corresponding shift in psychological focus around what to hold on to and let go of. Problems in this stage of development might result in a person who holds too tightly to neatness and order or conversely in a person who is very messy (i.e., lets everything go). The third stage also involves a shift in biological focus with attendant psychological lessons concerned with gender identification and finding one's sense of place in one's family of origin (the "phallic" or "oedipal" stage—more below). Between the third and last stage is a period of quiescence ("latency") before the emergence of the biological ability to reproduce the species (the "genital" stage which emerges with puberty) and psychological lessons on how one relates to and contributes to others in society. Problems at this stage might involve an (unconscious) drivenness in one's relationships or career so that one is unable to find joy or freedom in either (Freud, 1940).

At the center of the developmental stages is the oedipal conflict, in many ways the touchstone of Freud's (1905) developmental theory. Freud's elaboration of the Oedipus complex was tied to his abandonment of the so-called "seduction theory" (that sexual trauma was the cause of his patients' neuroses) and his articulation of an alternative theory to explain the pervasive influence of sexuality on his patients and their anxieties (Breger, 2000). That is, if the disorders he was treating were not due to his patients actually being seduced or abused in childhood, he then hypothesized that the source of their neuroses must derive from "sexual fantasies" in childhood. In the common explanation of the oedipal struggle Freud (1905) argued that the young boy (of about three or four) fantasizes about possessing the mother and replacing the father. Although Freud explained this as having sexual elements one must realize that the three- or four-year-old's grasp of sexuality is very rudimentary. It is perhaps helpful to think of oedipal desires as the wish to be the center of a relationship in which one's every need is met. One might even think of the oedipal wish as one for power such as one had as an infant with almost "omnipotent" control over the mother's actions in the first few weeks or months of life. The problem by the time one is three is a recognition that there is competition for this desired power and relationship by one obviously more powerful (the father) who also has a special relationship with the mother that somehow excludes him (see Blass [2001] for similar and other ways of explaining oedipal desires). What to do with such deep, powerful longings when one is three? For Freud, the successful resolution of the Oedipus complex was the "repression" of such fantasies (which inevitably involved mourning a sense of loss) and finding a way forward through identification with the father (and his power and capacity for relating). Conversely, Freud thought the unsuccessful resolution of oedipal desires the source of many neuroses. Potential problems in this stage might include excessive narcissism or a problematic guilt (perhaps unconscious) caused by usurping the father's power. Freud's theory of the oedipal struggle figures prominently in his writings on religion; he particularly ties certain religious attitudes to one's relationship with one's father (i.e., with how the oedipal conflict was resolved). We note in closing that although Freud thought this model well described male development he was never satisfied with his explanation for development in the female (see Freud, 1924, 1931).

How Freud's Religious Background Influenced His Life and Thought

Several people have documented the impact of Freud's early development on his work, pointing out how several of his central ideas are related to his own life experience. Such links include his ideas about the Oedipus complex and their connection to memories and dreams from his early childhood. Similarly, his idea that dreams express a wish comes from his analysis of his own dreams (Breger, 2000; Demorest, 2005; Elms, 1994). This section is an extension of this line of inquiry; it asks how the religious aspects of Freud's development may have influenced his theory (cf. Bakan, 1958; Homans, 1982; Rizzuto, 1998; Vitz, 1988).

The influence of Freud's religious background is seen in both direct and indirect ways. As noted in the Introduction, one sees this more indirect influence in the cultural religious notion of "development" (i.e., that life moves linearly toward some goal or purpose) and in the lingering influence of the ethical traditions of Judaism and Christianity. Not surprisingly, in Freud's case the ethical influence of his Jewish tradition is uppermost. We look first at these more indirect influences of Freud's religious background before turning to more specific ways this influence shows up in his life and work.

A Developmental Perspective

One can see the more indirect influence of Freud's religious background (via its cultural influence) in his adoption and elaboration of a developmental perspective on life (a view Kirschner [1996] identifies as derived from Jewish and Christian perspectives on the linearity of history). Freud was one of the earliest of psychologists to adopt such a clearly expressed developmental perspective in his work. The adoption of this perspective is most obvious in Freud's formulation of developmental stages. Freud's psychosexual stages of development chart a trajectory that takes one from infancy toward the goal of genital sexuality (which in its biological sense meant the ability to replicate the species but in its psychological sense pointed to mature expressions of one's sexual drives; Freud, 1905). The specifics of what one develops toward (i.e., Freud's vision of the good life) is taken up below in the more direct ways his religious background influenced his life and work.

One also sees the cultural religious influence of the developmental perspective in Freud's vision of psychoanalysis as working to right something awry (e.g., the superego overcontrolling the natural drives or of the id overriding the ego; cf. "where id was, there ego shall be" as a goal of analysis [Freud, 1932a, p. 80]). As noted in the Introduction this model of therapy as correcting something wrong reflects certain religious-cultural traditions indebted to the influence of Augustine on Western thought. Thus, Freud's adoption of a developmental perspective shows the influence of both his own Jewish tradition as well as elements of Christian influence on the Western intellectual tradition.

Ethical Legacy of His Religious Tradition

One also sees the indirect influence of Freud's religious background on his life and work via the ethical legacy of the Jewish and Christian traditions in Western culture. Freud (like all the psychologists in this book) was heir and participant in a culture influenced by religious traditions regarding notions of right and wrong, good and bad. Freud (1927, 1930) acknowledged that these traditions often made civility toward others possible, but he also found himself critiquing these traditions as well. In Freud's case his critique is often focused on the Christian ethical tradition in contrast to a Jewish one. One sees the indirect influence of the ethical legacy of these religious traditions in Freud's work in several ways.

Freud's Ethics and a Lifestyle of Restraint

As noted in the Introduction, part of the ethical legacy of both Judaism and Christianity concerns questions of moral or ethical obligation—what ought one to do? I want to suggest that one gets a better sense of the influence of Freud's Jewish tradition on this question not from his writings on this but by observing his own behavior toward others. Hence, one sees the ethical legacy of Freud's Jewish tradition especially in his own moral life. In trying to assess the nature of Freud's ethics, Browning (1987) follows Wallwork (1982) by arguing that Freud's particular version of ethics cannot be reduced to a simple ethical egoism (i.e., that one seeks to produce the most good over evil for oneself; this was Rieff's [1979] interpretation of Freud's ethics) but rather encompasses a more nuanced adoption of an ethic of mutual respect and reciprocity that accords well with Freud's Judaism (see Wallwork, 1991). Rieff (1979) makes a similar argument; that is, despite his Enlightenment rationalism and materialistic atheism Freud was personally a very ethical person and that behind his ethics lay the Jewish tradition. Freud (1960) once spoke of the life-affirming qualities of Judaism as being the source of a strong ethical tradition that influenced not only Judaism but the larger Western cultural tradition (Gay, 1988). This sense of ethics, as summarized by Freud's teacher Samuel Hammerschlag, valued autonomy but also included a concern for justice and rights for all (Rainey, 1975). One sees this sense of ethical responsibility in Judaism manifest in Freud's valuing autonomy in his patients, in his concern for unjust treatment toward Jews, and in his own ethical behavior. In terms of the latter, Freud's ethical restraint is even described as "puritanical" at times (Ellenberger, 1970, p. 427). For instance, he often reproached himself for his love of tobacco, books, and antiquities (Robert, 1977). Thus, though he is sometimes accused of not holding the reins on disciples (several of whom slept with their patients), and even though his ideas are said to be the source of a loosening of social morals, Freud himself maintained a high degree of moral and ethical sensibility throughout his life, due in large measure to the strong sense of ethics and the moral life bequeathed to him by his Jewish roots (Wallwork, 1991).

Goodness vs. Badness in Humans

One also sees the influence of this religious ethical legacy in Freud's reflections on goodness vs. badness in humans, questions long associated with the Jewish and Christian traditions. Clearly reflective of his Jewish tradition Freud did not see humans as innately good or bad as some Christian traditions do. However, it is interesting to note that he did see humans as rather weak (e.g., always in danger of being overwhelmed by their instinctual drives). We have noted that Freud took a dim view of human potential to be good and to do good toward others (Freud, 1930). Drives for preservation limit one's ability to consider others before oneself (Freud, 1920). For Freud (1927, 1930), although humans are rarely as bad as they could be, they are never quite as good as they imagine themselves to be either. Although it is interesting that some have noted the affinity of such a poor view of human possibility toward good with certain Christian traditions regarding a similar deficiency (e.g., Jones & Butman, 1991), it is highly likely that such pessimism regarding human nature was influenced by the horrors of WWI as well as Freud's experience of anti-Semitism. Freud had firsthand acquaintance of how the Christian tradition of love and forgiveness did not generally extend to him or his Jewish compatriots in the Austria of the early twentieth century (Cooper-White, 2018). This becomes one of the critiques Freud offers regarding the differences between a Jewish and Christian ethic. For instance, Freud (1930) is particularly critical of the Christian vision of the "love command" (i.e., to love one's neighbor as oneself) as not only unrealistic but as offering a kind of easy forgiveness to the Christians who ill-treated their Jewish neighbors.[1] Freud clearly saw his own Jewish ethic with a focus on justice in the present world as a superior ethic on this point. Thus, although Freud's reflections on the nature of goodness vs. badness in humans draw on his exposure to both Jewish and Christian experiences of these qualities in humans, it is the influence of the former that he finds more affirming and life-giving.

His Work Ethic

There is no true parallel to the Protestant work ethic in Judaism. References to work in Jewish sources such as the Talmud and Mishnah observe that while there is a commandment to *rest* (the Sabbath), there is no corresponding command to work. Although a few rabbis saw this as indicating one should only study Torah, a more consensual understanding was that work, while not commanded was often necessary, even honorable, and clearly preferable to idleness and dependency on others. Furthermore, it should be "clean and simple" (e.g., honest, not too hazardous or taxing) and allow time for attending to spiritual matters. It should allow accumulation of enough wealth that one could be generous to the less fortunate and it is better that work be loved than hated (Schall, 2001). One can see aspects of these Jewish perspectives on work in Freud's life such as generosity toward the less fortunate (e.g., to colleagues and patients as circumstances warranted; Gay, 1988) and the notion that it is better to enjoy one's work (e.g., choose it consciously and freely). However, the strenuous schedule of writing and case load that Freud maintained throughout his life (to prove he had made something of himself? [Freud, 1900]; Gay [1988] notes his typical workday began at 8am and extended well past midnight) suggest that Freud may have been influenced by the Protestant work ethic that would have been part of the cultural fabric of early twentieth-century Vienna as well as by Jewish perspectives on work.

Certain Key Ideas

In addition to these more indirect influences of religious traditions on Freud there also are more direct ways these traditions influenced his life and work, including certain key ideas in his thought. Although Freud's Jewish identity and background did not influence all his ideas, it did influence several. We begin by noting its influence on several ideas Freud had about his work in general.

Goals of Psychoanalysis and the Good Life

One sees the influence of Freud's Jewish background on his ideas regarding the goals of psychoanalysis; one might even think of these as Freud's vision of the good life (or perhaps for Freud the "good enough" life—to evoke a phrase from Winnicott [1971]). According to an oft repeated phrase, Freud is purported to have said that what one could hope for those who participate in a successful analysis is that they attain the ability to love and to work (Erikson, 1950/1963). Inherent in these goals is that people can love and work with a sense of freedom and pleasure. That is, people are no longer driven by unconscious instinctual forces in the choice of their love objects or their careers. Through psychoanalysis people uncover the hidden motivations for such choices, and thus can make more conscious, reason-based choices about continuing or changing relationships and career (Freud, 1932a). These goals also reflect ancient Jewish ideas. For instance, these goals mirror two key foci of the creation narratives in the book of Genesis (chapters 1 and 2). According to these chapters, humans are created for relationship to God and to one another (i.e., "to love") and they are to tend the garden (i.e., "to work").

Freud also spoke of these more ego-driven choices as being oriented toward the reality principle (vs. pleasure principle; that is, Freud saw the goal of psychoanalysis as the patient's need to accept reality (Freud, 1920). Often Freud's (1911) assertion that humans follow the "pleasure principle" is misunderstood in this regard; pleasure for Freud is more the reduction of tension or discomfort than an increase in satisfaction. In an oft quoted phrase, one summation of what psychoanalysis might achieve was the transformation of "hysterical misery into common unhappiness" (Freud, 1895, p. 335). Living according to the reality principle then is the goal of a mature life (Freud, 1920). This acceptance of reality is tied to Freud's religious background via the pursuit of truth.

Dreams and the Unconscious

In addition to these general ideas about his work, one can also see the influence of Freud's religious tradition on some of the key ideas noted above in the summary of Freud's thought. Ellenberger (1970) has shown that the sources for Freud's ideas regarding the unconscious were many. Freud had heard of the unconscious from Charcot when he studied in Paris and his own clinical work and self-analysis of his dreams further convinced him of a realm of psychic functioning beyond immediate awareness (Freud, 1900). But in addition to these sources one can point to aspects of Freud's religious background and exposure that influenced his ideas about the unconscious. For instance, Ellenberger himself suggests Freud likely heard of the unconscious at university from the Christian scholar Bretano, who taught that Augustine had been the first to speak of the unconscious, and others have suggested further connections between Freud's Jewish background and his notion of the unconscious. For instance, David Bakan (1958) tries to trace the impact of the Jewish Enlightenment (*Haskalah*) on Freud's emotional readiness to engage with certain ideas such as the multiple layers of consciousness. Bakan further argues that Freud's acquaintance with elements of the Jewish mystical tradition (Kabbalism) influenced his thought and likely lies behind Freud's superstitious preoccupation with numbers and his death. Philip Rieff (1979) also suggests that Freud's religious background influenced his notion of the unconscious as indifferent, impersonal, and unconcerned about the life of its creation. Personified this way, Rieff argues that the unconscious functioned like a hidden God for Freud. Given Rieff's argument, it is not hard to trace the characteristics of such an indifferent, impersonal unconscious to similar ideas about God that arose from interactions with his caregivers (Rizzuto, 1998).

Other connections between Freud's ideas about the unconscious and his Jewish background come from his comments on dreams. For instance, in his work on dreams Freud (1900) presented himself as a new Joseph, the famous biblical character known for interpreting dreams (see Gen. 40–41). Of even more importance is his way of interpreting dreams. For Freud, one interpreted a dream by looking for deeper meanings than appear on the surface of the dream (the latent vs. the manifest content). This concept that understanding is gained by looking for deeper layers of meaning is a Jewish idea long connected to the study of Scripture (Rieff, 1979). Some have noted that Freud's process of dream interpretation often treated patients as though they were a "text" whose various levels of meaning needed probing, much as the rabbis did with the Hebrew Scriptures in the Talmud (a collection of rabbinic interpretations authoritative in their own right; Bakan, 1958; Kradin, 2015). For the rabbis, one discovered the contemporary relevance of what happened to Abraham, for instance, by looking beyond the story itself for its essence, the enduring truths that the stories taught. Often one found this deeper meaning by discerning the ethical lesson being taught (but one might also find more esoteric meanings there as well [Bakan, 1958]).

The Drives and the Defenses

Another thing to note in seeking connections between Freud's ideas and his religious background is his concept of two drives that keep one in a state of tension and the attempts to defend against the anxiety this generates. Kradin (2015) notes the similarity of this idea of the continued tension between two powerful forces in the mind and an idea from Jewish tradition that speaks of two opposing forces in humans, the good and bad "yetzer" (or impulse); the former seeks the divine will while the latter seeks personal satisfaction. (This idea is often popularized in the depiction of an angel perched on one shoulder and a devil on the other, each giving advice while the hapless person tries to decide what to do.) Although Kradin also suggests other less likely connections between Freud's thought and his Jewish background (e.g., his concept of "transference" and the Jewish traditions of transferring sin by laying hands upon an animal; see Lev. 16), his reiteration of several points noted in this study (e.g., Freud's search for truth and the Jewish prophetic tradition, interpreting dreams similar to rabbinic interpretation of texts) shows just how often Jewish ideas and traditions lurk in the background of Freud's writings.

Oedipus Complex

In ascertaining how Freud's religious development influenced his conceptualization of the oedipal conflict, recall that Freud's own ambivalent feelings toward his father played a key role in his articulation of this idea (Monte, 1999). Freud saw his struggle with his father as a struggle that all humanity faced (Breger, 2000; Freud, 1905) and his elaboration of the Oedipus complex provided a way to explain and come to terms with these powerful emotions toward his father. In projecting this struggle back to primeval times, Freud's (1913) own experience gets projected back to the very beginnings of civilized life together; his own experience gets writ large upon the world, including God. That is, Freud has made the origin of religion (i.e., ideas about God) mirror his own religious development, wrapped up as it is with his relationship to his father. Bakan (1958) indicates how these connections work out in Freud's theory when he notes how the unconscious "desire to destroy the father can become conscious as doubt about the existence of God" (p. 280).

Freud's Theory of Religion

Finally, a crucial way that Freud's religious development influenced his work was in his theories about religion. We noted earlier that Freud tended to be mostly critical of religion and that this critique increased in severity over the years. Writing about religion for over 30 years Freud devoted three major efforts to the topic of religion along with several other essays (e.g., Freud, 1907b, 1910, 1913, 1927, 1939), often adding to and modifying his ideas about religion as his theory on psychic processes changed (Wallace, 1983a). Because Freud's ideas on religion are many, the exposition pauses periodically to consider how Freud's own religious development contributed to specific ideas about religion.

After an early passing comment about religion comparing it to the paranoid person's internal mental constructions which get projected onto the exterior world (Freud, 1901), Freud's (1907b) first formal treatment of religion was an essay in which he likened religious rituals to the obsessions of the neurotic, concluding that religion then was analogous to a cultural neurosis: "One might venture to regard obsessional neurosis as a pathological counterpart of the formation of a religion, and to describe the neurosis as an individual religiosity and religion as a universal obsessional neurosis" (p. 158). In this analogy Freud saw similarities between obsessional rituals and religious rituals in that both were driven by unconscious motivations, primarily guilt about sexual and aggressive thoughts and feelings. As the ceremonial acts of the obsessive (the compulsive rituals) are performed to defend against the anxiety caused by the obsessions, so religious rituals ward off anxiety connected with one's temptations.

Although Freud clearly draws on his experience with patients in formulating his ideas about rituals and neuroses (cf. Rat Man case; Freud, 1909), Freud's own struggles with superstitious obsessions (e.g., Freud, 1905, 1907a) also seem to have contributed to this early argument regarding the nature of religious rituals (Rainey, 1975; cf. Freud, 1919). As he did with other parts of his theory Freud here turns his own experience with superstitious obsessions and their function into a general insight about religious rituals.

However, Freud was not content simply to draw analogies between religion and obsessional symptoms. He wanted to understand how it was that religion came to be and how it held such power over humanity's consciousness. His next two theoretical statements about religion offered answers to these questions at the personal and cultural levels. In an essay on Leonardo da Vinci, Freud (1910) argued that the personal origins of religion (belief in God) were connected to one's relationship with one's father. Psychologically speaking, God is nothing more than an exalted father and so people lost their belief in God when the authority of the father waned. Freud further connected belief in God to the working out of one's "father-complex" (cf. the Oedipus complex) by noting that religion involved the projection of certain wishes about the father upon the larger environment (e.g., for his protection in one's helplessness). Such wishes for protections suffer inevitable failures; religion, he argued, compensates for such failures by positing an exalted father, God.

Freud's ideas about the origins of personal religious belief and relationship with one's father are clearly reflected in his own religious journey. His argument that religion loses its authority as the father loses his could not better describe Freud's religious movements following the loss of respect for his father recounted in the story of his father's hat and the playful yet irreverent way in which Freud treated religious topics in the letters from his early adolescence (Freud, 1910, 1969). God, like his father, got demoted there. There also seem to be parallels between the wish for the father's protection, the projection of this wish onto God and the compensation for the inevitable disappointments associated with such beliefs in Freud's own experience with his father (Rizzuto, 1998). When Freud (1910) wrote in his essay on Leonardo that "we naturally feel hurt that a just God and a kindly providence do not protect us better from such influences [the cruelties of fate] during the most defenseless period of our lives" (p. 137), he might well be describing his father's weakness. Certainly, when he wrote that "the unbeliever has to grapple with it [the loss of a sense of protection] on his own" (Freud, 1910, p. 123) he is describing his own approach to such losses.

The connection between belief in God and the "father-complex" (i.e., the Oedipus complex) is taken up again in Freud's consideration of the cultural origins of religion. In *Totem and Taboo* Freud (1913) explored both the cultural origins of religion and its psychological hold on humanity. In this book Freud extended his thinking regarding the father complex to the origins of forbidden behaviors (taboos) in civilization. Freud proposed that such prohibitions arose from a primeval enactment of the oedipal struggle (sons rose up and killed the ruling father figure because he had reserved the women to himself; then, feeling remorse the sons set up prohibitions as well as devised means for remembering and honoring the now dead father). Freud saw these restrictive actions as the beginning of civilization and the totemic remembrances as the beginning of religion. Thus, Freud thought he had explained not only how humanity came to establish religion as a cultural system but also how religions function: they defend against the anxiety and guilt generated by the instinctual sexual and aggressive drives. We have already noted a connection between Freud's articulation of the Oedipus complex and his religious background that need not be repeated here.

Freud's (1927) next major statement regarding religion was in *Future of an Illusion*. This book gathered ideas from his previous works to offer a new, comprehensive statement that took up the questions of why it is people are religious, what function religion plays in culture, how religion has failed in modern times and what is to be humanity's new hope in the place of religion. Freud repeated several arguments from his previous work (e.g., that religion was based in infantile wishes for a powerful father figure who can save one from the exigencies of life (Freud, 1910); that the cultural origins of religion are found in the efforts to symbolically restore the killed father). In this new statement he further described such infantile wishes as "illusions" because they originated in the yearning for a return to infancy when such protection was assumed. Thus, religion was an illusion because it was based on human wishes that the gods "exorcize the terrors of nature . . . reconcile men to the cruelty of Fate . . . and . . . compensate them for the sufferings and privations which a civilized life in common has imposed on them" (Freud, 1927, p. 24). Similarly, he extended his argument on the cultural origins of religion to claim that religion disguised the historical realities of humanity's guilt in its creeds and rituals of expiation and thus was more like a delusion (untrue) than simply an illusion (which can on occasion be true). Thus, Freud saw religious beliefs not simply as wishful thinking, but pathological thinking. Freud conceded in this book that historically religion had performed a positive function in that it helped restrain humanity's sexual and aggressive drives, allowing people to live together. But Freud also thought that after several thousand years, religion had lost its power to bind people together in common purpose (cf. Rieff, 1979). Having shown the infantile origins of religion and its motivations, Freud thought it simply a matter of time before people would give it up. In its place the more modern scientific understanding of human nature would provide a means for holding civilization together. *Future of an Illusion* is Freud's most optimistic statement regarding the future of humanity; aided by science, he saw the hope of a bright future. About three years later, in *Civilization and Its Discontents*, he has forgone such optimism as its own illusion (Freud, 1930). (It is interesting to note that in arguing so strongly about the illusory nature of religion, Freud does not seem to notice that the "science" he champions is also an ideology (and illusion); see Rieff, 1979; his friend Pfister had made similar remarks when the book came out [Freud & Pfister, 1963].)

How do the arguments in *Future of an Illusion* reflect Freud's own religious development? In addition to the previous connections to ideas also found in his other works one notes that Freud's charge that religion had failed modern people, that it had lost the power to bind them together in meaningful purpose clearly mirrored his own journey (Breger, 2000; Rizzuto, 1998). Similarly, Freud's argument that science provides the means for people to renounce their instinctual drives without the aid of religious illusions also mirrored his journey. Freud (1927) saw his ability to endure the fates without God as the model of maturity for all and psychoanalysis as the path that could make this possible (though it is important to point out that Freud was not as devoid of defenses against the exigencies of life as he supposed; his breaking pottery to ward off misfortune [Freud, 1901; Jones, 1957] and his antiquities collection both have defensive functions, even if the latter is thought a more mature defense [Rizzuto, 1998]). In addition, one also sees the influence of Freud's religious journey on his inability to imagine a mature religious function. He himself had had no such experiences (Freud, 1930), and it was hard for him to imagine them in others, even when confronted by them in people like Pfister. He cannot imagine religious motivations that derive from sources other than instinctual ones (Freud, 1927). Thus, this book knows nothing of a mature religion, nor of religion's potential as a bulwark against oppression (e.g., from the state—often called its "prophetic" function). Rather the religion Freud describes here is one that is itself an oppressor.

Of course, the religion Freud envisions here is primarily the Catholicism of his native Austria at the time (Vitz, 1988; Wallace, 1983b). Cooper-White (2018) speaks of a "Habsburg-Catholic" Vienna to call attention to the interwoven political and religious influences that provided a context not only for religious beliefs but the whole of civic life at this time; she argues that this environment with its undercurrent of anti-Semitism provided a "total context" that could not help but color Freud's ideas about religion (pp. 6, 8). She argues that Freud's aversion to religion cannot be understood rightly without taking this environment into account and that failure to do so tends to skew interpretations of Freud's views of religion more negatively than is warranted. Here then another aspect of his own experience informs his ideas on religion.

Freud's final engagement of the topic of religion (*Moses and Monotheism*) was published just before his death. In his final book-length treatment Freud (1939) explored a question that had troubled him for many years: what is it that makes the Jew unique? His oft stated attempts to define the "essence" of Judaism (e.g., its ethical approach, its power to resist common prejudices, its power to bind a people together) were attempts to answer this question. Now, near the end of his life, with cancer having taken a toll and the increase of anti-Semitism with Hitler's rise in power, Freud returned once again to the question of what had given the Jew this mystique. In brief he argued that it was Moses that had made the Jew unique. But in an ironic twist Freud argued that Moses himself was not a Jew but an Egyptian follower of the monotheism instituted by pharaoh Amenhotep. Thus, the arguments of this book are

Freud's strongest critique of the religion of his ancestors. In this work, Freud strips Judaism of one of its central heroes and makes his accomplishment a borrowed one. This book also reflects Freud's own religious concerns as he ponders how it is a religion of the "son" (i.e., Christianity) has replaced a religion of the "father" (Judaism) culturally. This puzzled him because as noted above he thought Judaism the better religion ethically in its concern for justice in the present world.

Other Ways

Freud's religious background also influenced his life and work in other ways; four of those are in the techniques employed in psychoanalysis, his dogged pursuit of the truth, his secularizing of certain religious ideas, and his general attitude toward religion.

The Techniques of Psychoanalysis

When one looks more specifically at some of the techniques Freud employed in his new science, one also sees the influence of his Jewish background. We have already noted how Freud's techniques of dream interpretation are indebted to the Jewish Talmudic tradition of looking for deeper layers of meaning in sacred texts (Bakan, 1958; Kradin, 2015; Rieff, 1979). Because of this technique of treating a dream like a text, others have noted how Freud's "science" looks more like a "hermeneutic" (Ricoeur, 1977); i.e., more like literature or the humanities than science.

One can see a similar connection in Freud's idea that psychoanalysis involves interpretation of the "transference" (i.e., the qualities in the relationship between the analyst and the patient whereby the patient transfers to the analyst those feelings or responses the patient has to other significant people in his or her life). We have also noted above how a focus on the relationship as a means of healing is also part of Freud's Jewish tradition.

Pursuit of the Truth and Thirst for Knowing

Another way Freud's Jewish background influenced his life and work was in his thirst for knowing. Gay (1988) and Phillips (2014) note that one of the driving forces in Freud's life was his "greed" for knowledge. This greed to know was influenced by his religious tradition in two ways. First, Phillips argues that Freud (e.g., 1905) links all desire, including the desire for knowledge to sexual desire and our curiosity about sexuality (e.g., how did we get here? How are babies made?). According to Phillips the question Freud set for himself was one regarding how knowing was related to desiring. Thus, one sees the influence of Freud's religious background in Phillips' conclusion that

Freud's greed for knowledge takes up in a new way the biblical conjoining of sexuality and knowing (cf. Gen. 4:1 "and Adam 'knew' Eve . . . and she conceived").

Another way Freud's Jewish background influenced his greed to know was that this greed included a desire for truth (Phillips, 2014). This notion that the truth is worth pursuing, whatever the cost, is an idea central to his Jewish faith (an idea also shared by the Christian tradition; Gay, 1988; Hoffman, 2011; cf. Freud, 1939). Furthermore, this pursuit of the truth regardless of cost casts Freud in the tradition of the Hebrew prophets (cf. his identification with Moses as one who would speak the truth even at the cost of being rejected by his own followers). Freud saw science as participating in this pursuit of the truth and his desire to make psychoanalysis a means to this pursuit is what drove him to identify psychoanalysis as a "science" (Freud, 1927, 1932b). Thus, for Freud, psychoanalysis became a modern way to pursue this ancient Jewish ideal.

Secularizing Certain Religious Ideas

Some scholars have spoken of psychoanalysis as providing secular versions of religious ideas (e.g., Browning, 1987; Rieff, 1966). Freud himself acknowledged on occasion that this was what he was doing in offering a secular alternative to religion (e.g., Freud & Pfister, 1963). One can certainly see aspects of this idea when one considers the structures of Freud's second model of the mind (i.e., id, ego, superego). Although some (e.g., Sall, 1975) have sought to offer a sort of one-to-one correspondence between Freud's notions of id, ego, and superego and certain religious ideas, the connections are more indirect. For instance, one aspect of the superego is the introjection of parental and social values. In the West these values are deeply influenced by the Jewish and Christian traditions to which Freud was exposed. According to Freud (1927), one of the critical functions of the superego was to induce guilt when one had violated these introjected values; he even valued some of religion's ability to restrain the instinctual drives in that it allowed people to live together in society. In this attempt to explain the origins of guilt Freud is dealing with an important legacy from his Jewish tradition. Furthermore, his suggestion that both religion and psychoanalysis seek to relieve guilt (though by different means) indicates his desire to replace this religious idea with a psychoanalytic one (i.e., the functions of the superego parallel religious ones; see Carter & Narramore, 1979; cf. Rieff, 1979).

There are two other ways Freud's structural model of the mind reflects a secularizing of religious ideas. For instance, when one turns to the ego as the more rational side of mental functioning one recognizes that this valuing of rationality also parallels Jewish ideas valuing the mind (see Freud, 1939; Jones, 1957). In addition, the ego's function of reining in the instinctual impulses also mirrors Jewish (and Christian) ideas of self-control (see Freud's [1914b] valuing his ability to keep his strong emotions in check as a reflection of his Jewish heritage [Rieff, 1979]. Furthermore, in Freud's articulation of the instinctual drives (i.e., the id) what one notes is their intractable quality, rooted as they are in biology. Such hereditary intractability in humans is usually spoken of religiously via the category of "original sin" (usually a Christian focus) and a few of Freud's followers have noted the similarity between these intractable qualities of the drives (especially the so-called "death instinct") and this religious idea (e.g., Klein, 1948; Winnicott, 1971). Thus, in this model of the mind one finds secularized versions of several religious ideas both from Judaism and Christianity.

His General Attitude toward Religion

Finally, we note that another important way Freud's religious identity and background influenced him was to create in him a strong negative attitude toward religion but an attitude also fraught with ambivalence (Wallace, 1983a, b). Throughout his work Freud (1910, 1913, 1927, 1939) addressed a series of questions regarding the origins of religion, its cultural roles and impact on civilization and its attraction to humans. His answers to each of these questions are essentially negative and his conclusions regarding the negative consequences of religion grew stronger with each new treatise, not so surprising given some of the experiences he had with religion noted above.

Concluding Comments

How then does one characterize the influence of Freud's religious journey on his work? The chief legacy is that it left him with ambivalence toward religion. Thus, though he becomes an atheist through the influence of various developmental and cultural factors, he ends up an atheist who could not get away from religious questions and interests (Rizzuto, 1998; Wallace, 1983a). If, in good Freudian fashion one inquired of the sources for Freud's atheism and ambivalence one must return to his childhood. What was it there that made it hard for him to believe and led him to conclude that life must be lived "without the gods"?

One recalls that there were three figures that influenced Freud's earliest religious experiences and provided his sources for his earliest conceptualizations of God. Freud's interactions with his mother during his earliest years were characterized by emotional distance (at least temporarily) and dominance (Breger, 2000; Vitz, 1988) so that one of the images of God that Freud takes from these interactions is that of a hard, emotionally distant God who demands and impinges (Rizzuto, 1998). This is not a God that one can trust or wants to get close to, leaving Freud without the foundation for the ability to believe in a benevolent power. Recall that Freud's (1900) childhood dream associations to his mother involve images of God (or Nature) that demand a death. As a mother substitute Freud's nanny also influenced his earliest images of God and religion (Breger, 2000; Rizzuto, 1998). Freud's associations with the nanny would have left him with images of God as both exciting (in positive and negative ways) yet abandoning (Rizzuto, 1998; Vitz, 1988). In many ways the images that arose from Freud's associations with his nanny seem to be the religion Freud had most in mind as an adult (e.g., in terms of its emotionality) and contributed to his inability to imagine religion as an adult activity. (No doubt the nanny's abandonment of him also contributed to the loss of a foundation for trust in a life-giving God and these interactions with both his "mothers" provide a psychological reason for his inability to believe in a benevolent God as well as for the observed neglect of the mother in Freud's formulations about religion [Rizzuto, 1998]; where the feminine does appear in his theory, it is not particularly complimentary [Rieff, 1979; Vitz, 1988].) When one turns to the associations Freud had between his father and God (recall Freud [1910] claimed that the father is the chief source of one's image of God) one finds, not the wished-for protector but a rather weak God, one that does not draw allegiance or reverence (Rizzuto, 1998).[2]

Thus, Freud's own early development drove him toward atheism, to a need to be self-sufficient. For the adult Freud (1960) then there is no kind and gentle God (or Nature), only a cruel fate before which one must resign. Since one cannot trust the goodness of God or Nature one had best learn to fend for oneself without God. And yet, Freud is ambivalent toward religion as well. The aspects of religion he most denigrated (its emotionality) were the aspects to which he found himself most attracted (cf. his comments that the essence of Judaism remains a mystery, yet one that held him fast at a deep emotional level despite his atheism; Freud, 1960). Freud cannot get away from religious interests and his own ways of acknowledging a "spiritual" realm though he would not name it such.

Notes

1. Wallwork (1991) summarizes five objections Freud (1930) had to what he saw as the Christian version of this ethic of loving one's neighbor as oneself: 1) It is impossible to keep given how one's instinctual leanings (e.g., aggression and narcissism) limit those to whom one can reliably extend love. 2) It is unjust to those with whom one has special ties, such as family. Freud sees as given that all social interactions require some level of reciprocity and therefore argues that those with special ties to us have greater expectations of consideration than those without such ties; to violate such expectations by loving indiscriminately he thought an injustice to those for whom such expectations were both natural and rational. 3) Not all are worthy of one's love. Freud notes that compared to family or clan, strangers are more likely to be hostile toward one; he thought an indiscriminate love command ill prepared one for such realities. 4) Its poor handling of aggression promotes hostility toward outsiders. That is, he saw the love command promoting denial and repression of one's aggressive drives. With no acceptable conscious expression of these frightening feelings (e.g., through a good-natured joke), these hostile drives go underground and emerge in overt hostility to those outside one's immediate social network. 5) Its extraordinary requirements create unhappiness in those who try to keep them. Wallwork further notes that Freud's interpretation of the love command is not the only way to understand the injunction to love one's neighbor as oneself. He reviews both Jewish and Christian alternatives to Freud's interpretation that it requires indiscriminate equal love toward all.

2. There is some possibility (some argue probability) that Freud was molested as a child though scholars disagree as to whether the person responsible was his father, his nanny, or both. These claims are often based on methods that require some level of speculation such as trying to read between the lines of certain passages from Freud's writings and letters (especially those to his friend Wilhelm Fleiss in what is often termed his "self-analysis") to ascertain the level of autobiographical disclosure they contain, trying to better understand what certain elusive phrases meant, and in some cases treating denials and perceived omissions as "defenses." Because of the historical distance, the elusive nature of the sources and the interpretive methods used, the level of certainty that can be ascribed to these claims remains open (e.g., see Krull, 1986; Kuptersmid, 1992; Partridge, 2014; Roudinesco, 2016; Whitebook, 2017). If Freud were abused as a child, this would add a significant layer of understanding to his rejection of religion.

CHAPTER TWO

Carl Jung

As a young child growing up in a pastor's home, Carl Jung was surrounded by the sights and sounds of varying religious activity. From the rituals of his father's parish life (e.g., baptisms, burials, etc.) to lively stories from his mother about wandering spirits, the young Carl found himself both attracted and excited as well as frightened and confused by these activities. One sees how deeply these experiences impacted him when one realizes that Jung spent the remainder of his life trying to understand and make sense of religious experiences, including his parents' and his own. This chapter follows that journey. It tells the story of Jung's early struggles with the religious sentiments of his parents through his own religious misgivings as a child and adolescent to his adult explorations of religious phenomena and his conclusion that religion is one of the most formative forces in human development (Jung, 1957; McGuire & Hall, 1977).

Few people who read this book will not have heard of Carl Jung. Even less will not have experienced his influence on contemporary culture which is multiple and varied. From the often unrecognized influence of Jung on everything from the spirituality of the Alcoholics Anonymous movement and its concept of a higher power that helps one overcome addiction (Finley, 2000; McCabe, 2015) to the blockbuster cinematic production of the Star Wars saga (e.g., with its concept of "the force" which is neither good nor evil in itself but can be turned to either and the well-known "archetypes" of the wise old man [Yoda], the hero [Skywalker] and the shadow [Vader]. See Ellerhoff, 2015; Ryback, 1983), people have drunk deeply from the Jungian well, whether they know this or not. Jung has further influenced contemporary spirituality through the contemporary pastoral counseling movement (e.g., Dittes, 1990; Perry, 1991; Sanford, 1989) as well as in a variety of "new age" religions (Tacey, 2001; see for instance the "Age of Aquarius" popularized in the song of that title and Jung, 1958a). Even the contemporary appreciation for "spirituality" but without tying it to historic or organized religion echoes Jung's influence. This chapter explores this influential psychologist and his enduring legacy by focusing on part of Jung's story: how his own religious background influenced his life and work.

In trying to summarize this part of Jung's story, one notes that the literature on Jung is almost as voluminous as that on Freud. As with the literature on Freud it is impossible to do it justice even when one narrows the focus to the literature on Jung and religion. Because religion and spirituality were central to Jung's background and work, this literature alone fills several bookshelves. Thus, this chapter is not exhaustive in its review of what is known about Jung's religious background, its influence on his work, and of what he had to say about things religious.

What Is Known of Jung's Religious Journey?

This section summarizes what is known of Jung's religious journey from his early years in the home of a Protestant pastor to his adult affirmations of the role of religion in his life. It draws from autobiographical materials as well as from materials amassed by his various biographers. It tells the story of a young man intrigued, puzzled, and sometimes frightened by the religiosity he experienced in both himself and his parents. It tells the story of how he came to understand these sometimes frightening experiences as full of grace and calling and of his unfolding understanding, embrace, and execution of a personal mission to revitalize the symbols of religious life for a new age.

Religion in Jung's Early Childhood Home

Jung is unique as the only psychologist in this book to grow up in the home of a pastor. Jung's father Paul was a pastor in the national church of Switzerland, the Swiss Reformed Church, part of the Protestant tradition in Switzerland that went back to John Calvin (Bair, 2003; Jung, 1961). Thus, Jung grew up in a household where religion and spirituality were central to the functioning of the family. As a pastor Jung's father was involved in the various tasks of parish life: study, preaching, parish visitation, and of course, the rituals associated with births, marriages, and deaths. As we shall see, the young Jung's observations and imaginings connected to these rituals played a key role in his own religious development.

The religious atmosphere in the Jung home had a long history. Not only was his father a pastor but both of Jung's parents came from families in which several of the men were pastors or theologians (Hayman, 1999). Although Paul Jung's father had been a doctor and a Catholic, he had a significant religious conversion to Protestantism under the German theologian, Friedrich Schleiermacher. Paul Jung showed promise as a scholar with his dissertation on a tenth-century Hebrew commentary of the Song of Solomon and seemed destined for a life of scholarship until financial concerns forced him into the pastorate (Bair, 2003). As part of a pastor's household, Jung was expected to attend church regularly, which he did up to his confirmation (Freeman, 1959; Hannah, 1991).

Jung was the fourth born but the first child to survive in this family (Bair, 2003); furthermore, he was an only child until his ninth year. Jung (1961) reported that his relationship with his father was characterized by two qualities: reliability and powerlessness. More will be said about Jung's sense of his father's weakness in the section on adolescence. For now, one notes that the sense of his father's reliability dates to very early in Jung's life and seems to have provided a steady, if somewhat mundane presence as well as predictability for the young child that was lacking in his interactions with his mother. But even though Jung described his father as reliable, he does not seem to have received from his father (or mother) the kind of consistency and reliability that are crucial to the young child for acquiring the solid psychological and emotional foundation on which further development depends (Atwood & Stolorow, 1993; Feldman, 1992; cf. Winnicott, 1964). Furthermore, the fact that by the time he entered grammar school Jung's parents had begun to sleep in separate rooms points to problems in the relationship between his parents which in turn impacted their interactions with their children. Jung began to sleep in the room with his father and from there he often observed his mother wandering the halls at night (Bair, 2003).

As noted above, Jung's mother, Emilie, also came from a long line of religious leaders and teachers. Her father and several of her brothers were either pastors or theologians (Hayman, 1999). Her father had been the chief bishop of Basel when she was growing up and possessed a curious spirituality. For instance, Emilie's father kept an empty chair in his study for his dead first wife with whom he continued to have conversations even after his marriage to Emilie's mother. He also required his daughters, including Emilie, to stand behind him while he prepared sermons to swat away various ghosts and spirits that tried to interfere with his preparations. To add to this, his second wife (Emilie's mother) was said to possess the gift of "second sight" or clairvoyance (along with several of her sisters) (Bair, 2003). Although such spirituality may sound strange to modern ears, Jung (1961) remarked that such superstitious aspects of religion were common in Switzerland well into the nineteenth century. Thus, from an early age Jung's mother developed sensitivity to supernatural happenings and seemed most alive when regaling others with stories of such happenings. Jung's mother (along with her sisters) was involved in and helped conduct several séances over the years, including some in the parsonage (Bair, 2003). Jung (1961) found his mother's spirituality uncanny and the source of several anxiety dreams (cf. Atwood & Stolorow, 1993).

In addition to her deep interest in spirits and ghosts, Jung's mother seems to have been a deeply troubled woman who also suffered from depression. She was hospitalized several months for her depression when Jung was about two. During her absence, Jung was cared for by two women—one a small, olive-complexioned maid who seems to have loved him (and whom he later used as an image of the anima—a central concept in his theory explained below). The other person was a girl from nearby who came regularly to the parsonage to play games and who would later become his mother-in-law (Bair, 2003). Because of his mother's absence at such a young age, Jung reported that he came to associate the word love with her absence and its attendant sense of her unreliability. Thus, he wrote that he came to suspect the word love whenever it was spoken, including references to the love of Jesus (Jung, 1961). These experiences also helped promote both an isolation and a self-reliance in the child along with a concentration on the inner life (Hayman, 1999; McLynn, 1996).

As with his description of his father, Jung (1961) also characterized his relationship to his mother by two words. In addition to her unreliability, he spoke of her being uncanny. This uncanniness seems to have manifest in several ways. One was Jung's experience of two personalities within his mother. What he called her "No.1" personality was most present by day and was that of the demure pastor's wife. Jung experienced this aspect of his mother as warm and nurturing. But especially at night she seemed to manifest another side of herself (what he called her "No. 2" personality). Jung experienced this aspect of his mother as dark and mysterious; it also seemed to be associated with other-worldly spectral images that he would see floating out of her room into the halls (Jung, 1961). Also, she would sometimes speak as if under her breath, but Jung understood these to be words spoken to him by her No. 2 personality. He experienced these words as cutting to the "core of [his] being" (Jung, 1961, p. 49).

Later, his mother's involvement with séances also contributed to his experience of her as mysterious (Bair, 2003). All of this gave his mother what Jung (1961) called a more earthy type of religion (in contrast to the institutional religion of his father). Jung found this uncanny side of his mother both attractive and repellant. His own later involvement in, and investigation of, séances testify to both his attraction and wariness regarding this type of spirituality in that though he participated in these events he wanted to understand them in naturalistic categories (Bair, 2003). This experience of his mother's uncanniness fueled Jung's interest in occult spirituality throughout his life and work.

In addition to being an only child for his first nine years Jung was a rather solitary, introspective child (Hayman, 1999), the kind of personality he would later describe as introverted (Jung, 1921). In addition to the impact of his interactions with his parents, such a child has an active inner life and so it was with the young Carl. To the impact of his interactions with his reliable but powerless father and unreliable but uncanny mother and how these influenced how he thought about religious things, one must give some attention to young Carl's own direct religious experiences and how they influenced both the way he thought about religious things and the way he engaged them. In his late life autobiography, he tells several stories that give insight to his religious/spiritual development during his early years (Jung, 1961).

One incident that Jung recounted from his childhood that was formative in terms of his religious development was a dream that he dated to his third or fourth year. In this dream he descended Alice-in-Wonderland-like down a hole in the ground where he encountered a treelike entity that was covered with skin, had a single eye, and sat atop a throne. As he gazed upon this terrifying symbol, he heard the voice of his mother state, "yes, just look at him. That is the man-eater" (Jung, 1961, p. 12). The phrase rendered "man-eater" in English comes from a German word that can indicate "to take unto oneself" (i.e., to occupy, eat, devour) and was a phrase that had several associations for the young Carl (Bair, 2003; Hayman, 1999). First, this phrase was associated with a childhood prayer that his mother sang to him at bedtime. In this hymn the Lord Jesus is asked to protect (or "take") his children from Satan (cf. the English prayer of children: "Now I lay me down to sleep; I pray the Lord my soul to keep. And if I die before I wake, I pray the Lord my soul to take"). The young Carl interpreted the lines from this song to indicate that Jesus would "take" (i.e., eat) the children before Satan could (Hayman, 1999; Jung, 1961). This notion of Jesus taking his children had further associations in the young child's mind from his inquiry about certain funeral rites with men in black coats and being told of the people lowered into the ground that the Lord Jesus had taken them unto himself. Jung recounted that this dream left him with a dread about the Lord Jesus (Jung, 1961). Later, as an adult he wrote of his associations to this dream that it was years before he recognized the phallic qualities of the object and that he was never quite sure of the referent for the man-eater comment. Nevertheless, this image of a "subterranean God 'not to be named'" gets mixed together with his childhood understandings of Jesus and so remained with him

> throughout my youth, reappearing whenever anyone spoke too emphatically about Lord Jesus. Lord Jesus never became quite real for me, never quite acceptable, never quite loveable, for again and again I would think of his underground counterpart, a frightful revelation which had been accorded me without my seeking it. . . . Lord Jesus seemed to me in some ways a god of death, helpful, it is true, in that he scared away the terrors of the night, but himself uncanny, a crucified and bloody corpse. Secretly, his love and kindness which I always heard praised, appeared doubtful to me. (Jung, 1961, p. 13)

Note that these associations point to both a duality and unreliability in Jesus, a description not unlike that of his parents, especially his mother (Atwood & Stolorow, 1993). One also notes that his experience of this dream fueled an early ambivalence toward Jesus as well as Christianity that remained with him throughout his life.

Jung's solitary, introverted nature was also evident in attempts to escape the periodic tension between his parents. For instance, Jung would often retreat outside to sit alone and to calm himself (Jung, 1961). Jung also seems to have been able to sooth himself by engaging in ritual-like behavior where he stuffed pieces of paper into a stone wall and lit them afire (when he was about seven and again at nine). An incident that gives witness to Jung's solitary self-soothing is his carving a little wooden man from a two-inch piece of wood cut from his school ruler. He painted the little wooden man to look like the funeral men in black coats and secreted it in a place known only to him. He brought the little man gifts, including a special stone, and would visit him when he felt anxious.

Perhaps because of his own solitary nature or perhaps because of his mother's duality, Jung early on came to experience himself as having two personalities as well. His No. 1 personality was drawn to science and reason, while his No. 2 personality favored more mystical experiences (Jung, 1961; Wehr, 1987). Indicative of the duality he often felt Jung (1961) reported that sometimes when he escaped, he would sit upon a certain stone. There he would play a game in which he was uncertain whether he was the boy sitting on the stone or he was the stone on which a boy was sitting. Another aspect of this duality was his experience of himself as both a schoolboy with lessons to do and of also being a wise old man. It will come as no surprise that Jung's introverted nature also showed up in his childhood religious experiences as well. For instance, he reported that his dream of the underground phallic symbol was a solitary experience suffered alone and not shared with anyone for over 60 years (Jung, 1961).

Religion in Jung's Adolescent Years

Jung continued to have significant yet solitary religious experiences as he moved into his adolescent years. Of particular significance is an event Jung related as having happened about his eleventh year. It is told here because it seems to illustrate Jung's being on the cusp of his adolescence with the new ways of thinking that come during this developmental period (though the literalness of the images points to pre-adolescent thinking as well; Piaget, 1970). He speaks of a certain consciousness of both God and self coming to him at around this age (Jung, 1961). The event involved a waking dream or vision that he had one day on his walk home from school.

He had this vision as he passed the cathedral that was at the center of the city. Suddenly, he was overwhelmed by a disturbing thought (or vision) that he willfully suppressed for several days. Finally, when he could no longer suppress these frightful thoughts, he yielded to them. In his vision he saw the cathedral bathed with glorious sunlight and saw God on his throne looking down upon it. Then, in his boyish vision God defecated, with the result that the glimmering roof was shattered, and the cathedral walls torn apart. This was the thought he had not been able to face. Jung found this vision so disturbing that he could not share it with anyone (and did not for over six decades). He pondered how it was that God would allow him to have such a thought. He eventually concluded that God wanted and made him have this thought as a kind of test of whether he was able to trust God's grace as sufficient to cover him despite such thoughts. Having given himself over to having the thought he reported, "I felt an enormous, an indescribable relief. Instead of the expected damnation, grace had come upon me" (Jung, 1961, p. 40).

This incident is interesting in three regards. First, Jung is hardly the first young boy to have imaginings about the elimination habits of God. What is unusual is that in Jung's case, he felt he could not share this thought with anyone, especially his parents. He thought his father would not understand and might only chide him for such questions and he felt his mother too dark and mysterious to approach (Jung, 1961). This left the child with a solitary struggle. Such solitary struggles would almost prove his undoing at a later point in his life.

Second, the vision of God, the cathedral and its aftermath also left Jung with a new understanding of God. This experience convinced Jung that God was a living reality, a God that could be encountered in gracious acceptance and not just an idea to which one gave intellectual assent. This God he had encountered could be experienced apart from the rituals and beliefs of the institutional church which seemed to hinder people from being able to experience God's living grace and presence (Jung, 1961). In fact, he came to distrust the institutional church's portrayal of God because Jung's encounter with God also made him aware of something different about God that he had not heard from the church's teachings: God had a dark side! After all, it was God who had forced Jung to have those thoughts of God destroying the cathedral. He wrote: "Consciously I was religious in a Christian sense, though always with the reservation: 'But it is not so certain as all that!' . . . And when religious teachings were pumped into me and I was told 'this is beautiful and this is good' I would think to myself 'yes, but there is something else, something very secret that people don't know about'" (Jung, 1961, p. 22). This new, secret understanding of God's nature would fuel Jung's interests and explorations for the rest of his life.

Third, in addition to the more immediate interpretation attached to the vision, its chief significance lies in the meanings that Jung attaches to it later in life. In many ways this vision is formative to the way the adult Jung came to view contemporary Christianity and his role in trying to revitalize the symbols of his childhood religion.

In addition to this singular vision which Jung continued to ponder the remainder of his life, there are two other related events in Jung's adolescence that give insight into his religious sensibilities during these years. The first involves several things that happened in connection with his confirmation in the Swiss Reformed Church. During this period, Jung reported that he mostly found discussions and questions about the teachings of the church boring. This was due in part because as a result of his vision noted above Jung felt he had received secret knowledge about God that was never discussed in church (Jung, 1961). However, since confirmation was an expected part of development, especially for the pastor's son, Jung grudgingly participated in this boredom until he saw that eventually part of what was covered in the catechism was the doctrine of the Trinity. Long puzzled by this doctrine Jung waited with eager anticipation for these lessons. His disappointment was palpable when his father announced that he himself did not understand this part of the catechism and would skip it. The disappointed Jung had only one other hope and that was the transformation that would attend his actual confirmation ceremony. Jung wrote of his hope that this experience would give him a special sense of God's wonder and work in the world. However, this ceremony also was a grave disappointment. He felt nothing special, felt that nothing had changed within him or within the others that participated in the ceremony. To Jung's eye, those who participated seemed to be going through the ceremony in a rote kind of way. In fact, seeing a laborer in formal dress for the occasion made both the man and the ceremony seem somehow foreign to Jung (1961).

The other event from Jung's adolescence that gives insight into his religious sensibilities concerns a series of observations of his father's religious life. The powerlessness that Jung associated with his father was primarily manifested in his father's faith (Jung, 1961). Jung thought several things associated with his father's faith made him weak. First, Jung thought his father had become rather unthinking about his faith, a position Jung felt his father also encouraged in him, i.e., to simply "believe" rather than to think about the things of God (e.g., his father skipping over the part of the catechism regarding the Trinity).

In addition to this unthinking quality Jung (1961) also thought his father had grave doubts about his faith (which contributed to his father's frequent irritability and sadness, common symptoms of depression). This belief was especially strengthened when Jung heard his father pray: "once I heard him praying. He struggled desperately to keep his faith. I was shaken and outraged at once, because I saw how hopelessly he was entrapped by the church and its theological thinking. . . . Now I understood the deepest meaning of my earlier experience [the vision of God destroying the cathedral]; God himself had disavowed theology and the church founded upon it" (Jung, 1961, p. 93). Jung (1961) came to see his father as a tragic figure about whom he could only feel sadness, a figure trapped in a religion he did not fully believe and in which Jung felt he had no experiential encounter with God or God's grace.

Obviously, these religious experiences from his childhood and adolescence left a lasting impact on Jung's later religious life and thought. On the negative side, Jung had struggled with some ambivalent feelings toward Lord Jesus since a young child. As an adolescent these ambivalent feelings were strengthened both by his perception of his father's ambivalent feelings toward the Christian faith and his own experiences of a darkness in God. Because he saw Christianity as so ineffective in his father's life Jung came to think of it as ineffective for most people; it certainly was for him. Furthermore, his vision of God destroying the cathedral left Jung with the conclusion that God also was no longer interested in the institutional church and that the institutional church knew little if anything of an experiential encounter with God (Jung, 1961). Thus, religion came to have a very private dimension for

Jung, not surprising given his strong introverted nature. How to address this ineffectiveness of the Christian church would occupy Jung later as an adult.

Finally, one can see the working out of the impact of these early experiences in Jung's adult religious life in two other ways. First, these experiences caused Jung to give great authority to dreams and visions. Second, Jung (1961) will later point to these experiences as fostering a self-awareness that his consciousness was bigger than himself, an idea that Jung will devote considerable attention to in his future work.

Religion in Jung's Young Adult Years

This period takes in Jung's time at college and his first years at the Burghölzli (psychiatric) Hospital. Jung's continued religious interests and development during this time are seen in several events. During his undergraduate days Jung occasionally spoke to his fraternity on various topics. These talks show his preference for spiritualism over materialism as he often raised the question why those who studied science refused to even consider such claims (Bair, 2003). In one presentation Jung argued for "the reinstatement of 'the mystery of a metaphysical world, a metaphysical order' to the center of Christianity" (cited in Bair, 2003, p. 46), a theme that would occupy him for years to come. (Ellenberger [1970] reports that Jung once told this group that he had never had an experience of God but the context [and his subsequent writings, e.g., Jung, 1961] suggest that this was an overstatement made to counter the remarks of another student.)

During Jung's time at college other events back home piqued his interest in spiritualism as well. One mysterious event involved his mother's attributing an ominous cause to the dining room table loudly splitting down the middle for no apparent reason. A similar event was the family hearing another loud noise only to find the cause to have been a kitchen knife that had shattered while lying in the drawer. Such events sensitized Jung to occult experiences and fueled a desire to understand what was happening in such experiences (Bair, 2003; Jung, 1961).

Most significant in this regard was that Jung began to participate in a series of séances conducted by his mother and her kin during his college years (Bair, 2003). He was especially taken with the abilities of a young cousin, Helene Preiswerk, who was a medium for contact with dead relatives, including his maternal grandfather (the one who had kept an empty chair for his dead wife). During his medical studies Jung would undertake to write up an analysis of his experiences during the séances for his doctoral dissertation. Titled "On the Psychology and Pathology of so-called Occult Phenomena," his task in the dissertation was one of investigating psychic phenomena from a scientific viewpoint; in this work he hoped to reconcile science and spiritualism (Bair, 2003; Hayman, 1999). In the dissertation he argued that such experiences were due to various states of mind in the medium and not to the supernatural (a position with which he did not always remain consistent) (Ellenberger, 1970; McLynn, 1996).

These séances seem formative to Jung's religious sensibilities in several ways. On the one hand this early involvement in spiritualism is something that Jung engaged in for much of his adult life as well (Bair, 2003; Hayman, 1999). No doubt Jung's interest in these kinds of spiritualistic experiences were connected to his early fascination with the mysterious and uncanny spirituality of his mother. It also seems that in both participating in such experiences as well as trying to analyze them scientifically, Jung was trying to understand his own experience of having dual personalities (i.e., his No. 1 with its feet in the scientific world and his No. 2 with its access to deeper realities) (cf. Jung, 1961). Similarly, Jung's observations of and experiences with his cousin seem to have attuned him to other divisions in states of the self (McLynn, 1996). Furthermore, that these spiritualistic exercises seemed to allow his cousin access to special knowledge might be seen as a precursor to his notions regarding what he came to call the collective unconscious (see key ideas; Jung, 1928).

When Jung took up his position as psychiatrist at the Burghölzli his continued interest in religion can be seen in his fascination with the religious language and symbolism of his patients (Hayman, 1999). Some of these experiences caused him to deepen his conviction that some of his patients might be accessing a deeper wisdom than they could have known from their own life experience. He saw such experiences in his patients as having a parallel to some of his own early experiences of access to a wisdom beyond his years (Jung, 1961). (Jung later explored such insights of his and his patients as examples of the collective unconscious; Jung, 1919). It was also during his early days at the Burghölzli that Jung began to read widely in the literature of mythology and began to ponder the presence of universal symbols in various mythologies and religions (Ellenberger, 1970).

Religion in Jung's Adult Years

Jung's adult years are rich and varied in terms of his religious development. His adult explorations of spirituality often involved new places and ideas while some explorations had continuity with the religious experiences of his childhood. One can characterize Jung's adult religious journey in two related ways. At times his adult religious development is that of someone trying to find an alternative spirituality to the ineffective Christian spirituality he observed in his father and the institutional church. At other times his seems a journey of one who longs to revitalize the symbols of the Christian faith of his youth so that a new generation might find life in them. This section is organized around several series of events that provide some insight into Jung's religious development over his adult life. Because this takes in such a long period this section is larger than usual. To aid in readability it is subdivided into his early years, middle years, and later years.

Early Adult Years

Jung (1961) disclosed in his late-life autobiography that religious ideas had occupied him his whole life though this preoccupation was often very private, unknown even to those closest to him. For instance, his daughter once stated: "when I was about twelve or so, I didn't pray anymore because I thought it wouldn't please him, because he always made fun of theologians. . . . I thought he wasn't religious at all, and it was only through reading his books that I discovered he'd been a religious man" (reported in Hayman, 1999, pp. 221–222; see the Rogers chapter for a similar comment by Natalie Rogers on her father).

During his time at the Burghölzli Jung sought to understand the often confusing and convoluted ways in which his psychiatric patients tried to communicate. Influenced by his supervisor, Eugen Bleuler, and coupled with his reading in mythology and religious symbolism, Jung began to interpret his patients' sometimes incoherent ramblings as symbolic language (Bair, 2003; Hayman, 1999). Jung noted that their speech often contained religious language and illustrations and he was sometimes struck by the correspondence between the utterances of his patients and his study of religious myths and rituals both ancient and contemporary. One correspondence in particular intrigued him. A patient with schizophrenia said to him one day that the phallus of the sun was the origin of the wind (Jung, 1911–1912). Although others might have dismissed this as the ramblings of a disorganized mind, Jung was struck by how much this sounded like something he had read regarding an ancient religion. Because of the patient's social and intellectual circumstances Jung was convinced the patient could not have known this information from books and yet the patient's pronouncement sounded to Jung as though it mirrored the Mithraic myth regarding a long tube that descended from the sun being the origin of the wind (Freeman, 1959; Jung, 1936a). Such incidents caused Jung to ponder again whether there might be a larger pool of wisdom available to humans if only they knew how to access it.

His work and reading at the Burghölzli also brought Jung into contact with the writings of Freud (Bair, 2003; Jung, 1961). From this reading and his subsequent correspondence with Freud a friendship developed around their shared interests in trying to understand their troubled patients. Space does not permit a thorough summary of the intricacies of this friendship, but it is worth noting that from the beginning there was a tension between the two over how to understand and work with religious material (Hayman, 1999; Jung, 1961; Kradin, 2015; McGuire & Hall, 1977; Palmer, 1997). From his early childhood experiences Jung was open to and explored a wider range of spiritualities than Freud was comfortable with. Although Jung thought one could bring a scientific viewpoint to the study of religious phenomena, Freud suspected Jung of having more than a scientific interest in religion and perhaps thought Jung's interest in religion gave more credence than was helpful to what Freud (1927) considered a competitor to the new science he was developing (Bair, 2003; Rieff, 1966).

Freud's suspicion of Jung was heightened during a face-to-face meeting in Vienna. They were discussing paranormal psychology and precognition and Jung had relayed his family experiences with the cracking table and breaking knife (Bair, 2003; McLynn, 1996). Freud expressed skepticism about supernatural causes but Jung, being ever sensitive to such happenings, felt a burning sensation in his diaphragm just before a loud crack occurred in Freud's bookcase. Both men jumped, startled that the bookcase might topple over on them. Jung identified this as a kind of precognition. Freud was skeptical. Jung told him that there would be another similar report shortly. No sooner had he said this when the bookcase gave another loud crack. Freud was visibly uncomfortable. Before they parted company Jung reported that Freud told him that they must defend psychoanalysis as a bulwark against the "black tide of mud ... of occultism" (Jung, 1961, p. 150). Hence, early on Freud seemed to fear Jung might substitute a mystical explanation for neurosis rather than the sexual one Freud (1905) proposed. This was partially confirmed by a major work on religious symbols and their transformation in the unconscious that Jung (1911–1912) produced during this period. In this book Jung concluded that neuroses may have religious as well as sexual origins (Ulanov & Dueck, 2008).

Such differences over the role of spirituality in neurosis and human life presaged a short-lived friendship between Freud and Jung. From his own experiences Jung felt that religious experiences could be powerful noetic experiences (i.e., experiences that give knowledge or insight) that tapped a wider reality than that which could be apprehended by conscious activity alone (Jung 1961, 1938). Freud remained suspicious and in the end Jung's interest in the occult and spirituality contributed to their parting company. One might note that Freud's reaction to Jung's mystical bent seems odd considering Freud's own interest in such phenomena (e.g., telepathy even to late in his life; see the Freud chapter). Nevertheless, their differences over spirituality contributed to the breakup of their friendship although this difference is by no means the entire story. There are a host of other personal and political reasons for the breakup that cannot be treated here (see Bair, 2003; Breger, 2000; Gay, 1988; Hayman, 1999).

The breakup with Freud portended a particularly significant period in Jung's life; it was a period of crisis rich in its impact on his personal and religious development (Ellenberger, 1970; Wehr, 1987). Jung called this period his "confrontation with the unconscious" (Jung, 1961). Ellenberger has called this a period of "creative illness"; others have been less charitable and attribute an active psychosis to Jung (McLynn, 1996). Jung himself wondered at times whether he might be descending into madness and had to frequently remind himself of the basics of his identity (e.g., I'm a husband, father, a doctor with patients, etc.) to help sustain him through this crisis (Jung, 1961, p. 189).

At the heart of this crisis was a journey of self-discovery. Why was he here on the earth? What was his purpose in life? What were the story/symbols that gave him meaning? Jung had concluded that Christianity and its symbols no longer provided a sufficient story by which he could live, but he did not yet know what would provide a sufficient defining story (or "myth") for his life (Jung, 1961; Wehr, 1987). During this period of crisis and self-exploration Jung received many visions and dreams that he felt guided him toward answers (some of these he would spend years trying to decipher) (Bair, 2003; McLynn, 1996). Jung also kept a journal (later published as the *Red Book*) of his experiences during this time and these reveal a time of various mystical experiences where Jung was often visited by various figures and spirits that conveyed information and insights (Bair, 2003; McLynn, 1996). One figure from his visions, Philemon, was a composite being with one part an old man that Jung described as of "Egypto-Hellenistic atmosphere with a Gnostic coloration" (Jung, 1961, p. 182). Jung had visits with Philemon over a period of about three years in which Jung received many utterances he did not understand. When Jung decided to write some of these conversations down a series of paranormal activities occurred in his household; Jung felt his house had become filled with spirits. When Jung asked them what this was about, they answered "we have come back from Jerusalem where we found not what we sought" (Jung, 1961, p. 191). Jung immediately began to feverishly write and the haunting ceased. He wrote for three days in a state akin to automatic writing (Hayman, 1999) and at the end had produced a manuscript he called "Seven Sermons to the Dead," a most curious collection of musings and aphorisms which Jung tended to keep secret most of his life though he occasionally distributed a copy privately to friends or colleagues (Bair, 2003; these were finally published as an appendix to *Memories, Dreams and Reflections*). One finds in these sermons the germ of several of Jung's later ideas. Because these experiences seem like those of Jung's psychiatric patients some have seen this time as a period of psychosis survived (McLynn. 1996). Jung (1961) concluded that these experiences had been a journey of spiritual enlightenment, that they had been a profound encounter with what he will come to call the collective unconscious.

A key therapeutic technique emerged from this period as well. It involved a kind of yielding to and exploring of the strange sensations and visions in what he came to call active imagination (Jung, 1916, 1921). He would engage in a kind of forced concentration on the various elements of the vision to see what might emerge from them. In submerging himself in his visions Jung had faced and conquered his fear that he might go completely mad and eventually emerged more integrated for letting these various aspects of himself manifest rather than resisting them (Jung, 1961). He would use a similar method with clients.

In terms of his spiritual development during this period Jung became more convinced of the ineffectiveness of Christian symbols. Thus began a search for religious symbols with more vitality; he found this in the ancient religion of Gnosticism (Jung, 1961). Gnosticism had arisen among the Greek philosophers and had influenced early Christian thought before being condemned as a heresy in the second to third centuries (Perkins, 2007). Jung (1961) thought Gnosticism's path to salvation or enlightenment through secret knowledge accorded with his own early experience of having been given secret knowledge of God and provided Jung further evidence that his experiences tapped a larger pool of knowledge that had been present through the centuries (i.e., the collective unconscious) (Hannah, 1974). Furthermore, Jung thought that the Western church had condemned Gnosticism because the Gnostics had addressed the dark side of God which the church did not wish to acknowledge but which he also knew from personal revelation.

Middle Adult Years

In the end Jung concluded that his studies of Gnosticism had been a dead end because he could not trace a historical thread to their connection with contemporary life (Jung, 1961). Nevertheless, he continued to look for vital symbols to guide one's life. A second place he looked was in other religions. For instance, Jung spent several months in Africa talking with various shamans about their varied beliefs about God and creation (Jung, 1961). A visit to the Pueblo Indians in the U.S. had much the same purpose. Jung also became interested in the *I Ching* from Chinese religion (a book on a method for discerning the fates) and came to consult it when he faced important decisions (Hayman, 1999; McLynn, 1996). In these religions Jung sought to discern the common themes and symbols that spoke to the journey of spiritual enlightenment. Jung saw in religions a symbolization of psychic forces and began to formulate religious ideas and symbols in psychological language (e.g., Jung, 1942a). For instance, his adaptation of religious rituals like the *I Ching*, were ways he sought to tap into the energy of a larger (collective) unconscious in humans. This larger unconscious became a manifestation for Jung of what others called God: "I prefer the term 'the unconscious,' knowing that I might equally speak of 'God' or 'daimon' if I wished to express myself in mythic language" (Jung, 1961, pp. 336–37; cf. Jung, 1921, 1952).

In his continuing search for vital religious symbolizations of the psychic life Jung began to study the writings of the alchemists, those medieval thinkers best known for their attempts to turn base metals into gold. However, Jung thought there must be more to their studies than this. He noted that the Western church had also condemned these writings and he wondered if it might be that they possessed a symbolic vitality similar to Gnosticism. Was it that alchemy also was open to the darker side of God, and this too contributed to its condemnation? As he studied various alchemical texts, Jung concluded that these studies regarding the transformation of physical elements were in reality explorations about the spiritual transformation of the self (Jung, 1944, 1961). Here, in the writing of the alchemists, Jung found a way beyond the impasse he had arrived at in his study of Gnosticism. The alchemical texts provided a historical bridge from the ideas in Gnosticism to ideas being expounded in contemporary Western (i.e., Christian) culture (Jung, 1961). At last Jung thought he had found what he was looking for: ancient writings that had symbolized the spiritual quest in the language of the science of its day. This was what Jung hoped to do for a new generation, to revitalize religious symbols and doctrines by reinterpreting them in his version of the language of a scientific psychology (Jung, 1938, 1957, 1961).

Jung's alchemical studies had again raised the issue of a dark side to God with the associated questions of evil and how this is to be accounted for in a religious system (Jung, 1944, 1961). Jung had not found the two main ways that Christianity answered this question satisfactory. Christians either defined evil as an absence of good—*privatio boni*) or appealed to a dualism that saved God from evil by personifying it in Satan (Jung, 1952). From his own experiences of God's dark side Jung also had come to believe there might be salutatory elements to this side of God—after all, his encounter with the dark side of God had been an experience of grace (Jung, 1942b, 1961). Thus, he sought a different answer that might more fully account for his own religious experiences. In his search he turned to examine the religions of the East (especially Hinduism and Buddhism) and on a trip to India this question of the presence of evil was uppermost in his mind (Jung, 1961).

Although he was attracted to the religions of the East because they did not appeal to a dualism to explain the presence of evil Jung nevertheless concluded that these religions did not take evil seriously enough, treating it as an illusion to be overcome by enlightenment. Jung thought evil to be a reality in the universe that must be directly addressed. This he felt the religions of the East did not do (Jung, 1961; cf. Stein, 1995).

Later Adult Years

Jung returned from India with a renewed appreciation for the religious symbols of the Christian West in which he had grown up. Although he thought Western Christianity given to a dualism in its doctrine of God, nevertheless he thought it to take the problem of evil more seriously and so Jung found a new purpose in trying to give renewed life to the religious symbols of the West. Thus, he turned his attention to revitalizing the symbols of Christianity in a new psychological language (i.e., that of the collective unconscious). In this way Jung thought he might renew an interest in spirituality for a new generation in the West. Thus, in the latter part of his adult life we see Jung engaged in reinterpreting a series of Christian doctrines concerned with God, Christ, the Trinity, and the problem of evil (Jung, 1961). Some of Jung's ideas on these doctrines are addressed in the sections that follow.

As Jung aged his reflections on his experiences, including those he deemed religious, took on an increasingly psychological framing; in similar manner his writings on religious topics as well as reflections on his religious experiences became applications of his psychological theory. For instance, an earlier reflection on the self as a symbol of Christ is later reversed to an interpretation of Christ as a symbol of the self (Jung, 1951; McLynn, 1996). Another example comes from his alchemical studies where he takes up an idea that had troubled him since his youth, the question of how one might reconcile the disparate elements of one's personality (e.g., conscious and unconscious, introversion and extraversion, dominant and non-dominant functions in personality types, his own No. 1 and No.2 personalities). In *Mysterium Coniunctionis* Jung (1955–1956) articulated the goal of life as the conjoining and balance of opposites (he also called this the "transcendent" function [Jung [1916], a psychological principle that is applied even to God who must conjoin both light and darkness, good and evil to be whole (cf.

Jung, 1952). Likewise, spiritual maturity in humans meant encountering and, in some ways, embracing one's "shadow" side.

Before bringing this section on Jung's adult religious development to a close, the question of anti-Semitism in Jung needs to be addressed. Freud had frequently made such accusations during their friendship (Bair, 2003), but such charges are inevitably overlaid with the bitter layers of personal and political disagreements between them and so become harder to judge at a distance (Roazen, 1975). However, an issue during WWII caused these concerns to be raised in a different context. By stating publicly during this historical period that he thought Jews were different from Germans (based upon their differing cultural heritage) Jung played into Nazi propaganda (Bair, 2003; McLynn, 1996). This incident was a blight on Jung's record which he found himself defending against for the remainder of his life. How the question of Jung's anti-Semitism is answered by those who write about it depends in large measure whether one is reading an assessment by a "Freudian" or "Jungian," for the disciples of both camps carried on the acrimony of their progenitors for several generations. Bair (2003), a Jungian biographer who seems to have given the most thorough attention to what can be known from documents of the time concludes that without further documentary evidence a cloud will always hang over this part of Jung's life.

In summary this section has charted Jung's adult religious journey as one that sought to infuse, if not replace, the ineffective symbols of the religion of his childhood. This quest took him down many and varied roads eventually leading back to a path that allowed him to integrate the disparate aspects of his past (and his self). Although Jung had long forsaken the institutional church as an adequate avenue for expressing his own religious impulses, preferring a more private journey, his various articulations of religion as symbolizing a living psychic reality meant that he considered all his later studies on the reality of what he called the collective unconscious to be a type of religious quest. What others called God he sometimes called the collective unconscious (Jung, 1961). Using this new language Jung continued to have enlivening experiences that guided his life, comforted him at times, and accosted him at times—the very things that are attributed to the work of God. Thus, the adult Jung continued to speak of "God" as an active force in his life (though what he meant by this term varied). When he built his well-known "tower of solitude" near his home in Bollingen he carved a Latin inscription over the door that stated, "called or not called, God will be there" (cited in Hayman, 1999, p. 110).

Some Key Ideas in Jung's Thought

In beginning this summary of Jung's key ideas an observation is in order. Those who write about Jung tend to agree that he is not always easy to understand due both to the volume of his writing as well as his writing style (e.g., Ellenberger, 1970; Hayman, 1999; Heiseg, 1976; McLynn, 1996; Maddi, 1996; Stein, 1995). In trying to summarize Jung's ideas on a given subject one often has the feeling of trying to hit a moving target. Any summary such as this risks oversimplification, distortions, and significant omissions (especially where his ideas are not as connected to his religious experiences); though I have sought to be accurate in what is described, these limitations should be kept in mind.

Collective Unconscious

As noted in the exposition of Jung's religious journey the collective unconscious refers to a cluster of ideas and images. One could say that Jung's notion of the collective unconscious is the lynchpin of his psychological theory with his other ideas coalescing around this. One way Jung described the collective unconscious is as pointing to a larger wisdom of the human race that lay beyond both conscious awareness and even one's personal unconscious (cf. Freud's [1912] ideas on the unconscious). One might think of the collective unconscious as a repository of wisdom found in the collective psyche of humanity (Jung, 1919, 1927a, 1940b). It is characteristic of the collective unconscious that it lies deeper than, and independent from, any personal history; there is both a universal and impersonal (or transpersonal) characteristic to the collective unconscious. It contains images and ideas common to the whole human race and is the reason behind the commonalities Jung found across times, cultural myths, people, and ideas (e.g., his reference to the ramblings of a patient with schizophrenia and Greek religious myths; Jung, 1928, 1936a). These shared primordial images and ideas are present in potentiality but gain some actuality through their manifestation in the archetypes which can appear in dreams and cultural symbols, especially religious ones. One draws energy or impetus from the collective unconscious in the engagement of life. In this way Jung (1961) sometimes equated the collective unconscious with the cultural symbol many call God. Jung also saw a unifying principle in the collective unconscious; that is, the collective unconscious works to conjoin any split off aspects that are present in the person's conscious life, thus moving one toward integration or wholeness (Jung, 1955–1956).

Archetypes

As Jung sought to describe the nature of the collective unconscious, he described certain deep, universal structures that gave shape to its contents. He called these structures the archetypes and described them as having a transcendent or numinous (spiritual) quality (Jung, 1911–1912, 1947). In describing the relationship of the archetypes to the collective unconscious one might think of the collective unconscious as water flowing along a riverbed; within the riverbed are various rocks that give structure to the water's flow. These rocks that structure the water's flow are the archetypes (Jung, 1936c) and they often reveal certain patterns. For instance, Jung found a preference for things to appear in groups of four among these structures; he will even speak of four as the number of the unconscious (Jung, 1938, 1942a). Archetypes themselves remain ineffable but find specificity through (though never fully captured by) various symbols found in culture, especially religious ones (Jung, 1958b). (One might note that Jung did not always maintain this distinction between the archetype and its image or symbol, sometimes treating the former as if they too were phenomena; Hayman, 1999.) Because the archetypes are universal structures they appear as common motifs in the literature, dreams, delusions, mythologies, and religions of all people groups (Jung, 1958b). Common recognizable archetypes include the hero, the old wise person, the boogey-man, the trickster, and the mother among others. Even "God" is an archetype in that all cultures have the "idea" of God (although Jung is clear that in speaking of God as an archetype he is not commenting on God's reality; Jung, 1961). Every culture has stories where these archetypes are symbolized (e.g., in the West various embodiments of the hero include Hercules, Beowulf, Superman, Luke Skywalker; personifications of the mother include not only actual mothers but Mother Earth and Mother Church). When an archetype appears in a dream, in a religion, or simply in life, it brings a certain influence that conveys a numinous quality or impels one to action. One feels as if something outside one's own conscious thoughts is giving one information, energy, and impetus (Atwood & Stolorow, 1993; Jung, 1917).

Shadow

Jung spoke of various archetypes throughout his work but devoted an extraordinary amount of space to three in particular. First is the shadow. This archetype pointed to disavowed aspects of human nature that Jung felt went unacknowledged or neglected and is usually the first archetype to be confronted in therapy (Storr, 1983). "The shadow personifies everything that the subject refuses to acknowledge about himself and yet is always thrusting itself upon him directly or indirectly—for instance, inferior traits of character and other incompatible tendencies" (Jung, 1939, pp. 284–285). A literary example of a person's shadow is the Mr. Hyde side of Dr. Jekyll's personality (Stevenson, 1886). Jung's reference to the shadow thrusting itself upon one points to how the shadow, like all aspects of the collective unconscious, participates in a conjoining of opposites (cf. Jung, 1955–1956). By thrusting itself upon the conscious personality, the shadow forces the conscious personality to acknowledge these repressed, inferior aspects that also belong to oneself. Thus, Jung (1938, 1951) also spoke of the positive qualities of the shadow as when he wrote that the shadow "does not consist only of morally reprehensible tendencies, but also displays a number of good qualities, such as normal instincts, appropriate reactions, realistic insights, creative impulses, etc." (Jung, 1951, p. 266). An illustration of this more positive side of the shadow might be an anxious person who finds new strength after acknowledging suppressed fears. However, such remarks make Jung's elaboration of one's relationship to the shadow hard to follow at times (McLynn, 1996; Sanford, 1989; Stein, 1995). One is never quite sure whether one is to embrace the shadow or simply acknowledge and manage it (e.g., Jung, 1917; cf. with Jung, 1951). What is clear is that one cannot deny such aspects of the collective unconscious without serious repercussions in both one's conscious and unconscious life.

Anima

The second archetype to which Jung devoted considerable attention was the anima. This archetype referred to the life force or life principle in living beings (Bair, 2003; Jung, 1921, 1961). The Greeks called this life force psyche, the Romans called it anima; in English it is often rendered by the word soul (Rollins, 1983). Like all the archetypes this one is best observed through the ways it is projected (Ellenberger, 1970). In men, the anima archetype takes characteristic form in projections onto the "opposite" sex (Jung was always interested in binaries) (Jung, 1921). Thus, the anima archetype has specific reference to unconscious personifications of feminine qualities in the inner life of the male: "Every man carries within him the eternal image of woman, not the image of this or that particular woman but a definitive feminine image" (Jung, 1925, p. 198). This image is composed of all ancestral experiences of the female and leads to both idealizing and/or demonizing the other as such images are unconsciously projected onto the beloved. The corresponding image of the masculine in females is called the Animus. Health comes in bringing these unconscious elements to awareness and into balance with one's conscious life (e.g., a female becomes aware of and acknowledges her animus; a male becomes aware of and acknowledges his anima). In this way one's interactions with others will not be driven as much by unconscious projections (Jung, 1921, 1955–1956).

Self

The third archetype to which Jung devoted considerable attention was that of the self. This archetype comes to represent the goal of human life for Jung. It is an expression of human maturity or wholeness and also is represented by mandalas (drawings of unified circles) that Jung (1955) found in various cultures. It represents a balance between all the various aspects of the person (e.g., anima—animus; conscious—unconscious; good—bad, etc.) (Jung, 1928, 1936b, 1940b). It is contrasted with two other concepts, the "persona" and the "ego." The persona is the public mask that all present to succeed and survive in social company. However, Jung (1940a) was clear that it was a mistake to live only as one's persona. The ego represents one's conscious personality and thus is only a part of one's life. In contrast, the self is primarily unconscious, a unifying potentiality for wholeness (Jung, 1936b, 1947). Jung (1940b) spoke of the movement toward the actualization of the self as a process of individuation whereby one can decenter from an ego-focused life to one that embraces all aspects of one's person and purpose. Individuation (the realization of the self) is a complicated process (more circular than linear) and for this reason Jung (1961) did not see movement away from the ego toward the self taking place prior to midlife. His thoughts about this movement toward integrative wholeness stand behind Jung's (1932) comment that the problems of his clients who were past midlife were religious ones (cf. Rollins, 1983).

Personality Types

The last key idea from Jung noted here is his ideas regarding different personality types. In some circles Jung is best known for this concept which was popularized through the Myers-Briggs Type Indicator (Myers & McCaulley, 1985). In distinguishing among personality types, Jung (1921) first divided humans along an axis of introversion and extraversion; this distinction he called one's basic attitude. This axis referred not so much to one's level of sociability as it did to where one found and recharged one's psychic energy. Introverts renew their psychic energy inwardly while extraverts renew theirs through external connections. In addition to one's basic attitude of introversion or extraversion Jung saw personality types distinguished around four functions or ways a person related to the world. Two of these he called the rational functions because they were ways of evaluating one's experience (either through thinking or through feeling) and the other two functions he labeled non-rational because they received experience (either through the senses or through intuition) without judging it. Jung argued that all these qualities were present in all humans but that in each category one orientation was dominant. Thus, by combining one's basic attitude with one's dominant functions Jung proposed eight different personality possibilities (e.g., an introverted feeling type or an extraverted thinking type). Furthermore, Jung (1921) proposed that one tended to neglect the non-dominant orientation in oneself but might feel drawn to it in another because at some unconscious level one wished for an integration or wholeness that required giving more attention to these neglected qualities. Jung saw these differences in personality types as contributing to many common human conflicts. For instance, in his own circles he saw clashes over psychological theory between Freud and Adler (that led to the eventual dissolution of their friendship) as manifestations of Adler's introversion in contrast to Freud's extraversion (Jung, 1921). No doubt Jung's own introversion in contrast to Freud's extraversion also contributed to their clashes.

How Jung's Religious Journey Influenced his Life and Thought

In the Introduction we noted that the religious backgrounds of the psychologists studied here had an impact that was both indirect (via its cultural influence) and direct. The more indirect cultural religious influences are seen in the adoption of a developmental perspective (i.e., life moves toward some purpose) and in the ethical legacy of their religious traditions. The more direct ways concern the influence of these psychologists' religious background on specific ideas in their thinking as well as the way they viewed their lives and work. Not surprisingly, these influences have a decidedly Christian cast in Jung's case.

A Developmental Perspective

Jung's adoption of a developmental perspective is less obvious in that he does not articulate a series of developmental stages one passes through as do Freud (1905) and Erikson (1950/1963). Nevertheless, one finds the notion of a developmental trajectory in Jung's (1932) comments that in midlife clients begin to think more about existential-religious issues. Such comments envision changes as one grows and matures as well as goals toward which one moves. As Kirschner (1996) has pointed out, this way of thinking about humans is indebted to the Jewish and Christian views of the linearity of history.

Another aspect of a developmental perspective concerns whether humans move toward the restoration of things gone awry or toward the completion of things already present in potential (see Introduction). Much of psychology has been influenced by the former goal due in large measure to the influence of Augustine on Western thought (Hathaway & Yarhouse, 2021). It is obvious in Jung's writings that he spent a great deal of his life researching and treating various psychopathologies in his patients; thus, he was well aware that much of therapeutic psychology is devoted to repair. However, it is significant to note that Jung's concepts of the collective unconscious and individuation focus primarily upon nurturing things already present within the person. Thus, Jung's theory of therapy has less of this focus on repairing something broken than one finds in others.

One can also see the developmental perspective in Jung's thought in his ideas about the goals of analysis and human life in general. What does life move toward for Jung? One might think of his answers to such questions as providing his reflections on the good life. The key thing to remember here is that the grand telos or purpose toward which life moves for Jung is becoming integrated or individuated; that is to say, one moves toward realization of the self archetype (e.g., Jung, 1928, 1939). This realization of the self involves a process in which one acknowledges, understands, and embraces the various dimensions of one's self (e.g., one's shadow, one's anima, one's non-dominant attitude and functions, etc.) (Jung, 1928, 1936b). Although this journey toward individuation involves some separation from aspects of one's previous embeddedness in family, beliefs, and/or culture, it also involves finding a myth or story by which to live. It is also significant to note that when Jung (1932) remarked that the second half of life is given to this notion of finding a myth to live out he characterized the movement toward individuation as a religious one (Jung, 1951).

Ethical Legacy of His Religious Tradition

The second way that Jung's cultural religious background influenced his work can be seen in the ways that the ethical legacy of his Christian tradition showed up in his thought. Some of the specific ways this occurred in Jung include the moral contours of his thoughts on good vs. evil in humans, his thoughts on what humans ought to do and to a lesser degree in his work ethic.

Goodness vs. Evil in Humans

One can see the legacy of the ethical traditions of his religious background in Jung's thoughts on good vs. evil in humans (often framed in ways indebted to his Swiss Reformed background). The problem of evil is an issue to which Jung devoted considerable attention (e.g., Jung, 1946, 1951, 1952, 1959). In seeking an answer to this problem, Jung engaged with both Western and Eastern thought. He had long been dissatisfied by the way the West (i.e., primarily the Western church) had addressed the problem of evil and argued that in banishing evil from God the church had lost something of the very essence of evil. For Jung evil, like good, belonged to the very fabric of the universe and to exclude it or cordon it off was to be in denial of the very nature of the universe. Jung also found himself dissatisfied with the answers in Eastern religions as well. Though some acknowledged a place for darkness in God (e.g., the Hindu god Shiva who represents a destructive deity; Flood, 1996), he concluded that in the end Eastern religions treat evil as an illusion. What is important to note here is that in Jung's discussion of these issues (e.g., in general and more specifically in his work on the shadow archetype), the framing of his discussion leans upon the traditions of his religious background.

What One Ought to Do

As Jung developed his thoughts on the goal of life (i.e., individuation/realization of the self), Browning (1987) points out that Jung moved beyond descriptive comments on psychological possibilities to argue for self-realization as a moral or ethical obligation. That is, for Jung (1932), movement toward becoming integrated or individuated is not simply what happens as we develop but what ought to happen in development. Although Jung will talk about this goal of development in various ways, what is of interest here is his appropriation of language from his religious background to describe this way of thinking about individuation as obligation. For instance, Jung (1932) wrote concerning the Christian ideal of the "imitation of Christ" that the need was not that of imitating Christ's life of sacrifice but in imitating Christ by living "our own proper lives as truly as he lived his in its individual uniqueness," further noting that "it is no easy matter to live a life modeled on Christ's, but it is unspeakably harder to live one's own life as truly as Christ lived his" (p. 340). One notes not only the sense of obligation in living one's own life present in this appropriation of the language of his religious background but also that Jung has radically changed the meaning of the terms he appropriates (e.g., the imitation of Christ; more on Jung's reinterpretation of religious language below).

Protestant Work Ethic

Jung's adoption of the so-called "Protestant work ethic" (that idea that one works for a larger purpose than survival; Weber, 1904/1958) is harder to assess because his wife's wealth eliminated the need for him to work. Although he kept a steady case load of patients which he mostly saw in the afternoons while devoting his mornings to writing, his attitude toward work seems more fluid and less compelling than in some of the other psychologists studied here (Baer, 2003; Hayman, 1999; McLynn, 1996).

Certain Key Ideas

In addition to the indirect influences of Jung's religious background on his life and work, there are more direct influences one can note in certain ideas Jung elaborated. This section summarizes several ways Jung's early religious journey is reflected in various ideas that have already been noted in describing his religious journey. These include his ideas about the collective unconscious and its expression via the archetypes, as well as in certain ideas about various personality types. As noted in the Introduction, such connections will have a tentative cast to them.

The Collective Unconscious and the Archetypes

Jung (1911–1912, 1919, 1936a, 1961) noted several sources for his ideas about the collective unconscious, including conversations with his patients, his readings in ancient mythology, and his own religious experiences. Some of the connections between Jung's religious experiences and his insights about the collective unconscious noted above include his experiences with his cousin's revelations during the séances, his experiences of his dual natures, as well as his own dreams and visions which he thought had sprung from a source beyond himself and granted him knowledge beyond his years.

One also can see a connection to Jung's earlier religious experiences in his description of the archetypes as a force from outside oneself that impels one to action (e.g., God making him have the vision of the cathedral destruction) as well as in his comment that the archetypes have a numinous or spiritual quality (Jung, 1911–1912, 1917, 1947). One also can see more specific connections between Jung's religious experiences and specific archetypes noted above. Jung's (1961) ideas about the shadow are clearly connected to early dreams and visions regarding a dark side to God. Similarly, one can see Jung's early experiences of his mother's spirituality influencing his ideas on the mysterious, sometimes subversive nature of the anima (Jung, 1921, McLynn, 1996) and his experience of a duality in himself as well as experiences of both his religious parents as not only being so disparate from each other but also with their own inner world, which provides a source for his ideas for a self that would be more integrated.

Personality Types

The last place we note the influence of Jung's religious experiences upon his thought is in his articulation of the personality types. These ideas drew on Jung's own introspective nature and desire to be alone (i.e., his introversion) as well as from his experiences of both himself and his mother as having two natures. Such experiences provided an early contribution to later conceptualizations of the differing attitudes and functions of the personality (Monte, 1999). Furthermore, his questions about God's two natures (e.g., light and darkness) point to his early religious experiences as also contributing to his thoughts about differing personality types (Jung, 1961).

Other Ways

One can also see the more direct influences of Jung's religious background on his life and work in the content and direction of his work, in the way he views his work, and in his theories about religion itself. This section looks at these influences.

Content and Direction of his Work

One sees the influence of Jung's religious background on his work in his life-long interest in religion, its nature, its role in life, its influence on the psyche, in what it discloses, and in what it conceals. In many ways Jung's adult life and work was devoted to understanding the religious experiences of his childhood and youth (Jung, 1961). Thus, religion became one of the key subjects of Jung's developing theory (e.g., 1937, 1938, 1944). This life-long interest in religion took two different but related paths.

On the one hand, Jung took from his childhood exposure and experiences a fascination with the more mystical side of religion, a journey which took him along many paths (e.g., Gnosticism, alchemy, religions of the East and West). This interest in the mystical side of religion was no doubt connected to his early experiences of the uncanny side of his mother and her involvement in spiritualism as well as his own sense of the uncanny within (e.g., his No. 2 personality) including his early religious dreams. Jung especially felt that these latter kinds of experiences had communicated to him something of the living God, making God more real to him than the liturgies of the organized church (Jung, 1961). After such experiential encounters with God, he was not content to "believe," he wanted to "know" (Ellenberger, 1970; Freeman, 1959).

On the other hand, Jung's life-long interest in religion was coupled with ambivalence toward Christianity, an ambivalence that went back to his childhood dream of the cavern and was especially evident in interactions with his father. Jung thought that the religion of his father (institutional Christianity) had domesticated the God he knew to be quite different and refused to engage certain questions about God. What is one to do with such a religion? Abandon it? Change it? Revitalize it? In the end Jung chose a combination of the latter options and so remained interested not only in religious issues in general throughout his life, but the Christian religion in particular as his attempts to address the dark side of God as well as his longing to revitalize the symbols of the Christian faith attest (e.g., Jung, 1938, 1952, 1957).

Seeing His Work as Like That of a Prophet

One also sees the influence of Jung's early religious background and experiences not only in the content and direction of his work but in the way he conceived the purpose of his work. Jung took away from these early experiences the notion that he had been chosen (Atwood & Stolorow, 1993; Jung, 1961); he had received a new "word" or revelation about the nature of God and the universe that others did not seem to know or understand (e.g., God has a dark side; there is a greater collective wisdom available to humans) (Jung, 1961). It is his purpose to convey this new understanding to others. This then is the story or myth by which he can live; his life project is to be the prophet of this new word from what others call God. He will help humanity, the West in particular, to encounter the living God who is active and always there if one but has the vital symbols by which to apprehend this (Hannah, 1991; Jung, 1961; Wehr, 1987).

For the West, this meant a revitalizing reinterpretation of the symbols of Christianity which had once given life to generations but in modern times had lost their moorings and vitality (Hayman, 1999; Jung, 1938, 1957, 1961). In carrying out this purpose Jung saw himself as a prophetic or messianic figure, writing at one point of a dream in which he envisioned himself as a kind of life-giving nourishment for humanity (Jung, 1961). Such ideas regarding his purpose draw heavily from the traditions of his religious background.

Jung's Theory of Religion

Jung's religious background also influenced his work in the way he came to think about religion. Since his religious life was so central to his development, it is no surprise that it played a role in the development of his psychological ideas about religion. Similarly, one also can see that Jung's development of psychological ideas gave him a new lens through which he viewed various religious experiences, including his own.

At the heart of Jung's ideas about religion is his idea that religion is a "natural" part of human life (Jung, 1938, 1957). Although Jung came to this conclusion from his wide readings in mythology, certainly the fact that religious experiences came naturally to Jung also contributed to his seeing them as natural to all humans. Jung (1938) postulated something within humans that caused them to not only desire but to look for and defer to powers greater than themselves. Interestingly, Freud (e.g., 1927) and Jung are not far apart on this point; however, they differ significantly both on the origins of such yearnings and on how one should respond to such longings.

This notion of humans as naturally religious has several implications. First, one's openness to the numinous becomes a measure of health for Jung. Consequently, Jung (1929) thought the absence of some sensitivity to the religious or spiritual was a sign of pathology (cf. Storr, 1983; note how different from Freud). Second, in the latter half of life, as attention turns from ego toward realization of the self, Jung (1932) described the problems he encountered in his patients as religious ones (that is to say, problems concerned with the larger purpose of one's life). In speaking of concerns with the larger purpose of life as religious issues, Jung is characterizing the journey toward self-realization as a religious quest (e.g., Jung, 1951; Storr, 1983). He thus reinterprets religious growth as the movement toward the integration of the self and, in speaking of religion as belonging to the very fabric of the world, Jung, at least at times, equates the collective unconscious with God (e.g., Jung, 1921, 1952 1961).

A second aspect of Jung's theory of religion is his description of God as a psychic reality (e.g., Jung, 1928; McLynn, 1996). By this, he meant to acknowledge that one cannot simply treat God as an idea, especially an idea that had no impact on one's life. By speaking of God as a psychic reality Jung wanted to say something about the inescapable religious dimension of human life. Jung was aware that the idea of God involved human projections (e.g., what he called the God-image; see Jung, 1952, 1955–1956), yet he did not intend this phrase to mean that God existed only as human projections. Rather, he argued that these projections were given to one or came to one from beyond one's consciousness; in his own words: "'God' already has a place in that part of our psyche which is preexistent to consciousness and that he therefore cannot be considered an invention of consciousness" (Jung, 1961, p. 347). Although the "idea of God" may be all the psychologist can prove exists, Jung was far from thinking the "idea" of God the only reality one encountered. He poked fun at such an attitude in his comment about those who thought it "all very well to speak of the Holy Ghost on occasions—but it is not a phenomenon to be experienced!" (Jung, 1961, p. 141).

However, one notes here that Jung's discussion of God as a psychic reality is one of those places where his ideas about God seem like a moving target. He wants to speak of God as a reality that is more than projections, yet his comments on the God-image hardly clarify things (Jung, 1952, 1955–1956). This conundrum is compounded by statements that seem to equate God with the collective unconscious (e.g., Jung, 1921, 1952, 1961). For Jung, God's reality was real enough (Ellenberger, 1970); he would leave others to sort this question of God's reality for themselves. This is one of those places where Jung "knows" and therefore does not have to "believe" (cf. Freeman, 1959). However, for those who do not know in the way he knew, it leaves the reality of God uncertain.

A third aspect of Jung's theory of religion is his argument that religious symbols need reinterpreting into psychological language if they are to find new vitality in the contemporary world (Jung, 1938, 1957). This is especially seen in the way Jung reinterpreted certain key ideas of the Christian faith (e.g., Jung, 1942a). We have noted his reinterpretation of religious growth as movement toward integration of the self (e.g., Jung, 1951; Storr, 1983). Jung bolstered this reinterpretation through his exploration of symbols of the self in the various religions of the world. From his own Christian tradition, Jung (1951) came to see the symbol of the Christ as an exemplar of the archetype of the self; for Jung, Christ's self-realization took the route of suffering and sacrifice. In the East Jung saw the Buddha as symbolizing actualization of the self through the route of reason (Jung, 1961). Mandalas could also be religious symbols of the self.

Jung also gave new meaning to other familiar Christian symbols that he thought had lost their vitality. For example, he sought to revitalize the Christian idea of God in several ways. We have already noted his reinterpretation of God as the collective unconscious. In another attempt to revitalize this symbol, Jung argued that four was the number of the collective unconscious; thus, Jung sought to envision God as quaternity rather than trinity (Jung, 1938, 1942a). He offered two ways for this revitalization. One was to incorporate God's shadow side more directly (Jung, 1952), the other was to redress the neglect of God's anima or feminine side (Jung, 1942a). In addressing God's shadow (often personified in Satan according to Jung) Jung stated that these shadow qualities belonged to the whole of the universe; the task was to acknowledge these aspects of the unconscious so as to tap their potential energy for becoming whole. (It is important to remember that Jung can be inconsistent in the way he speaks of the shadow, leaving one unclear as to exactly what to do with it.) In trying to redress the neglect of the feminine in God, Jung proposed that Christianity, particularly in its Protestant form, give more attention to Mary, the mother of Jesus and applauded the Roman Catholics in their elevation of Mary in the doctrine of her Assumption (though Jung is not always so complimentary of the feminine, thoughts likely influenced by experiences with his mother; Jung, 1927b, 1951, 1952).

A final illustration of how Jung sought to reinterpret Christian symbols was his reflections on how historical disagreements might be explained by way of personality types (we saw him do this with Freud and Adler). For instance, he attributed the conflict between Luther and Zwingli over the real versus the symbolic presence of Christ in the Lord's Supper as a reflection of Luther's extraversion (e.g., with preference for external sources of energy renewal—the real presence of Christ) over against Zwingli's introversion (with a preference for internal energy renewal—renewed via internal engagement with Christ's symbolic presence) (Jung, 1921).

Concluding Comments

What is one to conclude about Jung's religious life and its influence on his work? The answer is multifaceted much like Jung himself. People tend to have one of two reactions to Jung (although those with dual personalities of their own may have both)! Both reactions are found in religious as well as non-religious people. One set of reactions is basically negative. These take several forms. One series of thoughts clusters around the danger in reading Jung, or more specifically the danger in adopting Jungian thought (Buber, 1952; Hurding, 1985; Jones & Butman, 1991; Noll, 1994). Jung is obviously heterodox in his views of God and Christ when compared to traditional Christian teachings. Sometimes his ideas seem openly anti-Christian. Certainly, his embrace of spirituality takes in all spiritualities, including the occult. One can understand why Christians who embrace the historical, orthodox traditions of Christianity would find Jung troublesome (e.g., Hempelmann, 1986; Jones & Butman, 1991; Payne & Perrotta, 1988). Even for those who might recognize familiar terms in Jung, his clear project to find a more adequate reinterpretation of these traditional Christian symbols and doctrines make his ideas easy to misinterpret given his retention of the older terms.

A second set of thoughts clusters around the dangers of what might happen to one psychically if one adopts Jung or more specifically follows him down the path of complete openness to the collective unconscious. Is this to open oneself up to a potential if not actual psychosis, much like Jung himself experienced (McLynn, 1996)? Would one survive it as Jung did or are there dangers of getting lost? McLynn's remark on the larger number of suicides among Jung's patients than among other analytic approaches gives some weight to this concern (although the reasons for these suicides varied and include the trauma of two World Wars). Similarly, others have wondered whether Jung's encouragement to embrace one's shadow might foster greater inclinations toward evil in oneself (Payne & Perrotta, 1988).

Despite these concerns others have tended to have essentially positive reactions to encountering Jung (e.g., Hannah, 1991; Wehr, 1987). These reactions also take several forms. Since Jung (1935, 1961) described his work as the *cura animarum* (cure of souls), it is not surprising that he has been very popular in the pastoral care movement (e.g., Benner, 1998; Dittes, 1990; Moseley, 1990; Rollins, 1983). For instance, some Christians have taken an essentially positive view toward Jung's work by arguing that Jung may have gotten some specifics wrong but is mostly on target in emphasizing the centrality of religion/spirituality. For example, some think that Jung has simply gotten it wrong (based on the narrow sample of his father and himself) in stating that if one were an orthodox Christian one could not have a lively experience of God's grace (Ulanov & Dueck, 2008). Another way in which he seems to have gotten it wrong is in his characterization of the Christian Church's position on God and evil. Although he is right that certain Christians would not see any darkness in God (Jung, 1961; cf., Augustine's *Enchiridion*, chap. 11), others, including the Swiss Reformer Calvin attribute the origin of evil to God's providence (*Institutes*, 3.23.8) and Luther (1958) writes of the *deus absconditus*—the hidden side of God (see Dillenberger, 1953). In this same vein, the orthodox theologian Irenaeus wrote that God did not create a perfect world and that this lack of perfection was intentional on God's part (so that humans could grow in their love for God; *Against the Heresies*, xxxviii:1, xxxix:1). Such Christian theologies at least allow for variety in the way one thinks about God's relationship to the presence of evil in the world. Interestingly, although Jung (1951) is familiar with the work of Irenaeus, he does not seem to make this particular connection.

Finally, another positive reaction from both religious and non-religious people is a sense that one has found something truly freeing in Jung; one is now able to acknowledge aspects of the self long kept dormant or perhaps denied completely. One can embrace the whole of the self and not just parts (e.g., only embracing the persona). A similar cluster of thoughts is that Jung has made one aware that there may be deep treasures within the self that have been overlooked or neglected by one's restraint and that one may have missed something very precious within oneself (Ulanov & Dueck, 2008). When applied to religious life, this is the idea that one might be able to have a real experiential encounter with God.

CHAPTER THREE

Erik Erikson

When Erikson was a young child growing up in a Jewish home, he recalls playing under the dining table as the unsuspecting adults talked above. At one point the conversation caught his attention when a comment was made about his biological father. For a boy who suspected that the man he currently called father was not truly so, this conversation stirred something deep within. Who was his real father and what was meant by the comment that he was a Gentile (reported in Friedman, 1999)? This event is paradigmatic of a life-long journey for Erikson: who was his father and what was the nature of his parentage? The struggle over these questions caused Erikson's chief biographer to characterize Erikson's life quest as one in which he sought to find a benevolent father's face (Friedman, 1999). We defer for now an answer as to whether he ever found this or not but acknowledge that his quest to understand the impact of this absence defined much of his life and work. But first, we turn to the question of why include Erikson in this book; what is the story to be told here?

Erik Erikson is perhaps best known among the general public for his ideas regarding human development. Hardly anyone exposed to a textbook in psychology, counseling, social work, or education will not have seen an outline of his eight stages of the life cycle (Erikson, 1950/1963). Possibly even more ubiquitous is his concept of the adolescent identity crisis, something one is likely to hear referenced even if the speaker has no clue this idea originated with Erikson (e.g., 1956, 1968a). Thus, his theory has influenced not only the field of psychology, but his ideas have gained standing in popular discourse as well.

Like all the psychologists in this book, Erikson's early development, including his religious development, influenced his work. This chapter looks at what is known of Erikson's religious journey and how his religious development influenced various aspects of his work. It tells the story of how he came to embrace what he called a "stepson" identity that allowed him to live on the boundaries between various identities, never belonging entirely to one place or group all his life (Erikson, 1970, p. 744). This self-proclaimed identity has its roots in the absence of his biological father, and it is not surprising that this stepson identity shows up in his religious journey as well.

What Is Known of Erikson's Religious Journey?

This section draws from autobiographical materials as well as from materials amassed by his various biographers to tell the story of how a young man's stepson identity continued to be a driving force throughout his life, and which showed up in his religious identity in particular.

Religion in Erikson's Early Childhood Home

The development of Erikson's stepson identity in his religious life begins with events that occurred in his early years. The son of a Jewish woman from a well-off Danish family, he grew up without ever knowing who his biological father was. His mother, Karla, had been married for a short time to a Danish man who disappeared under mysterious circumstances shortly after the marriage. About four or five years later Erikson was born, the son of a different man whose identity his mother never disclosed to him. Because of the scandal of a pregnancy with no known husband, his mother moved to Germany to stay with relatives until the child was born and continued to live there after his birth (Erikson, 1970; Friedman, 1999).

For the first three years of his life, he and his mother lived on their own with support from her family. She was involved with a company of artists and would take young Erik there. In this group he seems to have felt a sense of belonging or at least a sense of place and he states that it was here that he had his first male role models (Erikson, 1970). It seems his mother may have been happy as well during this time, but this is not clear because she also seems to have wanted to find a relationship in which she and her son might be secure. This came in the form of a marriage to the pediatrician to whom she had taken Erik. As part of her marriage to Theodor Homberger, Karla Abrahamsen agreed to tell the three-year-old Erik that Homberger was his father (Friedman, 1999). Erikson (1970) wrote of those days "children then were not meant to know what they had not been told," adding "so I played in with this and more or less forgot the period before the age of three when my mother and I had lived alone" (p. 742). This collusion regarding his true parentage would play a key role in development of his own identity as well as in the development of his psychological theory.

Erikson reported two other memories of his early life with his mother that have a bearing on his identity development, including development of his religious identity. He remembered his mother as "pervasively sad" and "as deeply involved in reading" (Erikson, 1970, p. 745). Of this first memory we note that although her pervasive sadness may have given her a certain predictability, it also will have contributed to the quality of relationship that develops between the mother and the child. Welchman (2000) writes that his memory of his mother's pervasive sadness and deep involvement in reading "might be taken to imply a passivity that would push a child to find his own sources of stimulation rather than expecting it from his mother" (p. 16). D.W. Winnicott (1948) wrote about children who grow up with a depressed mother that such children may also feel sadness or take it upon themselves to try to cheer the mother and give her some reason for living. According to Winnicott (1960a, 1960b), such children might develop a false self and will inevitably feel that they have missed something important in the mutual exchange between mother and child, something Erikson himself also writes about (Erikson, 1950/1963, 1977). Erikson's daughter comments that her grandmother's refusal to tell Erikson of his biological father left him ambivalent and angry toward her (Bloland, 2005). Her refusal is overshadowed by reasons we will never know but one is left to wonder about its significance in terms of other withholding.

Erikson's (1970) other memory of his mother was that she was "deeply involved in reading" (p.745). One of the people she read and admired was a Christian theologian from her native Denmark, Soren Kierkegaard, often considered one of the fathers of the existential movement (Carlisle, 2019). Karla seems to have appreciated Kierkegaard both because he was from her native Denmark, but also for his ideas (Friedman, 1999). She passed on to her son what he described as an appreciation for the "existential core" of Christianity (Burston, 2007; Coles, 1970). What is remarkable about this earliest memory is that Erikson's mother was Jewish. Single for the first three years of Erikson's life, his mother later married a key figure in her Jewish community and reared her son in an observant Jewish home. We note some of Erikson's thoughts on this later but for now we simply note that the nature of Karla's Jewishness was one that did not exclude appreciation for certain Christian ideas. As further testimony of this general attitude among the Abrahamsen family, Friedman (1999) notes that Karla boasted that the family line included not only a rabbi but a church historian and a theologian, suggesting some mixed marriages along the way. Needless to say, Erikson's relationship with his mother impacted his religious journey and identity formation. This impact manifested itself in several ways and it is important to examine some of these as they unfolded in his adult years. Before turning more specifically to these influences it is helpful to note a few other things about Erikson's early life in the home of Karla and Theodor Homberger that have implications for his religious development.

Erikson's relationship with his stepfather was one characterized by an uneasy ambivalence from the beginning. From Homberger's side, his ambivalence can be seen in his delay of several years before completing the adoption process on Erikson (Friedman, 1999). From Erikson's side Homberger was an interloper who had taken his mother's attention from him (Erikson, 1970). This is likely related to the lie he was expected to acquiesce to regarding the notion that Homberger was his father. The falseness of these mutual roles seems to have left both Erikson and his stepfather unsure of their interactions with each other. Unsure of his and Homberger's true relationship Erikson (1975a) remembered early fantasies of coming from better parents, possibly fueled by his overhearing a conversation once in which some relatives spoke of his biological father as being a Gentile, a memory which further confused Erikson's speculations about his religious origins (Friedman, 1999).

Life in the Homberger home presented Erikson with further questions about his religious identity. Another requirement for the marriage between Theodor Homberger and Karla Abrahamsen (in addition to telling Erikson that Homberger was his father) was that Karla would keep an observant Jewish home (something she does not seem to have done prior to the marriage and even foregoes after the marriage when she visited her native Denmark; cf. Burston, 2007). This Karla did, keeping an observant and kosher household; Homberger himself was active in the local Reform Temple and was once its president (Friedman, 1999). Although remaining active in the Jewish community and Temple as well as observant in their home, the Hombergers had moved to a Gentile enclave within the city to aid upward mobility (Welchman, 2000). This created further strain between Erikson and his stepfather around questions of Erikson's identity. Although pretending that Homberger was his father, it was obvious to Erikson even early on that this was not so and as he became older it became even more obvious. Whereas Homberger was short and dark haired, Erikson grew tall and was fair haired and blue eyed. At Temple he was referred to as a "goy" (a derogatory remark regarding his Gentile looks), while at his school in a Gentile part of town he was known as the "Jew" (Erikson, 1970). Thus, early on Erikson's challenge in terms of identity is seen on two fronts. On the one hand was the question of whose son he was. But in addition to this aspect of his identity he also wrestles with a religious dimension to his identity: is he Jew or Gentile?

Religion in Erikson's Adolescent Years

As one might anticipate, a person who spent much of his life analyzing the stage of adolescence would have a story of his own adolescence worth exploring. This section looks at those portions of his adolescence that have a bearing on the theme of this book.

The first thing to note concerning his religious development during adolescence is Erikson's experience of his bar mitzvah in his stepfather's Temple. Erikson said this event in which the young male becomes an active participant in the Jewish religious services was a disappointment to him, providing no special feelings for him but rather having the feel of a "hollow ritual" (Burston, 2007, p. 8; Erikson, 1970; note the similarity to Jung's description of his confirmation ceremony). Although this comment comes from a much older Erikson looking back upon his early adolescence, Erikson may have had misgivings about this whole procedure because of his experience of being termed a "goy" (non-Jew) at his stepfather's Temple. (One also wonders if Erikson [1975a] had this or similar ceremonies in mind a few years later when he wrote of how some social rituals seemed to inhibit identity formation.) One continues to see Erikson's struggle with his religious identity in his later adolescence as Erikson drifts away from the Jewish Temple, writing a letter of "resignation" from it in the process (Friedman, 1999; Hoare, 2002). This drift has continuity with a trajectory observed earlier regarding his ambivalence to identify too closely with his stepfather and his religion. In its place he spoke of being drawn to the Christ of the Gospels during these years (possibly through his mother's conversations about Kierkegaard) (Erikson, 1970; Friedman, 1999). No doubt part of this attraction is Erikson's identification with one who is portrayed in the Gospels as welcoming all comers, both Jew and Gentile. Furthermore, the Gospels describe Jesus as conceived through the mysterious work of the Holy Spirit; this means that in being reared by his mother Mary's husband Joseph, Jesus does not grow up with his true father either, another point of identity for Erikson (Burston, 2007).

Erikson's adolescence is also characterized by an extended time for him to "find himself" and his purpose in life. With the support of his mother (perhaps unknown to his stepfather in terms of the financial amount), Erikson spent a year or so as a wandering artist in the mountains of Germany (Friedman, 1999). Erikson (1970) would describe this period in his life as a "moratorium" from having to make a lasting career choice (career choice being a key part of identity for the adolescent emerging into adulthood; cf. Erikson, 1950/1963, 1968a). An aspect of the moratorium for Erikson is that not only does he not have to decide about his career, but he also can explore other aspects of his identity. For instance, during this period Erikson recalled hearing a particularly moving recitation of the Lord's Prayer while visiting in the home of a friend. He wrote:

> In my youth, as a wandering artist I stayed one night with a friend in a small village by the Upper Rhine. His father was a Protestant pastor; and in the morning, as the family sat down to breakfast, the old man said the Lord's Prayer in Luther's German. Never having "knowingly" heard it, I had the experience, as seldom before or after, of a wholeness captured in a few simple words, of poetry fusing the esthetic and the moral: those who have once suddenly "heard" the Gettysburg Address will know what I mean. (Erikson, 1958, p. 10)

In this experience one sees another layer of the adolescent Erikson's attraction to Christianity. But more importantly, one notes that Erikson's adolescence and early adult years give him time not only to postpone the career question but to continue to explore the question of his religious identity as well.

One also can see the struggle with his religious identity (as well as struggles with other aspects of his identity) in some of his artwork from this period of wandering. Of particular interest is his woodcut of Mary and the baby Jesus. (Woodcuts seem to have been a medium with which Erikson worked a lot, partly because he was better with this medium than others, such as paints; cf. Friedman, 1999.) This particular woodcut points to his continuing fascination with the Christian religion that his mother had introduced to him via Kierkegaard. But there may have been more going on with this as well. Capps (2014) notes how this image of Mary as the mother of Jesus may have evoked in Erikson something of his earlier times with his mother (especially in those years when he lived alone with her, and his role models were her artist friends). Whether the adolescent Erikson would necessarily have made these connections consciously, Erikson's later embrace of Freudian theory is one in which the connection between unconscious forces and an artist's work can clearly be drawn (Freud, 1910; cf. Kris, 1952).

Finally, one notes one other remark Erikson makes regarding his adolescence. Erikson (1970) recalled of those years that he had a dear friend who "shared" his father with him, and it was this man that also first introduced him to the thought of Gandhi (more on Gandhi later). This is an interesting remark both in terms of Erikson's question of religious identity as well as his lifelong quest for a father figure. Not feeling especially connected to his stepfather, and not knowing his real father, Erikson was preoccupied for much of his life, and particularly in his childhood and adolescence, with the question of his paternity. Furthermore this father figure was a Gentile and perhaps Erikson felt some connection to him in this sense as well since he thought his biological father to have been Gentile. In terms of the larger question of identity it is also of interest to note that he and his friend both had Jewish mothers as well as Gentile fathers (Friedman, 1999).

Religion in Erikson's Young Adult Years

This period takes in the years from Erikson's first job until his immigration to the United States. Erikson's moratorium and thus his extended adolescence ended when he took his first job. This job came about when a childhood friend (the one who shared his Gentile father) invited him to come and help him in his job as a teacher at a school that had been set up by friends of the Freuds for the education of the children whose parents were in analysis with Freud. (It was not unusual for those in analysis with Freud to come from great distances and to settle in Vienna for a while, often bringing their children with them.) Erikson was invited to come and work with the children to teach them art and got along so well with the children that he was invited to join the staff at the school. Through this job he met the Freuds, both Sigmund, who by this time suffered a good deal from his cancer of the jaw, and Anna, Freud's daughter who both cared for her father's health and who had become an analyst in her own right and thus carried on her father's legacy in this way as well (Friedman, 1999).

Because Erikson got along so well with children, Anna Freud invited him to consider becoming a psychoanalyst for children, her own specialty, and so Erikson began a training analysis with Anna Freud as he pursued this goal. Among the things known about this analysis with Anna Freud is that she told him religion was an illusion, the classical Freudian approach to this topic (Friedman, 1999; Freud, 1927); this seems to have further facilitated his drift away from his Jewish religious roots and toward some negative ideas about religion in general (Burston, 2007).

Another aspect of this exposure to the Freuds was his coming to understand that Freud also had some ambivalence about his Jewish background, knowledge which gave Erikson some comfort as he struggled with his own ambivalence in this regard (Friedman, 1999). Although the reasons behind the ambivalences for each man were different (i.e., Erikson's also concerned his struggle over being half Gentile), Erikson (1970) noted that part of the comfort was that he found in Freud a substitute father figure. Given Erikson's ongoing struggle over identity and paternity, it is not surprising that Freud would have contributed to his struggle with his religious identity. During his time with the Freuds Erikson seems to have gone through a period of "non-religiousness" (Friedman, 1999). However, this non-religious part of his identity had its own ambivalences and began to waver under the influence of his new wife whom he also met during this period of his life.

Joan Serson was the daughter of an American mother and a Canadian father who was an Episcopal priest. As the daughter of a minister Joan had grown up in a practicing Christian family. Joan herself seems to have been very devout and though she had periods of struggle with the church, she seems to have remained a devoted Christian throughout her life (Capps, 2015; Friedman, 1999). As a believer she did not care for Anna Freud's comment to Erikson about religion being an illusion and the impact this statement had on him. It also did not help that Anna Freud had told Erikson that she did not think Joan a good influence on him (Friedman, 1999)!

In terms of Joan's influence on Erikson's religious identity struggles during this period one notes that when he and Joan were married there was a series of three wedding ceremonies. One was done in an Anglican chapel and seems to have been for her family and probably was Joan's choice as well. There was a civil ceremony since the Anglican ceremony would have had no legal standing in Austria at that time, and then there was a Jewish wedding for the sake of Erikson's mother and stepfather. As part of this Joan had to make some show of having converted to Judaism, but that she arrived at the ceremony with bacon for a celebration afterward signaled to some extent her true feelings about such a "conversion" (Friedman, 1999). Friedman reports that following his marriage to Joan, Erikson ceased any Jewish observances. One concludes that Erikson's drift from his Jewish roots in his adolescence and young adult years was widened not only by his marriage to Joan but by the Freudian critique of religion to which he was exposed (cf. Freud, 1927). Furthermore, this Freudian critique of religion is likely responsible for a short-lived dis-identification with religion in general since Erikson even made fun of Joan's religiousness for a time (Friedman, 1999). However, this derogation ceased as he came to see the strength and sincerity of Joan's commitment to her faith. It is Joan's influence that will further turn Erikson's reflections on religion and his religious identity toward Christianity (Hoare, 2002).

Religion in Erikson's Adult Years

Unlike some of the psychologists in this book, Erikson's personal growth as a religious person does not terminate with his adolescent or young adult years. Like Carl Jung, issues of faith continue to be important to Erikson throughout his life and much of his religious development, including further grappling with the question of his religious identity, took place during his adult years. Thus, there is a larger section devoted to the influence of Erikson's religious development in his adult years than for most in this book. In writing of Erikson's religious development in his adult years one is also addressing something of how his religious development influenced his work. Since both his own religious development and his thoughts about religious development occur in tandem, one understands that distinguishing between these two is somewhat artificial and done to aid readability.

Although there are several aspects of his religious journey as an adult that will need further elaboration, two main trajectories can be observed in terms of his religious identity: (1) one is that he gradually moves toward a clearer embrace of a Christian identity due in large measure to the continuing influence of his wife; (2) nevertheless, despite the move toward a clearer Christian identity, Erikson retains some identification with being Jewish (Burston, 2007; Friedman, 1999). One sees something of Erikson's penchant for identities on the boundaries (i.e., a stepson identity) in the very way he described these two identities.

"A Christian Apprentice"

When he was 74, Erikson wrote a letter to a friend the week after Christmas in which he described himself as a "Christian apprentice" (an appellation borrowed from his wife) who is "determined to live on the shadowy borderline of the denominational ambiguities . . . into which I seem to have been born" (quoted in Friedman, 1999, p. 453). But many Erikson scholars have noted that his "apprenticeship" to Christianity is evident much earlier than this and that his identification with the Christian religion is much stronger than the term apprentice implies (e.g., Browning, 1987; Hoare, 2002; Wright, 1982; Zock, 2004). One (Roazen, 1976) even sees his identification with Christianity as representing an outright conversion (though Roazen's conclusion seems primarily based on seeing some Christian symbols in Erikson's office at Harvard). What is obvious is that Erikson's attraction to and identification with Christian ideas and values deepened over the course of his life. In tracing the stages of Erikson's Christian apprenticeship, one might begin by noting some key events in Erikson's life that were formative in his opening up to Christian ideas. Interwoven with these events one can see several Christian themes that began to emerge and develop as Erikson thought and wrote.

The process of tracing the steps in Erikson's appropriation of a Christian identity begins by remembering his childhood exposure to the work of the

Christian theologian Kierkegaard by his mother (Erikson, 1970; Friedman, 1999). Karla Abrahamsen was attracted to Kierkegaard both because he was an intellectual from her native Denmark and because of some of the ideas he espoused. As an adult Erikson remarked that through this exposure his mother communicated to him her appreciation for the "existential core" of the Christian faith (i.e., that truth comes in the living of one's faith) (quoted in Friedman, 1999, p. 42). Erikson's attraction to Kierkegaard is thus multiply determined. First, attraction to Kierkegaard is one way to identify with and feel close to his mother. Similarly, he shares his mother's attraction to Kierkegaard because of his Danish heritage and identifying with Kierkegaard is one way to identify with this aspect of his own background. Perhaps his attraction to this well-respected Danish intellectual also is a way he can connect with the Danish father he never knew. In addition, Erikson himself appreciates this existential core of the Christian faith (more on the particulars of this appreciation later). This initial exposure to and attraction to the Christian tradition via his mother only deepens over the course of his life. One might recall that other events that favorably disposed Erikson toward Christianity included the adolescent Erikson's attraction to the Christ of the Gospels (Erikson, 1970) and his being moved by the Lord's Prayer during his youthful wanderings (Erikson, 1958).

When one turns to Erikson's young adult years, the most critical event in his ongoing attraction to the Christian faith is his marriage to Joan Serson, the daughter of an Episcopal priest (Hoare, 2002). As noted earlier, Joan was devout throughout her life, despite some struggles with the institutional church (Capps, 2015), and as a believer, she had an influence upon Erikson. Although Erikson made fun of Joan's religion early on in their marriage (possibly under the influence of Anna Freud who had told Erikson that religion was an illusion), her persistence in being a believer and her later encouragement of Erikson to accompany her to church services began to make a positive impact on him (Capps, 2015). Soon after their marriage he ceased observing any Jewish rituals left over from his upbringing in Homberger's home and when the children were born, Erikson agreed to let her raise them as Christians (Friedman, 1999).

Although Erikson spent the first couple of decades of his married life primarily in clinical work, he also was associated for about 10 years with the University of California (Friedman, 1999). Out of his clinical and educational work he produced his first major publication when he was almost 50 years old (*Childhood and Society*, a compilation of earlier work from his 30s and 40s). One sees little evidence of his Christian apprenticeship in this work, but by the time of his second major publication eight years later one is confronted with various Christian ideas front and center (Erikson, 1958). This second work was a major study of the Protestant Reformer Martin Luther's childhood and young adult years. In trying to trace Erikson's unfolding identification with Christian ideas, one must ask what lay behind the choice of Luther for his second major publication.

In his preface to this book Erikson (1958) identified several reasons why he was drawn to write this particular book. His chief professional interest at this time seems to have been the search for a means to further explore his understanding of identity formation (as proposed in his model of the life stages first articulated in *Childhood and Society*). From his work with troubled teens at the Austin Riggs Center and with combat veterans who had returned from WWII, Erikson (1950/1963) saw identity formation as critical to this time of development. Writing *Young Man Luther* (YML) a few years later gave Erikson the opportunity to devote further attention to this phase of development. This interest in identity formation was the chief impetus for restricting his exploration of Luther to primarily his adolescence (i.e., he wanted to look at Luther's identity formation. How was it that young Martin developed the identity of Luther the Protestant Reformer?) That said, one cannot help but note that although Erikson's professional concern with identity was driven primarily by Erikson's personal concern with his own identity (Erikson, 1970; cf. Roazen, 1976), Erikson could have pursued this interest in identity formation by studying any number of people. So, why choose Luther? Erikson (1958) stated that this choice also was determined by personal interests in religion, particularly the Christian religion and its influence upon society.

Erikson (1958) wrote in the preface to *YML* that for some time he had been thinking about his growing up in Germany and issues of faith. Behind this veiled comment lies the history of a young Jewish man who had grown up in Luther's Germany and had experienced first-hand some of the fruits of Luther's anti-Semitism. (In noting this quality in Luther, it would be unfair to him to think this aspect of his character the only defining quality of his life; he is much too complex for such reduction. But alas, this is not a book on Luther and so a more balanced presentation is left to his biographers). Furthermore, as a psychoanalyst, Erikson had heard from Freud's daughter how religion is like a sickness in humanity (Friedman, 1999). Writing *YML* gave Erikson opportunity to explore his more deeply emerging thoughts and feelings about religion and its role for both individuals and society. Recall again, that by this time Erikson had been married to a devout Christian believer and had seen a more positive side to religion, in particular Christianity, than he would have experienced as a Jew growing up in Germany in the first third of the twentieth century (see Cooper-White, 2018). Writing *YML* gave Erikson opportunity to explore his emerging ideas about religion and Christianity in particular. In studying the role of religion in society, one could not have picked a more obvious exemplar of how religion has influenced culture (as well as been influenced by cultural currents that were unfolding) than the Protestant Reformation. Writing *YML* seems to have had a formative influence on Erikson's developing ideas about religion in several ways for it is here that Erikson first explored the ethical dimensions of religion. Writing about Luther and the emergence of the Protestant Reformation gave Erikson opportunity to weigh in on how religion, particularly Christianity, had influenced the ethical tenor of Western culture. He also used this venue to elucidate and evaluate some of the ethical dimensions of Christianity. (More will be said on Erikson's thoughts on Christianity and the ethical tenor of Western culture below.)

In tracing the stages of his Christian apprenticeship, it is significant to note that Erikson (1958) spoke very positively of the Christian faith in *YML*. Yet, such a positive assessment seems to have come at a cost. Reviewers have sometimes pointed out that the overall positive tenor of *YML* toward the Christian religion caused Erikson to downplay the anti-Semitism in Luther (Burston, 2007; cf. Fromm, 1942). One way Erikson did this was to focus on "young Martin" and not the older, sometimes virulent anti-Semitic Luther. In fact, the older Luther interested him very little, and he did not care much for the man Luther became (Burston, 2007). In particular Erikson had some concern for the aggression that the adult Luther manifested (e.g., Luther's remarks about suppressing the contemporary peasant revolt through violence). Erikson did not value this part of Luther and did not expound much on this negative side of his development (though his own model makes much of how aspects of the negative pole are important in one's development as well; Erikson, 1950/1963).

How is it that Erikson was able to ignore such negative aspects of Luther? One could point to several converging influences that contributed to Erikson focusing on the positive in Luther over against the negative. First, one might note that Erikson's model of development emphasizes an overbalance of the positive over the negative for healthy development (see key ideas). Thus, in exploring Luther's development, Erikson may simply be following his penchant for emphasizing the positive over the negative. In addition, one would acknowledge the role his wife played in his positive attitude toward Christianity (Hoare, 2002). His wife was a devout believer and it was during the time he wrote *YML* that Erikson ceased to make fun of the Sunday services she so loved (Friedman, 1999). Through example and conversation, she helped him see the good in the Christian faith despite the negative aspects of someone like Luther. Also, during the time that Erikson was reflecting on the themes that frame *YML* he and his family moved back to Massachusetts to the Stockbridge area so that he might work with troubled teens at the Austin Riggs Center. A couple of his good friends in Stockbridge were his neighbors Reinhold and Ursala Niebuhr (Friedman, 1999). Niebuhr was professor of Christian theology at Union Theological Seminary in New York who wrote popular and influential books on Christian ethics and Christianity's influence on culture (e.g., Niebuhr, 1941, 1943). Niebuhr's conversations with Erikson also influenced him toward a more positive view of Christianity. Through this friendship Erikson began to deepen his understanding of the existential core of Christianity that he had earlier been exposed to as a child. Thus, this friendship with the Niebuhrs contributed to Erikson's deepening Christian apprenticeship (Niebuhr actually wrote a favorable review of *YML*).

Having finished his work on *YML*, in itself a formative experience in Erikson's Christian apprenticeship, Erikson soon found himself invited to teach at Harvard (Hoare, 2002). This position became another step along the way in Erikson's Christian apprenticeship, for it was at Harvard that he made the acquaintance of Paul Tillich, a German theologian who had immigrated to America during Hitler's rise to power (much like Erikson had) (Burston, 2007). Both Erikson and Tillich shared an interest in Kierkegaard; furthermore, Tillich's particular interest as a theologian was to make the existential core of the Christian faith relevant to a new generation by recasting the essence of the Christian faith into his new existential theological categories of "being" (Tillich, 1951). Erikson read everything by Tillich he could get his hands on and attended all of Tillich's lectures that he could (Burston, 2007; Friedman, 1999). His shared interests with Tillich and Tillich's own take on Christianity became further positive influences on Erikson's thinking about and turn toward Christianity; Erikson even displayed a crucifix in his office at Harvard (Friedman, 1999).

One might also note that in terms of his writing, Erikson devoted the decade he was at Harvard to writing his book on Gandhi, an early advocate of nonviolent protest who was educated at Oxford but returned to his native India to lead a nonviolent revolt against exploitative manufacturing practices (Erikson, 1969). Although not a book on Christianity in the way *YML* was, the relevance of this book to Erikson's Christian apprenticeship is seen in a couple of ways. First, one would note that the Christianity Erikson embraces is not a narrow kind in which insights from other religions would be excluded. This is obvious when one sees Erikson trying to correlate the teachings of Jesus with Gandhi's non-violent approach. Furthermore, one can see Erikson's recommendation of Gandhi's non-violent approach as something of an answer to the violence he abhorred in Luther (Johnson, 1977). Second, on a more general note, by the time Erikson had written *YML* and the Gandhi book, it is quite clear that his position toward religion had moved very far afield of a classical Freudian position on religion (Roazen, 1976). Unlike Freud (including Anna Freud), Erikson abandoned the notion that religion was an illusion and wrote favorably of the positive contributions of religion to society (more on this below). One notes that these two trends were occurring simultaneously in Erikson's adult development. As he was pondering the positive influences of religion in society, he was also investigating more deeply the Christian faith. Conversely, one might note that as Erikson became more acquainted with the Christian faith, he was simultaneously writing about the positive influence of religion in society (Erikson, 1958, 1977).

It is worth noting one last event in terms of charting Erikson's Christian apprenticeship. This occurred during Erikson's early retirement years and a move back to California. Here Joan began attending an Episcopal church and became friends with the rector, John Thornton (who would later do Erikson's memorial service). She became active in church activities and seems to have been an encouragement to the minister. Here Erikson started attending church with Joan and also became friends with the rector. Friedman (1999) notes that at Thornton's urging, Erikson took communion at least once for a ceremony in celebration of a mutual friend, an exercise that likely involved a token baptism. Furthermore, at Thornton's church Erikson taught a series of lessons on Kierkegaard to the Torah and Gospel group. In terms of Erikson's religious identity formation, one notes that the name of the class in which the lessons are taught signals both a movement toward Christianity for Erikson while also maintaining a location on the boundaries between his emerging Christian and his earlier Jewish identity.

Although Erikson's attitude and thinking toward Christianity changes over the course of his adult years, his growing identification with Christianity is not one in which his Jewish identity is entirely absent. It is also worth noting that the Christianity he espouses is one in which he can include thoughts from both Confucius and Hinduism though he clearly remains monotheistic (Erikson, 1969; Hoare, 2002).

Yet Still Jewish

Despite the obvious movement Erikson makes toward a Christian identity in his adult years, when he was pressed on this matter, he gave a rather paradoxical answer. One sees this reported on a couple of occasions by those who knew him well. Bob Lifton tells of a visit he had with Erikson during his retirement years in California. While they were enjoying a dip in Erikson's pool, Lifton said Erikson asked him what he knew about the "Jews for Jesus" movement that was beginning to make itself known about this time. Lifton explained that he understood them to be Jews that had been born again after the Christian fashion and identified Jesus as the Jewish Messiah. Lifton then asked Erikson to which side he belonged. He reports that Erikson laughed, thought, and then said with something of a grin, "both, of course" (Lifton, 1998, p. 99). This paradoxical answer regarding his willingness to identify with those who accept Jesus as the promised one (i.e., people who are Christian) at the same time contains an answer affirming his Jewish identity.

A second story comes from Don Capps who reports on visiting with Erikson at one point in the early to mid-80s to discuss work Capps (1985) was doing in which he correlated Erikson's developmental stages with the Beatitudes spoken by Jesus (see Matthew 5:1–12). Capps said that during these conversations he asked Erikson if he considered himself a Christian. He reports that Erikson replied, "yes, if that doesn't mean I have to be anti-Jewish" (Capps, 2015, p. 339). Here again one can see Erikson's growing comfort with a Christian identity if it does not require him to entirely relinquish his Jewish identity. But that he would even admit to such an identity shows the length of his journey away from the observant Judaism of his childhood.

In noting Erikson's movement away from his Jewish identity toward a more prominent identification with Christianity it is important to point out that one critic, Marshall Berman (1975) accused Erikson of trying to hide his Jewish identity in his (Erikson's) autobiographical reminiscences. Although Erikson clearly had ambivalences toward his Jewish identity (e.g., on occasions during his years at Austin Riggs when Erikson was asked if he was Jewish he often responded "partly so"; quoted in Friedman, 1999, p. 265), it is also significant that when asked about it he never completely denied it and even in the letter in which he identified himself as a Christian apprentice he remarked that "nobody who has grown up in a Jewish environment can ever be not-a-Jew" (quoted in Friedman, 1999, p. 454). One can note in this regard some evidence of the influence of his Jewish background in his writings (e.g., a citation of the Talmud [Erikson, 1963] and some references to Jesus' Jewish background in an article that recounted much of the Jewish history from the Bible. See Erikson, 1981).

In conclusion, one would note that Erikson's adult years are characterized by a continuing attempt to stay on the border between several identities (a continuation of his stepson identity). For instance, he stayed on the border between his German identity and his Danish identity (e.g., his adopted name of Homberger vs. changing his name to Erikson). He stayed on the border between his American identity and his European identity. This is especially more noticeable after America got involved in the Vietnam War and there were protests in the streets. His earlier ardor for and identification with America has dampened and his earlier interest in how the European temper led to WWII has modified (Erikson, 1950/1963, 1970; Friedman, 1999; Hoare, 2002). Finally, of most interest to this book is how he stayed on the border between a Jewish identity and a Christian one, not belonging entirely to either it seems (though the trajectory is clearly toward embracing the Christian faith). Nevertheless, one sees that the Christianity Erikson embraced was not a narrow one that tended to exclude but was more inclusive and allowing of boundary crossings.

Some Key Ideas in Erikson's Thought

In the section on Erikson's religious development as an adult we have already noted a few of Erikson's key theoretical ideas. This section is devoted to a more structured review of several key ideas in Erikson's thought before turning to some thoughts on how Erikson's religious development influenced his work. This can be no more than a cursory and oversimplified glance at Erikson's work, though hopefully one that is not too distorted. Furthermore, one cannot attend to all of Erikson's ideas even in summary and so the focus here is on certain ideas that will make the points in the next section more intelligible.

Psychosocial Stages of Development

Trained in and working from the Freudian tradition, Erikson's chief addition to Freud's focus on internal psychological development (e.g., the development of the id, ego, and superego structures of the psyche) is Erikson's focus on how the interaction between this internal development and the external environment contributes to one's unfolding patterns of growth (his so-called psychosocial theory—see Erikson's *Childhood and Society*, 1950/1963). The centerpiece of Erikson's theory is his positing a series of eight life stages characterized by varying patterns of interaction between developing psychological structures and environmental expectations that produce a psychosocial "crisis" that is associated with each stage (Erikson, 1950/1963, 1968a, 1982). These stages extend over the entire lifespan from birth to death. For Erikson life begins with a crisis over whether one will develop a sense of basic trust or mistrust toward the environment. Next is a crisis over autonomy versus shame and doubt that arises in toddlerhood and is especially seen in the battles over toilet training (and later law and order). The crisis of the third stage is that between initiative vs. guilt followed by a crisis between industry vs. inferiority in middle childhood. Perhaps the most well-known crisis of Erikson's model is that of adolescence where he proposes a crisis between identity formation or identity confusion (or diffusion). Once one has achieved a sense of identity one might then pledge this identity in fidelity to another; this is the crisis of intimacy vs. isolation. In the middle adult years there arises a crisis over whether one can be and remain generative (e.g., productive and/or creative) or become stagnant. The last stage of the lifespan sees a crisis between integrity over the life one has lived vs. a sense of despair that one's one and only life is about over, and it was not what one had hoped it would be. Of these life stages Erikson spent much of his energy on the stages of identity formation (e.g., the "identity crisis") in adolescence and generativity (how to remain productive and creative) in midlife and beyond.

Crises and Polarities

As one can surmise from the framing of the crises as one possibility vs. another, these crises evoke both positive and negative aspects of one's potential that manifest in the resolution of the various crises. Erikson sees healthy development a result of an overbalance of the positive quality though one retains aspects of the negative pole that also contribute to health. Thus, in the healthy resolution of the first crisis one is to be more trusting than mistrusting at a basic level, although being healthy also involves retaining some level of mistrust (e.g., being wary in strange places). According to Erikson each stage has its own crisis, its own set of positive and negative possibilities as well as its own preferred resolution even if not always realized. During each stage Erikson further argues that there are psychosocial processes that aid the negotiation of each crisis (or whose absence can hinder development). For instance, the process of mutuality aids the development of a sense of basic trust, the process of role experimentation aids identity formation, and so forth (more on some of these processes later).

Crises Resolution and the Emergence of Various Ego Strengths

As Erikson (1964) continued to expound upon his developmental stages, he described a series of ego strengths (or what he later calls "virtues") that emerge from the successful resolution of the crises of each stage. These include qualities such as hope, purpose, and love, among others. We will not enumerate these or explore them further here but will expand on certain of these as they become relevant for understanding certain points in the next section.

How Erikson's Religious Journey Influenced his Life and Thought

We noted in the Introduction that the religious backgrounds of the psychologists studied here had an impact that was both indirect (via its cultural influence) and direct. The more indirect cultural influences are seen in their use of a developmental perspective (i.e., life moves toward some purpose) and in the ethical legacy of the Jewish and Christian traditions to which they were heir. The more direct ways concern the influence of their religious background on specific ideas in their thinking as well as other things such as the way they viewed their lives and work and the major foci of that work.

A Developmental Perspective

One can see the more cultural influences of Erikson's religious background in his adoption of a developmental perspective and its elaboration via his articulation of the various psychosocial stages of the life cycle. This idea of a forward progression through stages of the lifespan is indebted to the Jewish and Christian traditions regarding the linear progression of history (Kirschner, 1996). Furthermore, Erikson's adoption of a developmental perspective is also seen in his idea that life is lived toward the acquisition of certain ego strengths or virtues that result from the successful resolution of the crises of the various stages. These strengths or virtues become goals toward which life moves. We look at the more direct influence of Erikson's religious background on his articulation of these strengths or virtues below.

The other indirect influence of religious culture on Western thought that was noted in the Introduction concerns the influence of Augustine regarding what one might move toward (i.e., toward the correction or restoration of something corrupted rather than toward the completion of something already present) that has influenced much of the thinking about therapeutic aspects of psychology (Hathaway & Yarhouse, 2021). In this regard, we note that one sees less of the focus on repair in Erikson than in Freud, his early mentor. That is, although Erikson is aware that things can go wrong in development and devotes some attention to how this can happen, Erikson is much more concerned to outline and concentrate on the normal unfolding of the more positive side of human development (cf. Erikson, 1958, 1977).

Ethical Legacy of His Religious Traditions

One also sees the more indirect, cultural influence of Erikson's religious traditions in various aspects of the ethical legacy of the Jewish and Christian traditions, both of which show up in Erikson's life and thought although there is an increasing appropriation of Christian categories as Erikson ages. Like the other psychologists in this book, Erikson is heir to a general moral framework derived from these traditions that is characterized by concerns about questions of good and evil, innate goodness or its absence, and obligation (what one ought to do) For instance, one can see the ethical influence of his religious traditions in his adoption of a strong work ethic that is directed by meaning and purpose and not simply survival (i.e., the Protestant work ethic; Weber, 1904/1958) as well as in his reflections on the question of goodness vs. badness in humans. Regarding the latter, Erikson (1969, 1976) occasionally spoke of his belief in sin, even "original sin" though he tended to give such remarks a psychological cast as well (cf. his comment that the absence of virtue is not vice but "weakness" [Erikson, 1964, p. 139]). Similarly, Wright (1982) points out that Erikson's discussion of the potential ascendency of the negative pole of each crisis is Erikson's way to handle the traditional theological categories of evil and sin. However, as we will see what one generally finds in Erikson's comments in these areas is an optimism regarding an essential goodness in humans (e.g., Erikson, 1977). Since Erikson's engagement of these ethical questions tends to reflect a more direct than indirect influence of his religious traditions on his work, the specifics of this influence are taken up below.

Certain Key Ideas

One sees a more direct influence of Erikson's religious background and development in certain key ideas in his thought (Browning, 1987; Hoare, 2002; Wright, 1982). This section looks at several ways that Erikson's religious background and development influenced key ideas in his work.

(Christian) Virtues as Goals of Development

We noted earlier that Erikson outlined a series of ego strengths or virtues that emerged as one negotiated the various developmental stages and crises. As Erikson increasingly called these qualities "virtues," one notes a shift from simple description of how things are to how they ought to be; Erikson's articulation of these virtues also become part of his vision of the good life as they outline qualities one moves toward (Browning, 1987; Capps, 1984). In his use of the word "virtue" Erikson appropriated the original meaning of virtue by the Romans who identified an animating principle in humans (i.e., Latin *anima*, sometimes translated as "spirit" in English). In referring to a spiritual or virtuous dimension in the human, Erikson sought to express something of a lost but basic unity of the person (cf. Erikson, 1964, p. 112). What is interesting for our concerns is to note that these qualities have a decidedly Christian cast (e.g., virtues of hope, love, integrity, etc.). For instance, several Erikson scholars have noted how closely Erikson's explanation of these virtues are to Christian ideas and attribute this connection to his own growing identification with the Christian faith (Browning, 1987; Capps, 1985; Roazen, 1976; Wright, 1982). Hoare (2002) also notes a connection of the ethical life to the Christian notion of *caritas* (love of neighbor); we will say more on this below but first we note how Erikson's progression toward a greater identification with the Christian religion is seen in his development of the concept of *mutuality*.

Recall that Erikson (1977) used this term to describe the quality of the earliest interactions between mother and infant. One way to think about this quality is the level of attunement between mother and child as they interact, each being able to read something of the other's reactions and to respond accordingly. Of course, early on most of the weight of this is borne by the mother though the infant has a role to play as well. Mutuality promotes healthy development in that if there is proper mutuality in these exchanges the infant can develop a sense of basic trust toward the world (i.e., mutuality is the "process" by which basic trust and hopefulness can emerge) (Erikson, 1977). If one can develop a sense of basic trust toward the world, then one can develop the ego quality of hopefulness. Without an overbalance of trust, one is not hopeful and withdraws from engagement of the world in a meaningful, growth-enhancing way.

In his further reflections on the concept of mutuality Erikson makes a significant shift in that he writes of mutuality not only in terms of the interactions between the mother and child at the beginning of life but in terms of a quality that needs to belong to relationships throughout life. Wright (1982) notes that this shift not only moves Erikson's reflections on mutuality from infancy to the whole of the lifespan but moves his description of mutuality from an "is" to an "ought." Thus, mutuality becomes a guiding ethical principle for all of life. In his comments on Erikson's concept of mutuality Browning (1987) further notes that although "Erikson writes a psychology imbued with an ethic of mutuality" he does not develop "his ethical views on strictly psychological grounds" (p. 205). He goes on to note that these other grounds included Erikson's growing identification with Christian ideas.

Perhaps one sees the influence of his conversations with the likes of Tillich and Niebuhr as Erikson (1963) begins to write more about the nature of mutuality and connects it to the Christian injunctions regarding love of neighbor as oneself. Erikson's (1963) interaction with and revision of the so-called "Golden Rule" where mutuality is interpreted as putting this rule into practice (Wright, 1982) clearly demonstrates his reflections on this aspect of the Christian tradition (i.e., *caritas*, the love of neighbor) (Hoare, 2002; cf. Niebuhr, 1941, 1943). It is interesting in charting Erikson's trajectory toward the Christian faith to note that although he begins his article on the Golden Rule with the Talmudic version ("what is hateful to yourself do not to others") it is what he identified as the Christian version ("love your neighbor as yourself"—noting a positive way of stating the rule over against a negative way) that he thinks most obligates us to others and is the version he ends up interacting with.

A second place one can see the growing Christian influence on Erikson's articulation of the virtues that arise from successful negotiation of each life crisis is in his expansion of the concept of *generativity*, the crisis that belongs to the years of middle adulthood (Browning, 1987; Erikson, 1950/1963). Recall that the crisis of this stage centers on whether one can be and remain creative and productive (generative) or will become stagnant. Erikson (1950/1963, 1977) noted several ways that one can be generative (e.g., having children, rearing them so that they might become productive citizens who find their place in the world, the production of creative works). With its concern about guiding the next generation, generativity is also about the legacy one leaves (i.e., can one leave the world a better place for succeeding generations; cf. Browning, 1987; Hoare, 2002). Thus, the virtue that arises from successful negotiation of the crisis of midlife is the ability to care (and here one sees a connection to the Christian concept of *caritas*). This focus on generativity and the ability to care plays a key role in Erikson's (1969) book on Gandhi's midlife years where Erikson (1969) wrote pointedly of Gandhi's ability to care for others such as the striking workers he represented. At the same time Erikson is deeply troubled by Gandhi's cruel treatment of—maybe inability to care for—his immediate family, a concern reminiscent of his concern regarding Luther's aggressiveness.

As with mutuality, in writing about generativity Erikson writes of it not only as an "is" of development but as an "ought" and like mutuality, generativity becomes an ethical principle to strive for and guide all of life (Browning, 1987; Capps, 1984; Roazen, 1976). As Erikson (1968a) developed his ethics of generativity and care he wrote that this care was to extend to all of humanity and not just to one's own tribe or "pseudo-species." Furthermore, this care is to encompass care of the earth and is especially manifest in care for future generations (Erikson, 1974). In Erikson's connection of this ability to care to the Golden Rule and his move to make generativity an ethical concern one can see further evidence of the influence of Erikson's continued gravitation toward more explicitly Christian ideas (Browning, 1987).

Revisiting Identity Formation

One can also see the influence of Erikson's religious background and development on his key ideas in his last reflections on his concept of identity formation, a concept he revisits in his last major theoretical paper (Erikson, 1981). What is of interest here is that he grounded his thoughts on this in the sayings of Jesus. Erikson (1974) had earlier written of Jefferson's attempt to find the authentic "presence" of Jesus in the various sayings attributed to him in the Gospels. In his article on Jesus Erikson also seems to seek after and identify with the "presence of Jesus" (Capps, 2014). In his articulation Erikson saw in the sayings of Jesus during his early ministry insight into early self-awareness (i.e., the sense of "I") and thus saw Jesus promoting a kind of growth of self-identity (Erikson, 1981). Hoare (2002) notes "to Erikson, Jesus was the model who showed 'the way' to a transcendent form of humanity, belief, and behavior"; that is, "the teachings and sayings of Jesus represent a 'leap' in human consciousness" (pp. 91, 93). For Erikson Jesus was an exemplar of one with clear self-identity. Erikson went on to write of Jesus' origins as a Jew and the history of the Jewish people guided by One whose basic identity is "I AM" (Ex. 3:14). Erikson thus grounds a sense of "I" (identity) in God. Capps (1984) remarks on this point: "Erikson says that God is One whose self-identity is eternal, and who is therefore the ultimate source of our consciousness of being an 'I'" (p. 125; cf. Erikson, 1968a, p. 220).

Erikson's Theory of Religion

One can also see the influence of Erikson's religious background and development in the theory of religion that he articulates. One key focus of Erikson's work is his evolving position on the role of religion in life and culture. To understand Erikson's theory of religion, it is helpful to first contrast it with Freud's theory of religion. For Freud (1927), religion was an infantile wish for a strong father figure that was projected upon the universe. Thus, for Freud religion was an illusion rooted in childhood. Not only did the child's understanding of God come from the child's early relationship with the father (Freud, 1913), Freud further saw religion as preying upon human fears of the unknown both in terms of one's own powerful drives but also of unknowable forces in the universe. Erikson was trained as a Freudian and for a while seemed to have adopted the classical Freudian view that religion was an illusion; however, after his marriage to Joan and through reflections on his own patients' religious experiences (Friedman, 1999), he modifies his understanding of religion in two significant ways.

Religion as healthy and adaptive. First, over against the Freudian notion that religion is pathological Erikson (e.g., 1958, 1977) argues that religion is an adaptive force for both the individual and culture. Although Freud (1927, 1930) conceded that religion may serve an adaptive function culturally in that it constrains certain negative or destructive impulses (drives) thus making it possible for people to live together in community, he saw religion as infantile and analogous to a collective expression of neuroses (Freud, 1907b, 1927). At the individual level he saw religion as developmentally regressive as well as thwarting one's "natural" (biological) instincts toward sex and aggression. Contrary to this understanding of religion Erikson argued that religion's cultural adaptability did not lie simply in its ability to restrain negative impulses. One sees this trajectory in Erikson's first major book, *Childhood and Society*. There he wrote, contrary to Freud, that one must avoid "the easy conclusion that our relatively advanced knowledge of neurosis permits us to view mass phenomena—culture, religion, revolution—as analogies of neuroses" (Erikson, 1950/1963, p. 15). One also senses that he is not willing to simply reduce religion in the way Freud did when Erikson (1970) writes that "what religion calls grace and sin transcends the comfort of adaptation and the management of guilt" (p. 758). From simple negation that religion can be equated with pathology, Erikson (1958, 1977) moves in his later writings to articulate religion's culturally adaptive aspects. For instance, in reading YML it is clear Erikson is not only concerned with Luther's pathology but also is interested in the powers of recovery and adaptability that are inherent in religion (Erikson, 1958). In this work Erikson also wrote of the connection between his first developmental stage and the capacity for religious experience, asking,

> must we call it regression if man thus seeks again the earliest encounters of his trustful past in his efforts to reach a hoped-for and eternal future? Or do religions partake of man's ability, even as he regresses, to recover creatively? At their creative best religions retrace our earliest inner experiences, giving tangible form to vague evils, and reaching back to the earliest individual sources of trust. (Erikson, 1958, p. 264)

For Erikson, religion is the socio-cultural force that fosters mutuality and hopefulness and is creative and adaptive in that it provides society a way to institutionalize the virtue of hope. Through its rituals and beliefs religion both promotes and nurtures mutuality within the whole of society, a reciprocal process in which religion promotes hopefulness and people with a measure of hope are those who are attracted to religion and thus keep religious practices alive for succeeding generations. This interest in the restorative powers of religion becomes part of a life-long quest for Erikson and becomes a theme that he returns to time and again (Erikson, 1963, 1969, 1977, 1981).

It is also important to note that although Erikson speaks of religion in generational and intergenerational ways, he makes his case for the individually adaptive aspects of religion. That is, to be a religious individual for Erikson (1958) is not only natural but healthy (cf. Burston, 2007, Hoare, 2002; Roazen, 1976). Furthermore, one might recall that religion is adaptive and creative on the individual level in that it is both an expression of and an organizer of what Erikson (1968a, 1981) called a "sense of 'I'" (an elaboration of his earlier ideas of "identity"). That is, religion is able to promote self-awareness and to help one find ways to both understand and express this self-awareness.

Another aspect of Erikson's (1958) positive and adaptive role for religion is his conclusion that humans are naturally religious (*homo religiosus*). That is, there is something within the human that seeks after something supernatural, something greater than the self, an Other to which one is connected and desires to connect (Erikson, 1968a). This point Erikson holds in common with Freud (1927), yet in Erikson (unlike in Freud) there is no connotation that such natural inclinations need to be given up as immature. For Erikson, this awareness of the spiritual has its foundation in the early interactions between mother and child (which establishes a capacity to experience the numinous or spiritual; more on this below). Such awareness may be invested in other pursuits in earlier life stages (e.g., gets invested in identity formation, expressions of intimacy, pursuit of an ethical ideology, etc.) but emerges particularly during the generative phase so that Erikson argues that everyone deals with the spiritual later in life (Erikson, 1969, 1984; Hoare, 2002; Zock, 2004). Awareness of our spiritual nature becomes part of what it means to be a mature adult (Erikson, 1958). As noted above, in Erikson's writings on this generative stage one sees his concern with ethics and religion merge. Part of religion's adaptive qualities lie in its promoting an "ethical" viewpoint (things to move toward) that moves us beyond the more primitive "morality" (things to avoid) of earlier development (Hoare, 2002; cf. Erikson, 1963, 1968b; more on this below). To mature for Erikson is to move toward ethical action. He writes that religion in midlife is concerned with ethical actions and explains the central virtue of this stage (that of care) in increasingly religious ways (see above) (Hoare, 2002; Roazen, 1976; cf. Erikson, 1969).

Finally, in summarizing this aspect of Erikson's theory of religion one notes that although Erikson takes a basically positive attitude toward religion, he is aware that religion can have its negative side (Erikson, 1950/1963, 1958, 1970). For instance, Erikson notes that organized religion could distort the human's primitive urge toward spirituality by turning one toward fear or subverting one's fears to its own use. Here Erikson (1950/1963) seems to lie closer to his Freudian roots, writing that "a religion, for example, may organize the nuclear conflict of sense of trust versus sense of evil, collectively cultivating trust in the form of faith and exploiting the sense of evil in the form of sin" (p. 277) and that "Christian ethics is based on a radical subordination of this world to 'the other world'" (p. 355). However, it is also significant to note that Erikson's negative assessments of religion tend to occur in his earlier writings and less so in later ones. Why this is so is not certain. Hoare (2002) attributes his negative comments about religion to a concern with "organized religion"; however, others (e.g., Friedman, 1999; Roazen, 1976) note Erikson also wrote of institutional religion as restorative (cf. Erikson, 1977). Wright (1982) is closer to the mark in his comment that Erikson is ambivalent toward organized religion. It is also possible that less negative comments about religion appear as Erikson's own religious journey takes him into a deeper appreciation for the positive aspects of religious faith.

Ontogenetic origins of religion. The second significant way that Erikson's theory of religion modifies Freud's is in the way Erikson re-conceives the ontogenetic origins of the child's understanding of God. (Ontogenetic refers to development within a person's life span; thus, here it would refer to how a particular individual comes to believe in and understand God). For Freud (1913, 1927) these origins lie in the child's relationship to the father (figure); thus, images of God are projections of these father images (including the wished-for father) onto the fabric of the universe. Erikson (1950/1963, 1977, 1981), by contrast, re-conceives the ontogenetic origins of our images of God to lie in our connections with the mother rather than the father (Capps, 1985; Wright, 1982). According to Erikson, the earliest interactions with caregivers tend to be those with the mother, and since these earliest interactions provide the foundation for hope (i.e., the prerequisite for religion or an experience of the numinous), it is the mother rather than the father that provides the template (and/or locus) for one's image of God. That one might think of God as nurturing, caring, loving and such, Erikson (1950/1963, 1977) argues, is drawn more from one's interactions with the mother figure than with the father figure though the father still has a role as well (cf. Capps, 1985; Wright, 1982). Thus, for Erikson, one's openness to and belief in an Other resides in the child's earliest connections with the mother, particularly in the mutuality that led to a sense of basic trust in one's environment. It is these early interactions with the mother that become the wellspring of one's image of God and the numinous.

As early as *Childhood and Society* Erikson (1950/1963) had written that "primitive religions, the most primitive layer in all religions, and the religious layer in each individual, abound with efforts at atonement which try to make up for vague deeds against a *maternal* matrix and try to restore faith in the goodness of one's strivings and in the kindness of the powers of the universe" (p.252, my emphasis). Note that for Erikson it is against a maternal matrix that one seeks to atone (vs. Freud [1913] who posits a father matrix in this regard). Erikson continued to affirm and elaborate this insight in his further writings on religion. For instance, in *YML* he wrote that "in the beginning are the generous breast and the eyes that care. Could this be one of the countenances which religion promises us we shall see again, at the end and in another world? Is there an ethology of religion?" (Erikson, 1958, p. 117). In *Toys and Reasons*, he re-visited this earliest interaction of the mother and the infant, writing that "this first and dimmest affirmation, this sense of a hallowed presence, contributes to mankind's ritual-making a pervasive element which is best called the numinous" (Erikson, 1977, p. 89). Here one cannot help but note the increased use of religious language to describe these earliest interactions. When he further wrote that "the numinous assures us of *separateness transcended* and yet also a *distinctiveness confirmed* and thus of the very basis of a sense of 'I,' renewed (as it feels) by the mutual recognition of all 'I's joined in a shared faith in one all-embracing 'I Am'" (Erikson, 1977, p. 90, italics in original), the religious language is front and center with its evocation of God's self-designation as "I Am"(cf. Ex. 3:14). Thus, for Erikson the face-to-face interactions between mother and child become the foundation for one's experiences of God. If one were to posit a source for this shift in Erikson's own life, one recalls that for his first three years he and his mother tended to fend for themselves, giving him a time where he and his mother can attach in important ways (although this period is not without some ambiguity in this regard). Conversely, when he is introduced to his stepfather at the age of three, he is not able to form a significant bond with him (Friedman, 1999).

In speaking about the developmental origins for a sense of the religious, it is important to note that Erikson does not intend to be reductionistic. Here again, he departs from Freud's (1927) reductionism of religion to a personal or cultural neurosis. In his last major theoretical paper regarding the origins of religious faith he wrote that

I do not mean to reduce such faith to its infantile roots. For the literal believer could well respond with the assertion that human childhood, besides being an evolutionary phenomenon, may well have been created so as to plant in the child at the proper time the potentiality for a comprehension of the Creator's existence, and a readiness for his revelations. And, indeed, the way the father can be experienced in childhood can make it almost impossible not to believe, deep down in (and indeed to fear as well as to hope for) a fatherly spirit in the universe. (Erikson, 1981, p. 480)

One cannot help but note the parallels between Erikson's emerging ideas about religion and his own religious development during his adult years.

Finally, in closing these paragraphs on Erikson's view on the ontogenetic origins of religion, one notes that there is an inconsistency in the way he speaks about the reality of God (Hoare, 2002; Wright, 1982). On the one hand, he expresses his classical Freudian roots in speaking of God in terms of God as a psychic reality (Erikson, 1970, 1975b) and in one sense he never seems to abandon this way of conceiving God. Yet, there are other places where Erikson leaves open the possibility that there might be a God who is real in addition to all the projections that humans have about God (e.g., Erikson, 1970, 1977, 1981). Don Browning recounts an interaction with Erikson in which Erikson reportedly said "in religion man does not just project something onto nothing. He is probably projecting something onto some reality which is actually there. There may even be an interaction between man's projection and this reality" (quoted in Wright, 1982, p. 183). One senses here that Erikson is no longer satisfied with the idea of God as a psychic projection as the only way to understand the goodness and benevolence he sees in the universe. However, in his published writings Erikson never quite grants a full reality to God; he always hedges his comments in this regard with words like "perhaps" and this is perhaps all one can expect from one speaking as a psychologist.

Other Ways

One can also see the influence of Erikson's religious background on his work in his increased emphasis on ethics, in his frequent turn to religious figures as he expands his earlier ideas on development throughout the lifespan, and in his emphasis on existential concerns.

An Increased Focus on Ethics

One of the ways one can see a more direct influence of Erikson's religious background on his work is in the focus on ethics that increasingly characterizes his work (Browning, 1987; Hoare, 2002). We have already noted aspects of this trajectory above (e.g., in the joining of the ethical and spiritual); this section expands on some of the specifics of this influence.

Distinction between morals and ethics. As Erikson rethought and re-worked various dimensions of his developmental model he distinguished between the related concepts of morals and ethics (Erikson, 1963, 1969, 1970; cf. Burston, 2007; Hoare, 2002; Roazen, 1976). This distinction shows Erikson's growth away from Freud's (1913, 1930) position which tended to speak of morality as a fierce, rather negative aspect of human development. In a simplified way one might speak of the Freudian tradition of the superego as one in which morality emerges as the inculcation of the various prohibitions that one learns from parents and society. Thus, morality focuses on that which one must avoid or is against. By contrast, Erikson (1963, 1968a) defined ethics as that for which one aspires or lives. It is the positive side of that aspect of human development for which morality might represent the negative side. Thus, while morality develops early in childhood, ethics does not begin to emerge until after adolescence according to Erikson. Ethics builds on the morality of childhood and the development of what Erikson called an "ideology" in adolescence. This ethical side of human personality continues to develop throughout adulthood and involves active engagement with others including subsequent generations (Erikson, 1963). Erikson also came to believe that these issues of morality vs. ethics eventuate as well in a consideration of what he called the spiritual (Erikson, 1969, 1976; Hoare, 2002).

Having defined ethics as something one aspires to or lives toward, one can see the outworking of this in his reflections on Gandhi and Kierkegaard. For instance, the Gandhi book gave Erikson a means to address some lingering doubts about the aggression he saw in Luther and which Luther had bequeathed to Western civilization (Friedman, 1999; Johnson, 1977). By the time Erikson wrote the Gandhi book, humanity's aggression toward both other humans and the earth had come into full relief (e.g., the Vietnam War and the violent protests against it; the Greenpeace movement to counter exploitation of the earth's resources). Erikson saw Gandhi's non-violent approach to conflict resolution a means and hope for all humanity. One also notes that Erikson (1969) devoted a good bit of space to exploring how Gandhi's generativity connected to ethical action especially in midlife. It also is significant to note that by the time he published this book, Erikson also was at a generative place in his own development and wrestling with issues of how to be a person of ethical actions in his own life (Hoare, 2002).

One also can see this increased focus on ethics in Erikson's (1975a) acknowledgement of Kierkegaard's influence on his way of thinking about the unfolding stages of life. This is seen particularly in the movement toward becoming an ethical actor as one moves through Erikson's stages. For Kierkegaard (1843/1987) the path to maturity is to move beyond the "aesthetic" stage in life (i.e., a concern for harmony and beauty in the world) to an ethical (right action) one. That one deals with religious dimensions of life later (by midlife and beyond) for Erikson also mirrors Kierkegaard's movement that beyond the ethical stage of life is a religious one (Burston, 2007; Erikson, 1975a; Hoare, 2002). In Erikson, his increased focus on ethics also shows a clear movement toward Christian ideas, a movement connected to Erikson's own religious development. Drawing upon both published and unpublished papers Hoare (2002) further summarizes a connection between Erikson's ethical theory and his focus on Christian themes: "Electing ethical adulthood as his primary vehicle, Erikson associated its development with the caritas of Christianity" holding "that the sense of self as a spiritual being is, necessarily, a concomitant of the ethical" (pp. 75, 79). This takes us to our next point.

Move from "is" to "ought." One also can see Erikson's increased emphasis on ethics in the movement from "is" to "ought" that was noted above. That is, in Erikson's elaborations regarding the ego strengths or virtues, they move from descriptive possibilities to prescriptive goals toward which life is lived, with each succeeding virtue building upon the previous one. This means that the whole of life is lived toward acquiring the virtues of the latter stages and that the qualities arising from the first of the stages become foundational for acquiring the strengths of the latter stages. He wrote, for instance, "will cannot be trained until hope is secure, nor love become reciprocal until fidelity has proven reliable" (quoted in Hoare, 2002, p. 101). Thus, for Erikson the end goal of life (what it is lived toward) as articulated in the last strength or virtue becomes the acquisition of "integrality" (a term he offered as perhaps more descriptive of what can be expected and achieved in old age than "integrity" given the diminishing capacities and resources of late life. This change of terms in his later writings [e.g., Erikson, 1982, 1984] often goes unnoticed in presentations of his model; Hoare, 2002). He noted that integrality pointed again to the holistic nature of the human and was more evocative of both the first stage and the increased focus given to the relationship between mutuality and generativity noted above; integrality and faith also get closer to the meaning of ego integrity as the end of development for Erikson (1984). This sense of continuity (perhaps completion) with who one was earlier means that the goal of human living for Erikson (i.e., integrality) might be framed in terms of becoming generative or able to care for succeeding generations in the way one had initially been cared for (see Browning, 1987 as well as the above discussions of mutuality and generativity).

An Increased Focus on Religious Characters

One also sees the influence of Erikson's religious background and development on his work in his increased focus on religious figures in his writing. It is significant to observe that in Erikson's most productive period (Hoare, 2002), his major work centered on two religious figures. As Erikson expanded his concepts of the life cycle through further reflections on adolescence (with its crisis of identity formation) and midlife (with its crisis of generativity) he did this via his studies of Luther and Gandhi respectively. Even in his later, less productive period (Hoare, 2002), Erikson still focused on religious characters: Kierkegaard and Jesus; even in his work on Thomas Jefferson, it is Jefferson's religious ideas that captivate him (Erikson, 1974). And although it would be inaccurate to think Erikson only used religious figures to advance his psychological theory, he does it often enough to make the point that his increasing interest in religion clearly guides significant portions of his psychological work. We also note that in looking at the religious figures on whom Erikson focused, one sees lines in his trajectory toward a greater Christian identity.

Luther. The reasons behind Erikson's choice of Luther have been noted above. In summary one recalls that Erikson could have expanded his concepts on adolescent identity formation in any number of ways and with any number of people. For instance, he could have written about some of the adolescents he worked with at Austin Riggs, which seemed his intent at one point (Friedman, 1999). He confessed he chose Luther as the means by which to expand and illustrate his concept of adolescent identity formation because he was also interested in some issues of faith and in choosing Luther, he was able to address both interests (Erikson, 1958). Thus, Erikson's interest in issues of faith and religion not only drove his choice of the person by which to further his thoughts on identity formation, this choice also afforded him opportunity to further explore his attraction to Christianity.

Gandhi. Erikson's (1969) book on Gandhi also illustrates Erikson's dovetailing interests in religion and human development. In this book Erikson looked at Gandhi not only as a political leader but as a religious leader as well. Thus, the theme of religion and religious leaders unites the two books, as does his exploration of the ethical impact of religion on society (Friedman, 1999; Hoare, 2002). In focusing on Gandhi as a religious figure it also is important to note the parallels Erikson draws between Gandhi and Jesus. He saw both as proponents of nonviolence and pointed to ways that Gandhi was influenced by Jesus' ideas in this regard. He also saw both Jesus and Gandhi as representatives of holy men; even more than this he saw them as key exemplars of the human as *homo religiosus* (as naturally religious; cf. Wright, 1982). These comparisons are important in a couple of ways. First, they indicate Erikson's increased interest in the figure of Jesus, and they also indicate Erikson's ability to negotiate various religious boundaries by pulling together ideas of the religions of the East and the West, especially around the theme of nonviolence.

Kierkegaard. One also sees Erikson's growing attraction to Christianity and its ideals in his later reflections on Kierkegaard. Erikson had admired Kierkegaard since his childhood exposure to him (Friedman, 1999). He was especially drawn to what his mother had called the "existential core" of Kierkegaard's Christianity, and he explored some preliminary dimensions of this in *YML* (Erikson, 1958). His friendships and conversations with the Niebuhrs and Tillich also deepened his interest in and understanding of this existential core of Christianity. In his later years it was Erikson's dream to develop his appreciation of Kierkegaard into a book devoted to this long-admired fellow countryman (Capps, 2014; Friedman, 1999). However, this was not to be; issues of language facility (he did not read Danish) and stamina were to prevent this. Knowing that he had limited energy for further writing in his later years Erikson instead turned his attention to the central figure of the Christian faith.

Jesus. Erikson's choice to stand on the boundaries of religious identity with a clear trajectory toward Christianity is especially noticeable in his last major theoretical contribution which was a work on Jesus (Erikson, 1981; Hoare, 2002). Conceived as a book, this project was thwarted by the same health issues that undermined his dreams of a Kierkegaard book. Erikson, with the help of his son Kai was only able to pull together the material for a substantial article (Friedman, 1999). In this article, Erikson (1981) noted that he had been interested in the teachings of Jesus from an early age (possibly through his early exposure to Kierkegaard and certainly since his adolescence). We might note that Erikson showed interest in Jesus and his sayings as early as *Childhood and Society* where he wrote:

> it is hard for our rational minds to comprehend . . . that frustrated wishes, and especially early, preverbal and quite vague wishes, can leave a residue of sin which goes deeper than any guilt over deeds actually committed and remembered. In our world only the magic sayings of Jesus convey a conviction of these dark matters. We take His word for it, that a wish secretly harbored is as good—or rather, as bad—as a deed committed; and that whatever organ

offends us with its persistent desires should be radically extirpated. (Erikson, 1950/1963, p. 149; cf. Mt 5:27–30)

Erikson's interest in Jesus and his sayings also had been evident in his earlier work on Jefferson where he had become intrigued with Jefferson's attempts to tease out the authentic sayings of Jesus (Erikson, 1974). Erikson chose for this last major theoretical paper to return to the concept of identity formation with a special attention to formation of a "sense of 'I.'" Focusing his thoughts on the sayings of Jesus during his early ministry in Galilee, Erikson brought together his growing interest in the founder of the Christian faith and his own work on identity and self-formation.

Interest in Existential Concerns
Finally, we note that the influence of Erikson's religious development shows up in his work through his increasing movement toward a more existential perspective on life (Hoare, 2002; Zock, 2004). This movement toward a more existential perspective has several influences. It has its earliest beginnings in his interactions with his mother around the writings of Kierkegaard and her appreciation for Kierkegaard's articulation of the existential core of Christianity (Erikson, 1970; Friedman, 1999). It was also influenced by Erikson's friendship with Paul Tillich whose "correlation" of traditional Christian categories with contemporary existential philosophy Erikson found quite intriguing. One can see this existentialism emphasized in Erikson's (1958) treatment of Luther's identity formation where he wrote on Luther's need to "mean it" (i.e., to really live it) when he said something. One also can see this focus on existential concerns in the distinction Erikson makes between existential dread and anxiety. Erikson wrote that all may suffer from anxiety, but all need not fall into a deeper existential dread. Erikson saw that many adults in midlife experienced a deeply meaningful spiritual sense, and this led him to distinguish this experience from a kind of dread rooted in fears of spiritual meaninglessness and the inevitability of death. Erikson further argued that each of these two states required a differing human response: "Anxiety may call for therapy; dread demands faith" (quoted in Hoare, 2002, p. 82; cf. Erikson, 1969, 1976).

Concluding Comments

Of the psychologists covered in this book Erikson's life work is more obviously connected to his own development than it is for any of the others. Erikson's main biographer describes Erikson's lifework as that of being the "architect" of the concept of identity formation (Friedman, 1999). It is obvious that Erikson's own quest to settle the issue of his parentage lies behind the question of identity (i.e., who am I; to whom do I belong). The search for his biological father is clearly formative for the heart of Erikson's work (maybe the whole?). He once remarked that his friends had accused him of inflicting his own identity crisis upon the whole of everyone's development (Erikson, 1970). Thus, when he worked with the troubled teens at the Austin Riggs center, he saw something of the troubled teen of his own youth. Even in his later life he sought to be the mature person he had described in his developmental model (Hoare, 2002).

When one turns to the more specific question of how Erikson's religious journey influenced his work, one notes that his search for identity clearly relates to his question of whether he was Jewish (like his mother and stepfather) or perhaps Gentile like his unknown Danish father. We see his ambivalence about these two identities play out for the remainder of his life (Friedman, 1999). Erikson's story is that of one forever on the border between identities; one who can never dwell irretrievably in only one identity. Thus, despite his clear movement toward a deeper Christian identity over the course of his life it was an identity in which his Jewishness, though deemphasized at times, was never denied.

Finally, if we return to the question posed by Friedman's (1999) comment that Erikson's life was a quest for the face of a benevolent father (Friedman, 1999) in the light of the theme of this book, one might say that he found something of this in the face of God, though only partially because for Erikson God's face has a decidedly maternal cast!

CHAPTER FOUR

B. F. Skinner

Skinner (1976) recounts a story from when he was around 12 years old in which he had lost a favored silver watch. Distraught over this event and after searching along the path where he thought he had lost it, he retreated to a favorite hideaway where he mused about his loss, finally concluding that there was an order in the universe in which good and bad balanced out. If fortune had come to his friends, it was inevitable that misfortune would come to someone else, perhaps him, and that misfortune would in its time yield to another time of fortune. Calmed by these thoughts Skinner began the journey home only to find the watch lying along his pathway! The young Skinner took this event as a sign that God had favored him and that all was right in the world. Although he would come to discount this explanation in later years, this story provides important insight into both the mind and environment of young Skinner. We will return to this incident below as we explore how aspects of Skinner's early religious environment lingered in his life and work. But first, who was Skinner and why include him in this book?

The days in which B. F. Skinner could be declared the most famous psychologist in America are long past (cf. Korn, Davis & Davis, 1991). Nevertheless, his legacy endures and continues to influence the fields of psychology, business, education, and mental health (Bjork, 1993). Skinner is most well-known for his development of a behavioral approach to understanding human experience. That is, for Skinner it is observable behavior (and not mental states or processes) that provides the best means for predicting a person's future actions or reactions. For decades Skinner (1953,

1971) devoted his time and efforts to observing various behavioral patterns (primarily in animals but also assuming humans as a higher order of animal followed these patterns as well). Many will have heard of his "Skinner box," a device he constructed to investigate the various ways and rates a pigeon might peck a target to receive a reward (Toates, 2009). Skinner called the various patterns he discovered in his box "schedules of reinforcement," distinguishing between reinforcement that was positive or negative. It is this concept of reinforcement schedules and how it is applied (e.g., in education or behavioral health) that probably defines Skinner's legacy best, and we will explore some of the particulars of Skinner's system below.

Although it may seem odd that religious development has anything to do with Skinner boxes and schedules of reinforcement, this chapter looks at ways in which Skinner's early years in a religious household influenced the development of his theory and his work. It tells the story of a young man who tried very hard to escape the influences of this early environment but was only partially able to do so. This early theme of escape from his constraining environment is noted by several of those who have written of Skinner and defines a key motif of his life (e.g., Demorest, 2005; Elms, 1994; Siegel, 1996). Late in life Skinner conceded that he was not as successful in escaping the influences of his early development, including religious ones, as he had hoped (Skinner, 1976; Wiener, 1996).

What Is Known of Skinner's Religious Journey?

This section looks at what is known of Skinner's religious background as a prelude to an exploration of how his religious background influenced his work. Although it makes some observations about his overall development, the chief focus is upon his religious development. It draws from both autobiographical and biographical sources.

Religion in Skinner's Early Childhood Home

Skinner grew up in a home characterized by Presbyterian piety. This theological tradition is an heir to the thought of John Calvin, the great Swiss Reformer. This form of piety spoke of God's order in the world and in people's lives (e.g., some were elected or chosen; Gonzalez, 1975). We also noted in the Introduction how this form of Christian piety is associated with the "Protestant work ethic" (i.e., one works hard in hopes of knowing one's part among the elect and to serve God; Demorest, 2005; Weber 1904/1958). Skinner (1976) noted that this was the religious tradition in which he was reared as a child.

The chief way Skinner (1967, 1976) described his mother Grace was controlling, but controlling in a way that was subtle and manipulative rather than overt. For instance, he reported that she only physically punished him one time, but that she found other ways of controlling his behavior because he became very sensitive to displeasing her (as well as his father), something he seems to have tried to avoid at all costs. He recalled that whenever he displayed any behavior that might be problematic his mother would say "tut, tut; what will people think" (Skinner, 1967, p. 391). (See the Rogers chapter for a similar experience he had with his mother.)

One gets the sense from reading Skinner's (1976) autobiography that he was not particularly close to his mother; Monte (1999) states that he was alienated by her emotional restraint and inhibition and that Skinner early on developed alternative activities that took him away from her presence and into the outdoors to engage in a variety of activities. Germane to his emotional escape from the psychological constraint of his parents was the variety of projects and activities the young Skinner engaged in. He was particularly fond of hunting and trapping small animals but was also fascinated to design and build a variety of objects. For instance, one biographer noted that

> he built roller-skate scooters, steerable wagons, sleds, rafts, slides, kites, model airplanes and tin propellers that could be sent high into the air with a spool and string spinner. He tried repeatedly to make a glider in which he himself could fly. It is tempting to see these devices as symbolic means of achieving both the progress that his parents valued and the escape from his constraining environment that he himself wanted. (Demorest, 2005, p. 100)

Of his interactions with his father William, one gets the same impression of a lack of closeness. Skinner's father seems to have been aloof and not well connected to his children or his wife (Monte, 1999); this may be connected to a depressive tendency Skinner (1976) saw in his father. When Skinner reports that it did not bother him that he felt his parents had shown more affection to his younger brother as they were growing up, one cannot help but wonder if his claim to being more independent and not too concerned with this disparity in parental love has the quality of protesting too much. As with his mother, Skinner attributed an aversive controlling nature to his father as well. Of his father, he said he never punished him physically, but that his father found more subtle ways to control him, including mocking his son's behavior. For instance, Skinner recalled his father mocking the way he walked stooped shouldered by hunching low and dragging his arms near the floor like a monkey to encourage his son to walk straighter. Of his father overall, Skinner (1976) saw him as generally lacking ability and ineffectual.

In turning to Skinner's (1976) early religious environment one finds several incidents in his autobiography that give insight into its nature. For instance, he noted that one of his earliest memories of religious teaching was an illustration of God's punishment provided to him by his paternal grandmother. She was trying to discourage lying in the young boy who was about four or five years old at the time. He remembers his grandmother opening the coal-burning stove to tell him that little boys who lied would one day be cast into a place that burned like the coals. Skinner reported being traumatized by this illustration and developing a great sensitivity to lying that troubled him at the slightest infraction even if he did not know at the time that something he said had been in error. He reported that it was years before he was able to manage the mental torments that the illustration produced.

When he turned to speak of his parents' religiousness, Skinner (1967) reported that his parents were regular attenders at a local Presbyterian church in the community in which he grew up, though they did not attend every Sunday, nor did they attend evangelistic revival meetings like most of their fellow Protestants (Bjork, 1993). They did, however, take him to Sunday school at a very young age (Skinner, 1976). When Skinner spoke of his mother's religiosity, he was not particularly charitable. He attributed a kind of sentimentality and pretentiousness rather than sincerity to her piety (Skinner, 1967, 1976). Of his father's religiousness he only reported a few observations. One was that his father played the cornet in church to help support himself. Skinner (1976) further noted that while his father occasionally worried about the state of his son's faith, he had decided that his son should not be baptized until he understood what it meant; Skinner stated that this time never came. (One notes that this is not the common Presbyterian position on baptism which tended to baptize children as infants [Gonzalez, 1975] and may speak to the level of his father's religiosity.) Although it is obvious from Skinner's biographers that his parents influenced him deeply (Bjork, 1993; Wiener, 1996), it is not always clear that it was their religiosity that lay at the heart of this influence. However, there are indicators that the influence of their religiosity got mingled with their general influence on Skinner.

Skinner's relationships with his religiously conservative parents naturally impacted his own religious development. When one couples the aloofness of his father and the coercive nature of his mother with the fact that they were religiously conservative, one can see the potential for a young man like Skinner to connect the two. One biographer (Wiener, 1996) notes that the connection between guilt and faith that arose from his relationship with his religiously conservative grandmother was even more obvious. Furthermore, it would be unusual if his sensitivity to disappointing his parents did not get connected emotionally to sensitivity with disappointing God as well (cf. Kirkpartrick, 2004; St. Clair, 1994). However, this negative religious environment was not all that the young Skinner was exposed to religiously. There also was a strong positive religious influence during the latter part of his childhood that extended into his adolescence.

In his autobiography Skinner (1976) writes with obvious fondness of Mary Graves who was to be both one of his schoolteachers and his Sunday school teacher for many years. Except for medical reasons he noted one five-year stretch when he did not miss a Sunday in her class. He recalled sitting in her Sunday school class week after week while she took her pupils through the Bible using materials supplied by the Presbyterian Church (he reports for instance that it took several years to get through the Pentateuch, the first five books of the Bible). Mary Graves also took a more liberal approach to religion than Skinner's parents. For instance, he noted that she taught her Sunday school class that the miracle stories of the Bible might be treated as metaphors and that the Bible could also be appreciated as literature (Skinner, 1976). He thus found her a moderating influence compared to his family's approach to religion. Through Mary Graves Skinner became aware of a kinder, gentler experience of religion (and possibly God).

When Skinner summarized what he took away from these earliest years it was the need to "fear God, the police, and what people will think" (Skinner, 1967, p. 407). This, of course, is only part of the story. In addition to the negative experiences of religion via his parents and grandparents Skinner also had positive experiences with religion from Mary Graves. Thus, there were several other influences besides fearing God, the police and what others think that stayed with Skinner. We will look at some of these lingering influences in the section devoted to this.

Religion in Skinner's Adolescent Years

The positive influence of Mary Graves on Skinner continued into his early adolescence (Skinner, 1976). Quite possibly under her influence, Skinner remarked that during his early adolescent years he took religion rather seriously, holding conversations with both Mary Graves and another teacher about this subject. He continued to attend Mary Graves' Sunday school class during these early adolescent years, noting that they had arrived at the gospels and the life of Christ at about the same time he reached puberty. He further reported that his awakening sexuality created problems for him in terms of the religious expectations that one not be forthright about these things (Skinner, 1976).

Skinner (1976) offered several illustrations of his attempts to take the Christian religion seriously during these early adolescent years. Two are quite humorous in the revelation of adolescent enthusiasm and naivety. One was an incident in which he tried to demonstrate the truth of the saying of Jesus that faith could move mountains (cf. Mt. 17:20). Skinner's attempt to verify this was to try to levitate himself. He attributed his failure to do so to the ineffectiveness of faith. In reading this account one senses that he never entertains alternate explanations for his failure. That the failure could not possibly lie within himself could simply reflect typical adolescent egocentrism (Elkind, 1967); alternately, it is possible that this reminiscing of the later Skinner is made to accord with his later position that causation lies outside the person (cf. Skinner, 1971).

A second illustration he offered of taking religion seriously was his decision to write an article for a Presbyterian magazine in which he would demonstrate the value of the Presbyterian faith by showing that more great composers came from that tradition than others. Once again one is struck by the adolescent naivety and egocentrism of such a pursuit. This too was a failed attempt, reflecting more the young Skinner's ignorance of music history rather than a deficit in Presbyterian theology. As an aside, one commentator (Shea, 1974) has noted that this need to demonstrate the superiority of his own position is present in Skinner's later writing where he tries to marshal verbal arguments against his various opponents. One thinks in particular of not only the points he makes but the tone he takes in *Beyond Freedom and Dignity* (Skinner, 1971; perhaps his most famous—or infamous—book).

Far and away the most illustrative example Skinner gave of his taking religious faith seriously is the story he recounted about the loss of his silver watch that opened this chapter (his "most valued possession" [Skinner, 1976, p. 110]). In his account Skinner described this incident as a mystical experience. As noted above his conclusion regarding the loss was resolved by a theory of compensation born out of perplexities regarding various injustices in his life and in the world. Skinner had concluded that somehow the universe must eventually balance the books between good and evil, between fortune and misfortune (even if this took place in the afterlife). Mollified by his theory of compensation he proceeded to walk back home. There, unexpectedly, he saw his watch laying in the grass. One senses the mystical nature of the experience in the language with which he spoke of the watch being "carefully placed" on the grass as if some invisible, benevolent hand had put it there. Skinner said this experience felt like a revelation to him and a sure confirmation of his theory of compensation. When he returned home, he recorded the experience in solemn biblical-like language and hid the paper away in a match box without telling anyone (cf. a similar experience in the young Jung). From notes he had written closer to the event Skinner recorded that because of this experience, he felt that "God has spoken to me . . . [and] I have heard him rightly and he has returned my watch as an indication of pleasure" (Skinner, 1976, p. 111).

One notes several things about this incident that reflect his religious upbringing. First, is the idea of order in the world, a key point of Christian thought, and especially Presbyterian thought (Grudem, 1994; Gonzalez, 1975); further this is an order regulated by God. In addition, the theory that life balances good and bad, if even in an afterlife, is part of Skinner's religious tradition as well. Finally, one notes the influence of his Presbyterian upbringing in the connection of this experience to signs that one might be favored by God. We will see that aspects of these beliefs survive in the adult Skinner's behavioral theory.

As far as other religious experiences of the adolescent Skinner, nothing further in the nature of mystical experiences seemed memorable and by the time he reached his later high school years he announced to Mary Graves (one of his high school teachers by now) that he no longer believed in God. He reported that she responded by saying "I have been through that, too" (Skinner, 1976, p. 112). Although Skinner does not note whether this remark was in sympathy or dismissal, the former seems more likely given the positive nature of his other comments about Mary Graves. (She may have been affirming common experiences of adolescent religious questioning; cf. Fowler, 1981). Although Skinner said on one occasion that this announcement of disbelief was within a year of his mystical experience (Skinner, 1967), he also acknowledged that it was a matter of some years before he was fully convinced that he no longer believed (1976).

In summary, Skinner's adolescent religious experience was characterized early on by a seriousness about his faith as well as by some early adolescent attempts to prove the soundness of his faith. As he continued through his adolescence Skinner became troubled by his emerging sexuality given the constraints he felt his faith placed on this and began, at least at times, to question whether he was still a believer (Fowler [1981] notes that such religious questioning is common during adolescence). In reflecting on the themes of restraint and escape noted above it is easy to see Skinner's movement away from religious belief as an escape from the constraining religion of his parents (Skinner, 1976; cf. Demorest, 2005). However, it is also interesting to speculate whether the earlier adolescent preoccupation with the more positive religiousness he experienced under Mary Graves might be its own escape from his parents' version of religion. As Erikson (1968a) has argued, the formation of one's identity during adolescence often involves protest against the identity of one's parents. Thus, a person with religious parents might become irreligious or vice versa. Alternately, one might become religious in ways other than one's parents (e.g., a child of Episcopalian parents might become a fundamentalist Baptist). Mary Graves' form of religion was certainly less restrictive and seems to have encouraged him in his taking religion seriously for a time.

Religion in Skinner's Young Adult Years

Skinner's religious development during these years encompasses his undergraduate years at Hamilton College and the years before his graduate work at Harvard. As typical of the later adolescent and young adult years, a central concern for Skinner was exploration and resolution of identity issues (Elms, 1994; cf. Erikson, 1968a). These issues centered primarily on vocational identity but also encompassed his religious identity. In terms of his vocational identity Skinner's chief early aspiration was to become a writer, an ambition encouraged by Robert Frost, the American poet to whom he had sent some of his work (Skinner, 1976).

In his early years at Hamilton College Skinner wrote poetry, short stories and essays that were occasionally published in various venues such as the college paper and small magazines (Skinner, 1976). Following his graduation from Hamilton, Skinner moved back in with his parents and younger brother with the intention of writing his first novel, setting aside a year in which to complete this project. However, this year did not prove fruitful in this regard and instead became a year of increasing tension, particularly between him and his father over whether his son might be a "loafer," certainly an identity of which people would not think well, and which did not fit well with the Protestant work ethic of his family. Skinner later described this as his "dark year," one in which his identity as a writer was seriously eroded and seemingly abandoned (Skinner, 1976, p. 265).

The lingering influence of the Protestant work ethic in Skinner brings us to the other aspect of Skinner's identity formation during this period, his religious identity. As noted above, by late adolescence Skinner had begun to consider himself a non-believer (at least at times). This journey away from the beliefs of his early childhood and adolescence into an identity as an atheist became solidified during his young adult years but does not occur without some bumps in the road. Evidence of Skinner's ongoing struggle over his religious identity is seen in several incidents he recounts from this period in his life (Skinner, 1976).

During his first couple of years at Hamilton Skinner noted that he came to think of himself as an atheist, yet despite these thoughts he also reported that during these years he "worried" whether he had "lost his faith" (Skinner, 1976, p. 220), suggesting there were other times his religious upbringing lingered. One sees other aspects of this struggle over his religious identity in his recounting the fact that he was troubled after finding out that one of his admired professors also taught Sunday school and he sought to make sense of how it was that one could be a college professor and still a believer in religion.

Skinner's choice of college also contributed to his religious identity struggles. Because Skinner knew little about colleges (other than that he wanted to go), he had chosen to attend Hamilton College on the recommendation of a friend. Hamilton was a rather conservative college in which there was compulsory chapel during the weekdays and compulsory worship service on Sundays. Skinner seems to have engaged in mild protest of these requirements by attending the compulsory chapels with a long coat thrown over pajamas, a behavior that was somewhat accepted since several other students engaged in this as well (Skinner, 1976). Skinner also found some resolution of his tension with compulsory chapel through conversations with an admired professor, who as Hamilton faculty, was also required to attend the compulsory services. From this professor Skinner came to understand that some of the faculty had ways of being present in chapel without fully participating. For instance, this professor helped Skinner see that one might appreciate the cultural forms of religion, such as its music and art without ascribing to its beliefs (Skinner, 1976).

Another interesting aspect of Skinner's religious development at Hamilton was his exposure to William Squires, a professor of philosophy deeply influenced by the Calvinist-inspired philosophy of Jonathan Edwards, an American Congregational minister from the eighteenth century (Shea, 1974). What is intriguing about this exposure to Edwards (through the mediation of Squires) is that several of Skinner's later psychological ideas show a strong resonance with certain aspects of Edwards' thinking. One scholar suggests this may be due to their shared Calvinist backgrounds (Williams, 1981). We will return to this question below.

Finally, one notes that Skinner's religious identity struggles seem to have involved his continuing sexual development and his exploration of various venues for its expression. From his autobiography, one senses that his emerging sexual experimentation conflicted with the religious strictures of his upbringing, perhaps producing further guilt and discomfort (Skinner, 1976).

By the time Skinner graduated from Hamilton his religious identity as an atheist was fairly solid though in his "dark year" following graduation one notes that his reading included books about mystical phenomena, providing evidence that he continued to think about religious phenomena (Skinner, 1976). As Skinner began to emerge from his dark year with its relinquishment of his identity as an author and his resolve not to be a loafer, Skinner's vocational identity struggles also took a decided turn with his decision to attend Harvard graduate school to study psychology (Elms, 1994).

Religion in Skinner's Adult Years
Skinner differs from the other psychologists in this study in that during his adult years Skinner reported no overt religious experiences. What positive influence religion may have had on his adult behavior is indirect; what one primarily sees in the adult Skinner is a negative reaction to religion. When he speaks of religion as an adult it is primarily through the lens of his new ideology, behavioral psychology, and generally these remarks are critical (more on this later). As an adult he no longer considers himself a religious believer and the remnants of his religious upbringing of which he is aware, he views as an inevitable and unfortunate residue of his early environment (Wiener, 1996). This view of the religious influence from his childhood resulted in his offering no religious training to his own children, having "suffered from the religious teachings" of his parents and grandmother (Skinner, 1979, p. 227). What religious education his children received came from their exposure to other children who took them to various churches. Skinner's identity as a non-believing adult might also lie behind some correspondence with Nathan Pusey, the president of Harvard at the time Skinner wrote to him about what he saw as several religious overtures in Pusey's presidential remarks. Skinner wrote to object to any "official attitude toward religion at Harvard" and added that he hoped belief would never be made mandatory at Harvard (Epstein, 1980, p. 127).

Although a confirmed atheist as an adult with an essentially negative view of religion by this time, it is interesting to note that Skinner reported a couple of more favorable indirect influences of religion during his adult years. For instance, Skinner recalled that during his post-doctoral years at Harvard he went with a philosopher friend to a Benedictine monastery for a weekend. He reported that he found his time there invigorating though he was not impressed with the discussions for the proof of the existence of God (Skinner, 1979). Another curious incident of religious influences on the adult Skinner is seen in his remarks about the various contributions to his quitting smoking. Among these influences he credited an evangelical radio preacher that he listened to because of the preacher's "fascinating . . . verbal behavior" (Skinner, 1976, p. 253). He recalled how this preacher spoke of the difference between being controlled and controlling oneself and noted that he found this latter idea helpful concerning his thoughts on self-management.

In concluding this section, we note again that the themes of restraint and escape identified by some of his biographers (cf. Demorest, 2005; Elms, 1994; Siegel, 1996) also show up in Skinner's continued efforts to escape from the religious influences of his childhood. One of the ways these efforts to escape the influence of his early religious experiences manifest is in several critical assessments of religion that he will make as a behavioral psychologist. These comments are dealt with in the section on Skinner's theory of religion.

Some Key Ideas in Skinner's Thought

Before turning to the question of how Skinner's religious background influenced his work, we review several key aspects of Skinner's thought. As with all the psychologists in this book the overview focuses on those parts of his theory that will make the next section more readable; thus, it does not cover all the important aspects of his work. Furthermore, it omits large parts of his work that have little or no bearing on the aims of this book. Thus, not only are these brief comments overly simplified, but they are also far from comprehensive.

A Behavioral Perspective

Early in his career Skinner adopted a "behavioral" perspective on the person and the world (Skinner, 1979). In psychology, this approach went back to people such as Ivan Pavlov (whose theory of why dogs salivated to the sound of a bell formed an entire paradigm for understanding behavior), as well as people like John Watson (whose conditioning of a fear response in "little Albert" made him infamous) and E.L. Thorndike (well known in the fields of educational and organizational psychology and a direct influence on Skinner's thought). Skinner understood his own version of behaviorism to be an improvement over Pavlov's "stimulus-response" behaviorism and preferred to call his own version of behaviorism "operant conditioning" (Skinner, 1953, 1974).

Operant Conditioning and Patterns of Reinforcement

In contrast to Pavlov, Skinner (1953, 1974) emphasized that behaviors in organisms were not always responses to stimuli in the environment. Rather, some behaviors were voluntarily "emitted" and that whether those behaviors would occur again was dependent upon the consequences that followed them. The following summary is greatly oversimplified of course, but for Skinner, if an organism found certain consequences pleasurable or rewarding, the behavior that preceded was apt to be repeated; conversely, if certain consequences were not rewarding, the preceding behavior was less likely to recur (although we note that Skinner preferred not to use such terms as pleasurable because they might be thought to refer to mental states). Skinner's pigeons in his box are the prototypical examples of his approach to studying behavior. If following a peck on a disc a pigeon was rewarded with food the pigeon was apt to peck again. Alternately, if pecking the disc resulted in no food pellet the pigeon was less likely to repeat this behavior (of course, this explanation omits many of the particulars under which a pigeon might or might not peck again, including distinctions between negative reinforcement and punishment). By varying the ways and times by which a pigeon might obtain a food pellet (Skinner kept the pigeons at about three-fourths their normal weight so that they would always be responsive to food), Skinner was able to elaborate various particulars about how and when reinforcements occurred (e.g., under positive versus negative consequences) as well as varying schedules by which reinforced behavior might occur. These patterns of reinforcement were the centerpiece of Skinner's work, and he developed a vocabulary of specialty terms to explain them (e.g., positive reinforcement, negative reinforcement, punishment, extinction, variable schedules, etc.; Skinner, 1953, 1974).

Absence of "Mentalist" Constructs

In what Skinner (1971) called a "radical" behaviorism he argued that it is only what is observable that is key to explaining behavior, including human behavior. Thus, any mentalist explanations such as appeals to motives or intentions, while common ways of speaking about behavior, offered no explanation at all according to Skinner (1957, 1971). Skinner sought instead to simply describe observable behavior. For instance, one does not act because one is "angry" (an internal thought or feeling) for Skinner, but perhaps because one has found that loud, forceful speech and gestures result in others giving in to requests made in such a manner. Being reinforced in this way, such behavior is likely to recur.

Environmental Determinism

Skinner's thoughts on behavioral patterns are further linked to his notions of environmental determinism. For Skinner, the world that has come to be is the product of evolutionary natural selection. Furthermore, what survived natural selection shaped the social environment that emerged. For instance, survival in the natural world became more successful when humans lived in groups but living in groups only became possible with the development of vocalization, a later development in human history according to Skinner (1974). This social environment in turn shaped various human behaviors. Since human behavior is environmentally determined it is not accurate or helpful to speak of culpability and responsibility regarding human actions whether these are misdeeds or laudatory achievements (Skinner, 1971, 1974). Both are products of what has been reinforced by the various contingencies that one has met in life. He offered illustrations of a concert pianist and a thief. The concert pianist is the product of an environment that was reinforcing of those behaviors that made possible these achievements. Beyond the genetic possibilities to nimbly move one's fingers, say, the achievement is the result of an environment that made engaging in such activities reinforcing and not because of some inner quality of diligence or tenacity within the human. Conversely, thieves are such because different contingencies were reinforced in their lives. This is not to say, however, that environments will continue to exist if they allow certain actions that are detrimental to their survival (i.e., thieving is generally punished in most environments that survive or, said differently, an environment that reinforces thievery is not apt to survive long while one that reinforces great piano playing might) (Skinner, 1948/2005, 1974).

Contingent Reinforcers

Although individuals are a product of both the biological and social environments that brought them into being, Skinner also spoke of the probabilities of what evolved out of all the possibilities that could have evolved. Thus, Skinner (1974) spoke of "contingencies of survival," a term that referred to what survived in the species; in speaking of the ways the environment shaped the individual Skinner spoke of "contingencies of reinforcement" (pp. 39, 44). In Skinner's language, what survived both at the species and individual levels was what got reinforced. Any uniqueness one sees in humans emerges because there are variations in what got individually reinforced. However, all humans are alike in that all are shaped by what was reinforced in their (particular) environment (Skinner, 1974).

These ways of thinking about behavior and the circumstances under which it will occur has several implications for how one approaches a variety of issues, but especially issues of what behavior one "ought" to engage in. We explore Skinner's thoughts on such topics in the next section which takes up the question of how his religious upbringing influenced his work as a behaviorist.

How Skinner's Religious Background Influenced His Life and Thought

We have noted that the religious backgrounds of the psychologists studied here had an impact that was both indirect (via its cultural influence) and direct. The more indirect cultural influences are seen in the concept of a developmental perspective (i.e., that life moves toward some purpose) and in the ethical legacy of their religious traditions. The more direct ways concern the influence of the psychologists' religious background on specific ideas in their thinking as well as other things such as the way they viewed their lives and work. In Skinner's case these influences draw heavily from Christian traditions.

A Developmental Perspective

Under the influence of the more indirect, cultural aspects of Skinner's religious background, he like the others in this book adopted a developmental perspective. Kirschner (1996) has argued that such a perspective is the result of Jewish and Christian traditions regarding the linearity of history. Although this developmental way of thinking is so ubiquitous in those who grew up in the West as to go unrecognized at times, it is always present. Even though it is less visible in Skinner's articulation of his environmental determinism, it is there nonetheless. That is, even with his environmental determinism, one sees that the outcome of one's responses to the contingent reinforcers that one has met does not come all at once but unfolds over the course of one's life (cf. Skinner, 1948/2005, 1974). Thus, even in Skinner one has the notion of a developmental trajectory.

As noted in the Introduction, another aspect of the developmental perspective concerns whether psychology (and therapeutic approaches in particular) envision their task as one of correcting or restoring something that has gone awry or of nurturing to maturity something already present. The former option is indebted to the influence of Augustine on Western thought (Hathaway & Yarhouse, 2021). This aspect of Skinner's thought also shows up occasionally. Although Skinner does not talk so much about correcting what is broken as about how one might reinforce a different future, such visions of improvement as the work of psychology reflect this influence of the Christian intellectual tradition in the West (cf. Skinner, 1971)

Ethical Legacy of His Religious Tradition

The other indirect, cultural way that Skinner's religious background influenced him was in the ethical legacy of the Christian tradition. One sees this lingering effect in Skinner's work in several ways.

Goodness vs. Badness in Humans

Skinner's interest in the question of goodness vs. badness in humans is one of the ways the ethical legacy of his religious tradition lingers in his work. As noted in the Introduction such questions have a long history in both Jewish and Christian traditions and have influenced discourse on these topics for centuries. It is significant to note that Skinner raises these issues of good vs. bad in humans primarily in dialogue with Christian ideas. Skinner's (1971, 1974) comments concerning these questions are in large part reactionary toward this tradition, arguing for instance that it makes no sense to speak of any innate goodness or badness in humans as though these were something that humans possessed. Goodness or badness are not qualities that humans possess but are actions that are environmentally defined and determined. "Things are good (positively reinforcing) or bad (negatively reinforcing) because of the contingencies of survival under which the species evolved" (Skinner, 1971, p. 104). That Skinner makes such arguments is partly attributable to his thinking he is correcting ideas that are obviously outdated and wrong but that he raises such issues at all shows the lingering influences of religious traditions that Skinner feels obligated to address.

What People Ought to Do

Browning (1987) has argued that all psychological theories of the human have a theory of moral obligation embedded in them, implicitly if not explicitly. This legacy of Skinner's religious tradition is also present in his work. At one point Skinner is quite explicit that not only is it within the purview of the behavioral scientist to define the good life, he further argued that the technology now existed to bring about this new world (Skinner, 1971, 1974). What is significant in these comments is that one senses that Skinner believes that if a behavioral scientist has such knowledge, the person ought to act on it. Although Skinner is most prone to speak of the mechanics involved in bringing about a better world, Browning points out that Skinner's vision of this more nurturing environment betrays an indebtedness to Christian ideas about what such a world would look like that goes unacknowledged by Skinner. We will look at the specifics of Skinner's vision of a better world below.

Protestant Work Ethic

One also notes the influence of Skinner's early religious tradition in his adoption of the Protestant work ethic (Bjork, 1993; Skinner, 1976; Wiener, 1996). This ethic focuses on hard work as the way to get ahead and change the circumstances in one's life. We have noted above Weber's (1904/1958) quintessential argument for how this Protestant work ethic emerged from the Reformed theology of John Calvin. As those in the industrial West equated prosperity with signs of God's favor, the prosperity that eventuated from their hard work made such work more rewarding (to use Skinner's concepts).

As noted above Skinner's religious upbringing was in the church traditions that were direct descendants of Calvin's theology (the Presbyterians) and his parents also had adopted and fostered this ethic (Bjork, 1993; Skinner, 1976; Wiener, 1996). Skinner's adoption of this work ethic was deep, and he carried it with him his entire life (e.g., he often wondered if he was being productive enough and kept journals of future projects; Epstein, 1980; Skinner, 1976). Its adoption helps one understand the guilt and discontent he felt during his "dark year" over the fact that he was not engaged in productive work (Elms, 1994; Skinner, 1976). The adoption of this ethic also is apparent in Skinner's (1948/2005) utopian novel *Walden Two*; in this community Skinner clearly valued worthwhile work, treating it not only as desirable but as something people "ought" to do (cf. pp. 50–51, 245); everyone, including visitors must do their share of daily work.

Certain Key Ideas

In turning to more direct ways in which Skinner's religious background influenced his life and work, one can see several of these. Chief among these ways include his views on orderliness in the world, human freedom, and the good life.

Order in the World

Skinner's view of the world is obviously influenced by his early religious development. For Skinner the world is first and foremost an orderly environment. In an early review of his method he wrote, "of course, I was working on a basic assumption—that there was order in behavior if I could only discover it" (Skinner, 1952, p. 227), and a biographer (Wiener, 1996) observed that throughout his life he was "determined to find the lawfulness, the order in nature" as the basis for his work in the prediction and control of animal behavior (p. 35). This presumption of order becomes the basis for his scientific method (cf. Bufford, 1981) and it was this presumption of order that lay behind Skinner's articulation of the various patterns of reinforcement he charted (Skinner, 1953). We have noted above that Skinner's early religious background exposed him to the idea of order in the world though there it was determined by God.

However, one must also acknowledge that there are aspects of the adult Skinner's (1971, 1974) view of the orderliness of the world that do not align with his religious upbringing. For instance, Skinner argued that what is here is what has survived in the natural evolution of the world and no further explanations are needed, including supernatural ones. In similar manner, the natural environment that survived was key in shaping the social environment that emerged which in turn contributed directly to shaping the kinds of humans that developed.

Although the adult Skinner finds no need for a God to explain the order of the world, one cannot help but notice that Skinner's description of the world that evolved, despite certain "contingencies," remains a highly determined one. As odd as it seems, such orderly determinism does not lie as far afield from the Presbyterian theology of Skinner's religious upbringing as one might think (cf. Gonzalez, 1975). Although Skinner himself does not make this connection between his scientific method and religion, others have made the case that science could only have arisen from the ordered view of the world present in the Jewish and Christian religions coupled with the freedom to explore the creation over which God had given humans charge (Glover, 1984; Kirschner, 1996). Thus, as odd as it might seem, apart from the absence of acknowledging God's role in such orderliness, in several ways the world Skinner envisions bears a striking resemblance to the world that Calvin and the Presbyterians would have recognized (see Cosgrove, 1982; Gonzalez, 1975; Jones & Butman, 1991)!

Human Freedom

One also sees the influence of Skinner's religious background in his ideas regarding human freedom. One recalls that for Skinner (1974) animal and human behavior is determined by the environment in which they live; he found this to be empirically true in his study of animal behavior and he speculated its applicability to human behavior (Skinner, 1953, 1957). However, in extending his findings about animals to his analyses of human behavior Skinner's view of the human becomes severely reductive. In his efforts to address human problems Skinner argues that it is only observable behavior that is useful for determining answers (Skinner, 1953, 1957). Cognitions, feelings, and volition, while obvious aspects of everyday human conversations, are more misleading than helpful categories for Skinner (1957). For him, much like rats and pigeons who find themselves in a maze or box, human behavior is shaped simply by the consequences that attend to it. Rats, pigeons, and humans engage in more of the behavior that they find reinforcing and in less of the behavior that is not reinforcing.

Thus, Skinner (1974) understands the human to be a biological organism that acts, nothing more, but nothing less. The cause of human action is the environment; the human is not an agent who chooses his behavioral model. The patterns of these actions are categorized in terms of the nature of the environments that call them forth. Threatening environments call for evasion actions; non-threatening environments allow a wider range of actions (Skinner, 1948/2005, 1974). That is, if the environment is threatening, the human must act to escape the threat; if the environment is not threatening, humans repeat whatever actions have been reinforcing. Understanding the environment which gave birth and nurtured a given person allows one to both control and predict a person's behavior. Since humans are the products of biological and social evolution, any sense of "freedom" must be carefully circumscribed (Skinner, 1971); freedom for Skinner is not the ability to do as one pleases but is rather the absence of any kind of force that might constrain human action.

It probably comes as no surprise that such a deterministic and reductive view of the human has earned Skinner much criticism (e.g., Bufford, 1981; Cosgrove, 1982; Jones & Butman, 1991; Kirschenbaum & Henderson, 1989; Monte, 1999). People especially object that Skinner's view of the human has rendered discussion of ethical behavior moot. Skinner (1971) responds to such criticism by noting that people find his ideas regarding the "radical" role of behavior (over against cognitions, feelings, and volition) objectionable because it erodes deep-seated beliefs about human "freedom and dignity."

Yet, one also encounters a conundrum in Skinner's view of determinism. Although humans are determined by their environment, he wrote that it is an environment of their own devising and can be changed (Skinner, 1971). What is one to make of this claim? It is important to note that this claim comes near the end of Skinner's most controversial book, *Beyond Freedom and Dignity*, a book in which he spent almost 200 pages trying to redefine the concept of human "freedom" through the lens of his radical behaviorism. For Skinner, human freedom is to be understood as the language used to describe escapist survival behavior evoked by aversive environmental conditions. For instance, though one might think one "chooses" to eat to escape hunger or chooses to avoid unpleasant or dangerous people, Skinner argued that such choices are predictable behavioral responses that have proven successful to personal (and species) survival in the past and this survival reinforcement ensures their future repetition in similar circumstances.

Thus, human freedom as the notion of being able to do what one wants is an illusion for Skinner. Although one might be forced to work under the threat of physical punishment, Skinner noted that even when people think they are choosing to work, what actually keeps this behavior going is its positive consequences (e.g., the reward of money that can be exchanged for any number of pleasant or reinforcing behaviors later). What Skinner pointed out was that both ways of sustaining work are forms of control; the latter is just less noticeable as a form of control because it does not evoke escapist behavior from aversive circumstances. Thus, freedom for Skinner is not about doing what one wants but is really a way of speaking about various means of control (an odd way to speak about freedom for most people). "Freedom" then is better defined as the ability to arrange one's environment in ways that increase positive consequences and reduce aversive ones (e.g., if the television is interfering with one's ability to study, one turns it off; but here again this seems a very limited understanding of freedom for most; see also, Skinner, 1948/2005, 1974).

One notes that despite Skinner's verbal gymnastics there remains an assumption of a biological or genetic preference for non-aversive environments. Although this makes sense in terms of survival, it does not entirely erase the conundrum of how one might change the environment if one's preferences for environments (positive or negative) were determined by earlier environments (cf. Williams, 1981). Similarly, Skinner's (1974) category of spontaneous, emitted behavior seems to fall outside the purview of a strict environmental determinism as well.

Although a search for the antecedents of Skinner's view of human freedom does not resolve this paradox, it does provide some interesting parallels to this idea from his early religious environment. Similar ideas about the limited nature of human freedom are found in the theological tradition in which he was brought up. For Calvin and the Presbyterians after him, human freedom is limited by the sovereignty of God. The notion that humans could freely choose to do what they wished was foreign to this way of thinking. It is God, not humans, who does any real choosing; all other choices are derivative in nature (Gonzalez, 1975). This was the view of human freedom Skinner encountered through all those years of exposure to the literature supplied to Mary Graves' Sunday school class (Skinner, 1976).

Another interesting possibility arises in terms of the religious influences on Skinner's ideas about human freedom, from his college exposure to the work of Jonathan Edwards, himself deeply influenced by Calvinist thought. Williams (1981) has written a helpful article comparing some of the ways in which Skinner's thought is pre-figured in Edwards. At the risk of oversimplifying (and perhaps distorting Edwards' thought given the lack of context) some of the similarities that Williams notes between the thought of Edwards and Skinner include the idea that at the human level cause and effect are part of the natural order of creation (of course for Edwards [1754/1957], it was God as First Cause who created this order). Thus, even human knowledge is continuous with natural processes and does not signal a break with the natural order (Edwards, 1980). (One should note that contemporary Edwardian scholars disagree on this point, but it seems the position of Squires, Skinner's teacher from whom he would have learned Edwards' thought and continues to be held by several Edwardian scholars [McClymond, 1998].) In noting the parallel with Skinner, Williams notes that for Edwards human mental activity does not cause sensory perception but is rather the product of sensory experience (cf. Edwards, 1754/1957); that is, consciousness is not self-generated but arises from sensory perception. Edwards also understood what are commonly expressed as "desires" as arising from prior experiences in the environment that have been found reinforcing (ultimately for survival). Williams further points out that Edwards argued for an innate or genetic predisposition in humans for self-preservation.

One sees correspondence between all these thoughts in Edwards and Skinner's theory. For instance, Skinner (1953, 1957) would certainly agree that so-called mental activity is the product of, rather than the cause of, sensory experience. Skinner also relies upon cause and effect to explain human consciousness and further argues for genetic predispositions in humans for self-preservation that is reinforcing. Williams (1981) attributes these correspondences to the common Calvinistic heritage of both Edwards and Skinner.

Perhaps even more telling in its correspondence are Edwards' and Skinner's comments on human freedom. Edwards (1754/1957) wrote that although freedom is commonly understood as the power to do as one pleases what is often ignored is how one's pleasures or desires come to be what they are. Here Edwards prefigures Skinner (1953, 1957) in his argument that such pleasures (or desires) arise from prior experiences all of which have their root in experiences that led to survival. For both Skinner and Edwards, humans, like lower animals, respond with behavior that has been habituated by reinforcement and not chosen by free will (Williams, 1981). For both Edwards (1754/1957) and Skinner (1948/2005, 1971), thinking oneself free is not the same as being free.

Thus, Skinner's deterministic view of the human has a close affinity with certain strains of the Calvinistic tradition in which he grew up. One *thinks* oneself free simply because one is following the natural results of what one has found reinforcing in one's environment (Skinner, 1971). Skinner himself seemed to recognize this convergence between his view of the world and a theological one when he wrote "theologians have accepted the fact that man must be predestined to do what an omniscient God knows he will do" (Skinner, 1971, p. 20). One hears a similar idea expressed in *Walden Two*. When one of the characters worries aloud about the conflict between control and freedom, Frazier (the chief protagonist with whom Skinner most identifies) replies: "Doesn't he know he's merely raising the old question of predestination and free will? All that happens is contained in an original plan, yet at every stage the individual *seems* to be making choices and determining the outcome. The same is true of Walden Two" (Skinner, 1948/2005, p. 279; my emphasis). As Browning (1987) summarizes, "all this suggests that Skinner believes that his perfectly planned operant environment is the secular counterpart to Presbyterian obedience to the providence of God" (p. 112).

Thoughts on the Good Life

One also sees the influence of Skinner's religious tradition in his thoughts on what an ideal world might look like. Skinner's vision of such a world is most clearly outlined in his novel *Walden Two*. There Skinner envisions an ideal environment created through behavioral engineering. In one passage Frazier, the central character, spells out what the "good life" would look like, describing what it is humans want out of life and presumably act toward when such actions are not thwarted by forces exerted by the environment. Frazier defines the good life for most humans as consisting of health, a minimum of unpleasant labor, a chance to exercise talents and abilities, intimate and satisfying relationships, and relaxation and rest (Skinner, 1948/2005). It is interesting that in this vision Skinner assumes most of these items to be self-explanatory and so offers no justification for their enumeration. He can only assume the self-explanatory nature of these values because they are so deeply embedded in Western thought via the influence of the Jewish and Christian traditions to which he was exposed that he does not even seem to notice from whence they are borrowed (cf. Browning, 1987; Glover, 1984).

Even more significant in this regard is to note that the world Skinner envisions is not merely a pleasant one but a "just" one. Browning (1987) writes that Skinner "unknowingly invokes time and again the idea of justice and uses it as a genuine ethical principle to guide his allocation of social reinforcement" (p. 106). Browning then calls attention to Frazier's remark in *Walden Two* that "you may have noticed the complete equality of men and women among us. There are scarcely any types of work which are not shared equally" (Skinner, 1948/2005, p. 123) before commenting that "here equality and justice between the sexes is unwittingly presented by Skinner as a presupposition guiding the organization of reinforcements, not the products of such reinforcements" (Browning, 1987, p. 106). It is particularly interesting that Skinner offers no rational or scientific justifications for how the ideal behaviorally engineered world ends up being a just one. If this assumption about a just world is not a product of the environment of Walden Two, where does it come from? Skinner leaves this question unanswered. What is now obvious is that such assumptions about a just world are a clear expression of the early theology to which Skinner was exposed (Gonzalez, 1975).

Other Ways

Other ways that Skinner's religious background influenced his life and work include his view of himself as a prophet, his tendency not to celebrate, the number of religious references in his writings, and in his theory of religion.

Skinner's View of Himself as a Prophet

One notes the influence of Skinner's religious background in his view of himself as something of a prophet akin to the prophets of ancient Israel (Shea, 1974). In biblical Israel, prophets were spokespersons for God, announcing God's truth to kings and ordinary people alike without regard to the consequences for themselves (Seilhamer, 1977). In the Christian tradition, Jesus is often thought of as a prophet in this sense (Hawthorne, 1992). What is interesting about Skinner's view of himself is that he seems to have thought of himself as such a proclaimer of truth (about the principles of behaviorism) who would speak to the power centers of psychology, education, and religion without regard to what such insistence might cost him in terms of people's opinions (Shea, 1974). He especially takes on the fiery mantle of the biblical prophet, for instance, when he waxes most stridently about the need to give up our illusions of freedom and to embrace the environmental determinism of his behavioristic model (cf. Skinner, 1971). Note his evocation of religious language to make this point: "The defender of freedom and dignity may then, like Milton's Satan, continue to tell himself that he has a 'mind not to be changed by place or time' and an all-sufficient personal identity... but he will nevertheless find himself in hell with no other consolation than the illusion that 'here at least we shall be free'" (Skinner, 1971, pp. 181–82). Here he appears as a prophet out to change the world and its view of itself even at the cost of being thought a crackpot or unpopular and he is not beyond overstating his own view to get people's attention for his point. One can see further illustrations of this prophetic mantle in Skinner's comments about self-deception, which draw some of Skinner's harshest comments; of his own life he will note that he has "fought hard against deceiving myself" (Skinner, 1967, p. 407).

Skinner's Lack of Celebration

One of Skinner's biographers reports that Skinner tended not to engage in celebrations much, whether it was birthdays, achievements, or milestones (Wiener, 1996). In this regard it is highly likely that Skinner's religiously tinged upbringing in which hard work was valued, and frivolity was not, contributed to his tendency not to celebrate. Moreover, it is interesting in the light of Skinner's reluctance to celebrate to note that Skinner's (1971, 1974) behaviorism is one in which one is not directly responsible for one's achievement (or failure); because these are all the result of environmental forces one cannot claim too much contribution to one's successes. Developing a psychology in which there is a lack of pride over one's accomplishments fits well with the theology he had been exposed to growing up.

Religious References in his Writing

Another way one can see the influence of Skinner's religious background is all the religious references and allusions that appear in Skinner's writing. As a result of his exposure to Mary Graves Skinner gained an appreciation of the Bible as literature, having gone through most of the Bible with her (Skinner, 1967). In this regard it is interesting to note that in Skinner's writings he shows a good literary acquaintance with the Bible, often dropping references and allusions to its contents throughout his books and articles. For example, he points to St. Paul's recommendation of marriage to reduce temptations to certain sexual behavior (cf. 1 Cor. 7:9) as an illustration of the behavioral technique of arranging "circumstances under which behavior may occur without being punished" (Skinner, 1971, p. 65), a point that corresponds with aspects of his behavioral approach. He also observed that "some religions teach that sinful behavior will be followed by eternal punishments of the most horrible sort" (Skinner, 1971, p. 61) and he often portrayed heaven as a collection of positive reinforcers and hell as a collection of negative ones (e.g., Skinner, 1953, 1971; Kirschenbaum & Henderson, 1989), positive and negative reinforcers being another key point of his behavioral theory. In another place he quoted St. Jerome on going two miles when asked to go one (cf. Mt. 5:41) to prove his point that "we conceal coercion by doing more than is required" (Skinner, 1971, p. 49). In its context Skinner's comment is about coercive elements in religion and our tendency to attribute the causes of behavior to mental states; thus, it is not intended as a compliment though the religious allusion still makes the point regarding this influence in Skinner's work.

Skinner's Theory of Religion

The last way we note that Skinner's religious upbringing influenced his work is in his view of religion. Although Skinner will speak of religion in positive ways on occasion, most of his comments about religion have a negative cast to them, usually having to do with the aversive controlling dimensions of religion (e.g., Skinner, 1953, 1971). In reflecting on why this might be one recalls Skinner describing his first exposures to religion as "torture," and only later in his childhood did he encounter a more positive aspect of religion (Skinner, 1976, p. 60). Perhaps because his religious parents were controlling and restrictive in their interactions with Skinner, his chief way to speak of religion is in terms of its socially controlling functions (e.g., Skinner, 1953, 1971).

Interestingly, while Skinner's writings are liberally dotted with religious illustrations and allusions, he only addresses religion topically in an early essay in his book on *Science and Behavior* (Skinner, 1953). There Skinner includes a chapter that looks at religion primarily as one of several social systems (e.g., government, law, ethics, etc.) that seek to manage and control social behavior. The bulk of the chapter is devoted to identifying various techniques for behavioral control as well as the types of behavior religion seeks to control. From Skinner's way of thinking, one is not surprised to find that the chief techniques religion uses for behavioral control are those of reinforcement and punishment. As a social system religion identifies certain behaviors as desirable or undesirable and rewards or punishes accordingly for compliance or noncompliance. The chief differences Skinner sees between religious and governmental control, for instance, is that religion appeals to a more powerful and ultimate set of rewards and punishments (i.e., heaven and hell) which often have the sanction of a supernatural realm. According to Skinner heaven and hell are made contingent upon one's behavior (e.g., sinful behavior is punished). Religion provides an escape from such aversive threats through beliefs and rituals of expiation and absolution, thus reinforcing, if not an increase in virtuous behavior, the reduction of sinful behavior. Furthermore, like other controlling agencies, religious ones often seek to arrange environmental conditions to reduce opportunities to engage in undesirable behaviors or to increase opportunities to engage in desirable behaviors. For instance, Skinner (1953) noted that religions might provide a list of prohibited books, movies, beverages, or clothing. Conversely, religions might suggest alternative behaviors such as St. Paul's encouragement to marry as an alternative to undesirable sexual behavior (cf. 1 Cor. 7:9).

In terms of the type of behaviors religions seek to control, Skinner saw religion as essentially promoting pro-social behaviors and punishing "selfish" behaviors. Skinner acknowledged that the promotion of such behaviors need not have religious backing (e.g., ethical groups can also promote such behaviors). Furthermore, since most religious systems rely on belief in a supernatural realm to sustain their powers of reward and punishment, once humans began to identify causes for behavior and its consequences within the natural environment, Skinner (1971) argued the need for religion also became reduced. It is interesting to note here that in the utopian community Skinner (1948/2005) imagines in *Walden Two*, there is no formal religious system (the controlling forces of Walden Two are much more subtle)!

Skinner's more positive remarks about religion emerge from the above analysis. Since all systems of social control are inevitable for Skinner, the main question is whether such control is positive and obvious rather than punitive and hidden (Skinner, 1971). Thus, Skinner is most complimentary of religion when he describes its positive reinforcing methods of control over against its use of punishments. For instance, he noted that whereas in a former day religion may have emphasized God's punishment and the threat of hell (recall his experience with his grandmother), in more recent times it had shifted to emphasize God's love, a shift he saw as a good move (Skinner, 1971; Evans, 1968). Similarly, Skinner connected the Christian belief in love and grace with desirable pro-social behavior: "Being good to someone for no reason at all, treating him affectionately whether he is good or bad, does have Biblical support: grace must not be contingent upon works or it is no longer grace. But there are behavioral processes to be taken into account" (Skinner, 1971, p. 99). One also finds several positive comments about this aspect of religion in Skinner's (1948/2005) novel, *Walden Two*. As it turns out the Frazier character (who is the chief spokesperson for the new behaviorally engineered community that Skinner advocates and the character with which he has the most sympathy and identification) is an admirer of Jesus as one who had great psychological insight. For Frazier, Jesus' greatness lay in his being the "first to discover the power of refusing to punish" (Skinner, 1948/2005, p. 245) As Woefel (1977) notes, "what Frazier is talking about is positive reinforcement as a means of changing behavior; he seems to equate it with what Jesus and Christianity are trying to get at with the notion of agape" (p. 1113).

In summarizing and assessing Skinner's view of religion one notes that there is a rather reactionary or aversive tone to it. In looking for the sources of such a reactionary attitude toward religion one can go all the way back to the subtle ways in which Skinner experienced the controlling nature of his religious parents (Skinner, 1976). Thus, one need not be surprised that the way his parents expressed their religion in combination with their controlling, aversive nature, gets associated with religion in general for Skinner. Having "suffered" from religion in his childhood (Skinner, 1979, p. 227) he is sensitive to this aspect of religion. Like his parents, religion becomes something restraining and oppressive, and from which one wants to escape. As an adult this is his primary view of religion. However, one cannot help but note that his support for this view is not simply from his behavioral view of the world but was also a prior conviction left over from his early religious environment.

Concluding Comments

The story of how B. F. Skinner's early religious development influenced his life and work is the story of someone who tried to escape the influence of his restrictive religious upbringing but was only partially successful in doing so (cf. Demorest, 2005; Siegel, 1996). Skinner concedes this partial success to one of his biographers in a remark about the lingering influences of his childhood. To Daniel Wiener (1996) he disclosed that "I am to some extent still Presbyterian" and though he does not find this admirable, he sees it as "inevitable after a given history" (p. 177). In this regard one might recall Freud's (1910]) observations that childhood casts a long shadow onto one's adult life; however, Skinner himself might simply acknowledge that what survived is what got reinforced. We note that the language of his Presbyterian upbringing would have framed such determinism differently than either of these.

On the negative side some of the influences that Skinner was not able to escape include his mother's emphasis on what others might think (Skinner, 1967; Wiener, 1996). Skinner (1967) himself connected this concern with "theological ghosts" from his past: "my position as a behaviorist came from other sources. Perhaps, like Jeremy Bentham and his theory of fictions, I have tried to resolve my early fear of theological ghosts. Perhaps I have answered my mother's question, "What will people think?" by proving that they do not think at all (but the question might as well have been "What will people say?")" (p. 409). His caveat at the end reveals his doubts as to whether he has truly been successful in this regard. One finds a similar doubt about his success in this regard in his confession that though he no longer made self-management choices for Protestant *rewards* the lingering influence of his religious upbringing is seen in his concession that he still made them for "Protestant *reasons*" (Skinner, 1967, p. 408; my emphasis).

Another possible aspect of his religious upbringing that Skinner has not escaped is his lack of emotionality. Although his biographers (Bjork, 1993; Wiener, 1996) point to the influence of his parents' restricted emotionality as contributing to a similar lack in Skinner (for instance, his descriptions of his brother's and his grandfather's deaths in his autobiographies seem singularly lacking in emotion) this restriction of emotions may also have religious overtones. There is within the Presbyterian tradition an emphasis on orderly behavior patterned after the Apostle Paul's advice that "all things be done decently and in order" (I Cor. 14:40; cf. Clarkson, 2017). This sense of all things being done decently and in order often takes the practical form of an emphasis on reason over emotions in this tradition (Wheeler, 2006).

On the more positive side, other aspects of his religious upbringing that Skinner was not able to escape include his concern for justice and equality noted above. From his treatment of these concerns in *Walden Two*, it is clear Skinner saw these as good qualities of his community despite his failure to explain where such assumptions came from. The connection of his concern with justice to his Presbyterian upbringing has been noted (see Browning, 1987).

Second, it is obvious that Skinner has not escaped the influence of the Protestant work ethic to which he was exposed early on. One senses that he does not actually want to escape this part of his upbringing (i.e., in his own way of explaining things, it was so reinforced by his upbringing that he could not do otherwise than value it). Skinner's value of work was deeply embedded and even influenced the subsequent way he thought about religions. He wrote in his notebooks that "it is not good if a religion doesn't make people productive" (Epstein, 1980, p. 44).

Finally, Skinner was not entirely successful in his attempts to eliminate attributing interior motives to human behavior, an attribution he associated largely with religion (Skinner, 1971). For instance, although he made great effort in his autobiography not to attribute inner motivations to his own actions, he cannot refrain from attributing such motives to other things like the Susquehanna River and even a minnow (Siegel, 1996)! For instance, in the opening paragraphs of his autobiography, Skinner (1976) wrote of the river that it "abandons," "attacks," "succeeds," even "tackles Pennsylvania at a more vulnerable point"—a mental motivation if ever there was one (p. 3). Such metaphors are virtually alive with inner emotions and in *Walden Two* he cannot refrain from attributing a deep *inner urge* in humans to push forward (Skinner, 1948/2005). Similarly, Skinner's assumptions about concerns for justice and benevolence in the engineers and managers of Walden Two reflect more than external influences and raise the possibility of inner motivations. Thus, despite Skinner's (1971) claim that inner or mental explanations are no explanations at all, he has not entirely escaped this kind of explanation associated with his religious past.[1]

Note

1. Such connections cause one to ask whether there also may have been internal qualities that contributed to the person Skinner became. For instance, although his sensitivity to breaking rules and expectations (cf. Bjork, 1993; Wiener, 1996) could simply be the result of a punishing environment over these issues, one cannot dismiss completely the idea of temperamental qualities within Skinner himself that contribute to such behavior. That is, one can imagine other responses to such an aversive environment besides the development of sensitivity; interestingly, those who consider explanations that draw upon the possibility of such inner motivations provide powerful alternative interpretations of Skinner's behavior (e.g., Elms, 1994; Siegel, 1996).

CHAPTER FIVE

Carl Rogers

As a teenager Carl Rogers once wrote that "the most wonderful promise in the Bible for me is: Ask, and it shall be given to you; seek and ye shall find; knock and it shall be opened to you. Lord, I ask Thy guidance; I am seeking the kingdom of Heaven" (Kirschenbaum, 2009, p. 20). As an adult he later wrote "neither the Bible nor the prophets . . . neither the revelations of God nor man—can take precedence over my own direct experience" (Rogers, 1961c, p.24); that is, his own experience is the highest authority he acknowledges. One could not have a clearer alternative to his childhood view that God directed his life (Rogers & Cornelius-White, 2013). What might have caused such a reversal in Rogers' thinking? How does one move from putting God at the center of one's life to banishing God to the periphery if present at all? Such questions stand behind the story this chapter seeks to tell. Thanks to two brief autobiographical pieces written by Rogers (1961c, 1967) at the height of his success, many people are aware that he grew up in a conservative Christian home with what he called loving but subtly controlling parents. What is less known are the particulars of that upbringing and how it influenced his life and work. This chapter traces the trajectory of Carl Rogers' religious journey, charting some of the forces and events that shaped his life and thought.

But first, who is Carl Rogers and why include him in this book? Rogers is considered one of the founding figures in psychology and counseling, due in large part to his role as a primary architect of the so-called "third wave" in psychology (behind Freudianism and behaviorism) (Demorest, 2005;

Homans, 1982; Monte, 1999; Slife, 2012; Thorne, 1992). Rogers was a pioneer in the scientific study of psychotherapy, being perhaps the first to film actual therapy sessions and to empirically study what types of counselor responses were or were not helpful for having people continue to share their thoughts and emotions. Rogers' work continues to influence the fields of psychology and counseling (e.g., motivational interviewing) as well as education (e.g., student-focused learning). It can be discerned more widely in everyday conversations about the importance of "feelings" and being oneself.

What Is Known of Carl Rogers' Religious Journey?

This section traces what is known about Rogers' religious journey from his early childhood until his death. Information about this journey comes from Rogers himself as well as from those who knew him. The trajectory of Rogers' religious journey begins as one in which he uncritically adopted his parents' views of religion in childhood to an adolescence in which Rogers embraced for himself the evangelical religion of his parents to a more questioning adaptation of his faith in young adulthood. As an adult Rogers eventually abandoned his faith along with any concerns for things religious before turning to an interest in spiritualism during the last decade of his life. This trajectory can further be characterized as a movement from a conservative Christian faith to a kind of Christian humanism with a keen emphasis on faith as something one lives rather than simply professes to a more atheistic humanism that lasted most of his life before his late life interest in spiritualism.

Religion in Rogers' Early Childhood Home

By his own testimony and that of others, both of Rogers' parents were highly religious and involved in various church activities (Cohen, 1997; Kirschenbaum, 2009; Rogers, 1967; Thorne, 1992). Rogers' father, Walter, was a successful businessman who gave generously to his church and was involved in several of its activities. He served on the Board of Trustees of the First Congregational Church in Glen Ellyn, Illinois (near Chicago), and donated the church organ for this congregation. This congregation also built a "Rogers' Chapel" in honor of Walter's generosity. Having grown up in a family active in the Congregational church, Walter also had long been active in this denomination including his time as a building contractor in the years they lived in Oak Park, a suburb of Chicago, before moving his family to Glen Ellyn. In college he had been president of the university chapter of the Young Men's Christian Association (YMCA).

Rogers' mother Julia also came from a religious background, a Baptist one more conservative than the Congregational background of Walter. After marriage to Walter, she attended the Congregational church with him, and this was the church in which Carl was reared though his mother seems to have remained more religiously conservative than his father (Kirschenbaum, 2009). According to Rogers (1967), she became even more conservative as she aged. Rogers reported that his mother had two Bible phrases that she was fond of repeating, "come out from among them and be ye separate" (2 Cor. 6:17), an affirmation of her belief in being part of God's elect, and "our righteousness is as filthy rags in thy sight, Oh Lord" (Isa. 64:6), an affirmation that even at their best, humans are deeply flawed. Rogers' sister Margaret reported other common sayings from their mother including "keep the standards high," a reinforcement of the religious affirmation of being separate and superior, and "scrubbing floors will cure most ills,' an affirmation of the strong work ethic of the Rogers household (Cohen, 1997).

Both of Rogers' parents took their faith seriously and were committed Christians. One gets some flavor of their conservative faith through a sampling of activities. Within the household there was a daily ritual of family worship which consisted of each child taking turns reading a few Bible verses followed by each member of the family kneeling at their chair for prayer while one of the parents said a final blessing before the day's activities began (Kirschenbaum, 2009). The Rogers' religious conservatism can also be seen in the list of the prohibitions for the children: no card playing, dancing, smoking, drinking, or attending movies among others (Rogers, 1961c, 1967). A further aspect of the conservative religious values of the Rogers household was in their choices regarding living arrangements. At the time Carl was born the Rogers lived in Oak Park, a suburb of Chicago which prided itself as being "the place where the saloons stop and the churches begin" (Hemingway, 1990; quoted in Kirschenbaum, 2009, p. 3). Oak Park had ordinances against things like boxing matches, uncensored movies, distribution of information on venereal disease and birth control, gambling, and the consumption of alcohol. Children under 18 could not buy cigarettes, play billiards, drive a car, or be out of the house after 9pm. Even with such an environment in which to rear the family, Walter decided to move the family 25 miles west of Chicago to a 300-acre farm in Glen Ellyn because he thought it might be a better place to shield his children from the evils of the city (Kirschenbaum, 2009).

What do we know of Rogers' interaction with his parents during these formative years? As an adult Rogers remembered this environment as subtly oppressive yet one in which all the children participated (Rogers, 1967).

Rogers' own participation in the family religion seems to have been as an obedient child. An early reader Carl read through a special children's edition of the Bible several times (Kirschenbaum, 2009; Rogers, 1967). Of the morning worship ritual, he noted participating from "as far back as I can remember" until he went off to college (Rogers & Russell, 2002, p. 24). Though describing his parents as loving, Rogers also described them as masters of subtle control. Of the prohibitions for the children, he remarked that he could not remember overt commands about these, just the understood expectation that the Rogers family did not engage in these activities (Rogers, 1967).

Rogers (1967) also reported that he did not feel much loved as a child and that his interactions with his family left him feeling hurt and isolated. He described his mother as withholding her affection at times (the subtle control?) and able to wither him with a glance. He described his father as somewhat insensitive to the needs of his young son. He remarked that one of the chief ways that the family interacted was through teasing, and while all members experienced something of this, Carl seems to have been especially negatively impacted by this kind of interaction. Furthermore, the move to the farm seems to have been especially isolating for Carl though also a source for adventure and learning (Kirschenbaum, 2009; Rogers, 1967).

Since the picture of the early religious atmosphere in the Rogers home comes primarily from the memories of the adult Rogers, how is one to evaluate this? Two observations might help. First, in contrast to Rogers' memories of subtle control and insensitivity, his siblings offer glimpses of fond, even fun-loving parents. As an illustration of the family's ability to have fun his sister Margaret recalled that following a fright she had in trying to ride a horse, the verse she was given to read from the Bible the next morning was "a horse is a vain thing for safety" (Psa. 33:17), at which point all the family had a good laugh (reported in Kirschenbaum, 2009, p. 9; cf. Cohen, 1997). While one can allow that Carl would have experienced the teasing differently than his sister, this report nevertheless paints a variant picture of family interactions. However, the second observation is also telling in terms of family atmosphere and that is Rogers' (1967) report that three of the six Rogers children suffered duodenal ulcers, including Carl.

Rogers' Religious Development During Adolescence

Although little is known of this period Rogers' adolescent years seem to have been ones characterized by a Christian faith that mostly mirrored that of his parents. This is gained from comments he made in a journal that he was given for high school graduation. Following his graduation, Rogers spent the summer in North Dakota at a lumber yard run by his uncle (Rogers, 1967). He lived alone on the premises and each day after work he spent his leisure time reading a series of classical books he had taken with him. Among those he read were Emerson, Dickens, Poe, Twain, Dumas, and Hugo. He reported that his reading helped him pass the time and ward off homesickness. Kirschenbaum (2009) writes that this summer was symbolic of Rogers' youth as one filled with rich intellectual life but rather socially and emotionally isolating.

Of significance in tracing his religious journey it is important to note several things about this period. A later recollection about this time shows he had fully embraced the religious prohibitions of his earlier childhood: "I didn't smoke or drink or have soda pop or go to the movies or contact girls" (Rogers & Russell, 2002, p. 45). Also illuminating of his adolescent faith is a comment he made regarding Hugo's *Les Misérables*. So transported was he by Hugo's narrative of Jean Valjean's redemption that he had something of an out of body experience. In a summary comment about the summer Rogers noted that he had had a lot of time to think and as a result he felt he had grown closer to God even though many things still puzzled him (Kirschenbaum, 2009).

Thus, the picture one gets of the young Carl Rogers who goes off to college is that of a devout young Christian, an image that continues throughout his first two years of college. When he arrived on the campus of the University of Wisconsin (all the Rogers went to Wisconsin, he notes of his obedience) he roomed at the dorm of the university chapter of the YMCA where his older brother Ross was the president (like his father before him) (Kirschenbaum, 2009; Rogers, 1967). In those days this association was dedicated to forming character in young men and involved them in acts of Christian service. Rogers later noted that this environment would have been pleasing to his parents (Rogers & Russell, 2002).

Rogers' first college major was in agriculture, spurred in large part by his activities on the farm. As an agricultural major and given his religious interests it is not surprising that Rogers became involved with a Sunday morning group run by Professor George Humphrey under the auspices of the YMCA for the religiously minded agricultural students. This group was involved in various social, educational, and religious activities and became a closely knit group. Rogers noted in a diary that his first semester had been one of the most enriching experiences of his life, not least because he had made his first friend, a telling disclosure given his earlier isolation on the farm (Kirschenbaum, 2009).

As the adolescent Rogers discovered new dimensions of relationships in his personal life he concurrently writes of God in more relational terms

(Rogers & Cornelius-White, 2013). Entries from his diaries give the flavor of this budding relational focus. In one entry a 17-year-old Rogers is much taken with finding the will of God for his life, writing that "it's wonderful to feel that God will really lead me to my life work, and I know He will, for never has He deserted me" (quoted in Kirschenbaum, 2009, p. 20). This same entry shows a young man also anxious lest he make a wrong decision or that his ambition thwart his pursuit of the will of God, typical struggles of adolescent faith (Fowler, 1981). In an entry marked "Plans for 1920" Rogers further wrote of his desire "to live closer to God, to form a more intimate relationship with Him and to spend more time and effort in communion with Him" (quoted in Kirschenbaum, 2009, p. 20). In a comparative comment that time spent cultivating friendships is time well spent, he mused how much more ought he then to spend time cultivating friendship with God (Kirschenbaum, 2009). In his comments about God's love and loving God in return one senses that Rogers' adolescent faith provided some compensation for what he missed in the love he desired from his parents.

Another diary entry records Rogers' reaction to an evangelism conference sponsored by the YMCA. In attending this conference on "Evangelizing the World in Our Time," Rogers began to consider Christian work rather than agriculture as his vocation (Rogers & Russell, 2002, p. 52). He wrote of his experiences in the conference that he had found a peace that he had not known before, noting "I never dreamed that simply enlisting for Christ could make me feel so right with the world" (quoted in Kirschenbaum, 2009, p. 21).

Rogers continued to be much involved with activities of the YMCA including several summer camps and reflects several times on his seriousness regarding his obligations to teach aspects of Christian character to the young men in his charge (Kirschenbaum, 2009). Because of his involvement in these various activities Rogers came to be known among the leadership of the YMCA and at the end of his fall semester 1921, the 19-year-old Rogers discovered that he was to be one of 10 young people selected from the U.S. to attend a World Student Christian Federation conference on missions in China during the spring semester (Rogers, 1967). This six-month trip became a clear turning point in the development of the young Rogers' faith. As a result of this trip Rogers' personal and relational faith takes on new social and humanistic dimensions (Kirschenbaum, 2009; Thorne, 1992).

Religion in Rogers' Later Adolescence and Young Adulthood

As Rogers moved from adolescence to young adulthood there were changes in his religious faith. His faith became more "liberal" than the evangelical faith of his parents as it became more action focused and socially conscience-oriented (Kirschenbaum, 2009; Rogers, 1967; Thorne, 1992). There are several phases to this growth beginning with his trip to China and continuing through his graduate work in seminary.

About six months prior to the China missions trip Rogers had written following another YMCA conference that Christian evangelization might need to include bringing the influence of Christianity not only to the saving of souls but to changing industry, politics, and relationships whether social or international (Kirschenbaum, 2009). When he sailed for China in February 1922 these thoughts became considerably expanded through conversations with his traveling companions (who were often from the more "liberal" churches and seminaries of the day) as they discussed the nature and purpose of Christian life and missions (Kirschenbaum, 2009; Rogers, 1967). We know something of the impact of this trip on the developing faith of the young Rogers because of a diary he kept during it as well as writing hundreds of letters to family and friends (Rogers & Cornelius-White, 2013). Several things are worth noting.

On the trip over Rogers reported his engagement in a discussion on the nature of Christ, particularly as to whether he is divine or simply a good man (Rogers & Cornelius-White, 2013). Rogers is particularly stirred by a conversation on whether one must believe in the divinity of Christ to be a Christian and confesses himself as something of a "doubting Thomas" regarding Christ's divinity (Rogers & Cornelius-White, 2013, p. 42). During Rogers' diary entries, one sees him clearly shifting his view of Christ to that of a great man but not someone divine. By the end of the six months, he wrote in a letter home:

> I have changed to the only logical viewpoint—that I want to know what is true, regardless of whether that leaves me a Christian or no. Since taking that attitude (and it has been a gradual step, starting before I left home) I have found the most wonderful new riches in the life of Christ and in the Bible as a whole. It is a tremendous relief to quit worrying about whether you believe what you are supposed to believe and begin actually studying Christ to find whether he is a personality worth giving your life to. I know that for myself that method of approach has led me to a far deeper and far more enthusiastic allegiance to Him. (quoted in Kirschenbaum, 2009, p. 25)

This quotation is notable in several particulars. First, it is important to note that it is Christ's "personality" and "life" (i.e., his earthy existence and not his divinity) that are the key to his new enthusiasm. Second, note that the young Rogers wants to believe the truth no matter the cost. Third, one notes that Rogers wants to know this truth for himself; it is not sufficient to believe something because others believe it or desire you to believe. Such observations remind us that such questioning of the faith in which one has been reared is quite typical in later adolescence and young adulthood (Fowler, 1981); it is a way of making one's faith truly one's own and is often interwoven with aspects of identity formation (Erikson, 1958) and individuation from one's family of origin (see his aside that these changes in his faith had begun in a context connected to "leaving home"). But more to the point of this book, we note that the pursuit of truth is connected to issues of honesty and integrity both to oneself and to others for Rogers and that all of these are deeply Christian values, values that Rogers will espouse even in times when he no longer considers himself a Christian (Kirschenbaum, 2009; Thorne, 1992).

In addition to his shifting beliefs about the nature of Christ's divinity, it also becomes clear from his diary and letters that Rogers is shifting to a more socially focused understanding of the gospel (Kirschenbaum, 2009; Rogers & Cornelius-White, 2013; Thorne, 1992). This more socially conscious understanding of the Christian message takes the form of reflections on the "unChristian" nature of war, industrial exploitation, and social and political oppression. He wrote at one point: "Thank God Christianity is always a force to be feared by autocratic power. I hope it always will be a force to be feared by autocratic power, whether that power is found in the industrial world, the social world, or the political world" (Rogers & Cornelius-White, 2013, p. 80). Rogers' shift to a more socially conscious Christianity is strengthened further by his numerous encounters with Christian workers and students from the various countries and cultures that were participating in the China conference along with his keen observations of the citizenry of the various places in Japan, China, Korea, and Indonesia that he visited. For instance, after conversations with leaders in the labor movements in Korea he reflects on how unchristian it seemed to him that churches in England and the U.S. had worked to outlaw aspects of the labor movement, writing that "there is no question that its [the labor movement's] theoretical aim is entirely Christian, and it is our duty to see that it is as nearly as possible always Christian in practice" (Rogers & Cornelius-White, 2013, p. 157).

This more socially conscious faith that was developing in Rogers also had a decidedly existential cast in that Christianity was something to be lived and not just believed or professed. This shift in his thinking is well illustrated by his comments about the binding of the young girls' feet who worked in the factories in China. Rogers remarked, "anyone who could see those little kids, and say that such things were all right, is not a Christian, by my definition.

I don't care whether he believes the whole Bible from beginning to end or whether he believes every orthodox doctrine there ever was—I wouldn't call him a Christian" (Rogers & Cornelius-White, 2013, pp. 155–56). So, the faith of the young adult Rogers developed into one in which it is actions more than beliefs that define whether one is a committed Christian or not.

A final thing the China trip did for the young Rogers was solidify his decision to go into Christian ministry. As a result of his new thinking about Christ and being a Christian Rogers wrote at the end of his China trip: "for the first time in my life, I find myself anxious to tell people what I believe about Him, and about His wonderful Kingdom that he came to establish. I don't wonder that His early disciples simply couldn't keep from telling the 'good news'" (quoted in Kirschenbaum, 2009, p. 25).

Following the China trip Rogers returned to the University with a change in major. He switched from agriculture to history with the intent of studying the history of Christianity as a better preparation for Christian ministry (Rogers & Russell, 2002). One can continue to trace the shifts in Rogers' faith through some of the papers he wrote for his college classes. One sees the existential emphasis on living one's faith in a paper on St. Francis of Assisi where Rogers argued that Francis focused more on doing good and following the example of Christ's life than on a mystical union with God. His concern that war could not be an activity for Christians found confirmation in a paper on the pacifism of John Wycliffe. He wrote that a summary of Wycliffe's principles would show that killing was wrong whether out of fear or hate, concluding that war was irreconcilable with Jesus' teaching on love and that it was worse for the institutional church to endorse war than any other entity (Kirschenbaum, 2009).

Particularly telling, in terms of future ideas from Rogers is a paper he wrote on Luther and religious authority. In this leader of the Protestant Reformation, Rogers found a staunch supporter of the principle of setting the individual conscience of the Christian above all external authorities "be it Church, or Pope, or a rigid interpretation of the Bible" (quoted in Kirschenbaum, 2009, p. 33). As Rogers (1967) noted of this paper, its theme was one that stuck with him; the importance of people trusting their own experience became a foundational principle of his theory and work (Rogers, 1961a). Rogers later said of the Luther paper "I'm sure I was working out a personal problem with authority and coming to be my own source" (Rogers & Russell, 2002, p. 76).

Of course, one embodiment of that authority was his parents. Despite his parents' distress over his changing beliefs, they do seem pleased with his decision to go into the ministry (Kirschenbaum, 2009); however, they were not pleased with his choice of seminary! Rogers (1967) himself seems in later years to have taken some delight in his choice of "the most liberal [seminary] in the country," Union Theological Seminary in New York City (p. 353). Rogers' parents wanted him to attend Princeton, a leading conservative seminary at the time and in what Rogers (1967) later characterized as an attempt at bribery, offered to pay all the expenses for Rogers and his new wife if he would attend there. Exulting that he could not be bought, Rogers and his new wife, Helen, instead departed for New York City with a conciliatory wedding gift of $2500 (Rogers, 1967), roughly equivalent to three years wages for the average earner at the time (Cohen, 1997).

At Union Seminary Rogers was exposed to a much more liberal Christianity than that of his time at home. It was much more in line with the theology of those he was exposed to during the China trip and continued to expose him to the social dimensions of the gospel prevalent among the liberal Christian churches of that time. The so-called "Social Gospel" (see Rauschenbusch, 1917) movement was very much a part of the Union curriculum during Rogers' time there and promoted bringing love and justice into the present world as a central focus of the Christian faith. Rogers would have been exposed to this version of Christian humanism in which theologians tried to wed the best of contemporary science and the humanities with the tenets of the Christian faith to help bring in the kingdom of God on the earth (Kirschenbaum, 2009; Nicholson, 1994).

One sees certain emphases in Rogers' faith during his two years at Union. Among these is the continued emphasis on the lived nature of Christian faith over against something that is simply professed (Kirschenbaum, 2009). One sees this in the classes in which he enrolled and in the practical activities he engaged in outside the classroom. Among the course offerings Rogers was drawn to the courses in psychology that the seminary had recently begun to offer. One of his first and most loved classes was entitled "Working with Individuals" taught by Goodwin Watson, a psychologist who would later become a mentor to Rogers (Cohen, 1997; Kirschenbaum, 2009). In this class Rogers (1967) said he discovered that one could help people change and grow in ways other than through the ministry. Rogers' activities outside the classroom included a summer pastorate between his first and second year where Rogers said he got his first real exposure to people and their problems (Rogers & Russell, 2002). Other work outside the classroom included serving as director of religious education at a church in Mr. Vernon, New York, where Rogers sought to make social commitment among the congregation an increasing part of what he did. Kirschenbaum (2009) writes of these efforts: "During the week the children would tackle real problems in their lives and in their community. On Sunday the worship service would be a time of sharing and reflection on these efforts, a time for renewal of faith in their ethical mission, and a time to build a sense of community" (p. 48).

Perhaps the key turning point in Rogers' religious journey while at Union was a student-directed seminar he and other students convinced the seminary to allow (Rogers, 1967). In this seminar Rogers and his fellow seminarians engaged meaningful questions as to why they were pursuing careers in Christian ministry. Is it to please someone else, to satisfy some external standard, or is it because this is their true personality? Important questions indeed and as a result Rogers remarked that about half of the people in the seminar talked themselves out of Christian service, himself included. Having decided to leave the Christian ministry Rogers followed his inclination toward a practical approach to people and their problems and enrolled in Columbia University (across the street from Union; Kirschenbaum, 2009; Rogers, 1967).

Before addressing the shift in Rogers' religious journey that the move to Columbia signals, a few comments about Rogers' time at Union are in order. I have sought to characterize the nature of Rogers' faith at this time as Christian humanism. This is seen in his shift toward a theology that focuses more on concerns with justice and peace in the present world; he argues that it is the duty of the Christian (and the Christian church) to make a better world for the humans that inhabit it (Kirschenbaum, 2009). These are clearly humanistic concerns but the fact that they are framed as theological concerns points to a Christian dimension in Rogers' humanistic vision during his time at Union. Furthermore, at Union Rogers encounters a theology that is open to the goodness that remains in humans despite their fall from grace (Nicholson, 1994), a theology that contrasts in important ways to emphases of his mother. Although he will eventually drop the Christian framing, it is interesting to note that Rogers will continue to affirm this more positive vision of the human (Thorne, 1990).

Religion in Rogers' Adult Years

In leaving Union Seminary and the pursuit of a career in Christian ministry Rogers made a clear break with his previous vision of religious faith (Rogers, 1967). Even before he left Union one can see shifts taking place in the way Rogers considered his faith. In papers written for his Union classes Rogers was questioning whether Christianity was the only true faith and whether one could speak of Christian faith at all if what one meant were some unified system of beliefs to which all Christians subscribed (Kirschenbaum, 2009). Although Rogers' break with his Christian past does not appear as clean as he later portrayed it (Rogers, 1967), one must admit that for several decades what most characterized Rogers' religious life as an adult was its virtual absence. When he mentions his Christian past, it always is in the past; furthermore, he primarily casts it in a negative way (e.g., Rogers, 1961c, 1967).

During this longest period in his life Rogers abandoned talk of God so that his formerly Christian humanism gives way to an empirically grounded humanism (cf. Kirschenbaum, 2009). So complete is Rogers' abandonment of talk about God that he becomes reluctant to initiate conversations around religious issues and does not openly invite such questions from others (cf. Barrineau, 1990; Thorne, 1992). When long-time colleague Elizabeth Sheerer was asked whether there were areas that Rogers' person-centered theory did not address, she remarked that it did not address spiritual dimensions of the person. When asked why she thought this was, she responded "That's Carl. This was an area of difficulty for Carl. We learned early in the game not to talk about religion with Carl. That was a taboo subject because it was uncomfortable for him" (Barrineau, 1990, pp. 423–24).

Rogers' disuse of religious language during this period also is seen in his preference for reframing religious questions from others in the language of science. He once remarked to theologian Paul Tillich that although they were interested in similar ideas "I prefer to put my thinking on those issues in humanistic terms, or to attack those issues through the channels of scientific investigation" (Rogers & Tillich, 1966/1989, p. 72). Furthermore, during this period, he not only did not speak of religion at a personal level, but he also offered no psychological theory of religion, nor any formal statements about its role in life and culture. For all practical purposes, Rogers had become an atheist.

What has happened to move Rogers from his early positive attitude toward the role of religious faith in his life to what becomes a decades-long aversion to it? How does one account for such a reversal? Perhaps Rogers simply gave up his faith. Having begun a journey away from the conservative beliefs of his early adolescence to a more liberal, questioning version of the Christian faith, by the time he is at Union some of his papers suggest that Rogers further moved to a position where he questioned whether religious belief was necessary at all (Kirschenbaum, 2009). In this regard, Fowler (1981) has noted that sometimes people lapse from their faith in response to the questioning that arises in young adulthood.

However, a second possibility is that Rogers was so taken by the beliefs of his new profession that religious beliefs were no longer persuasive or relevant as an explanatory system (cf. his comment to Tillich). The Enlightenment-driven rationalism he would have encountered at Columbia (Kirschenbaum,

2009) had no need for God and the Freudian psychology of his early clinical training had declared religion a cultural neurosis and illusion (cf. Freud, 1927). Perhaps Rogers' aversion to his former religious faith is explained as a kind of "reverse conversion." In conversions, one's previous way of construing reality is often despised as being so far from the truth that one can hardly believe one used to see things that way. One is often then hostile to others who profess what one used to believe but no longer does. The converted person wonders why others do not see the light that the convert sees (cf. Hoffer, 1966; James, 1902). Rogers (1967; Rogers & Russell, 2002) clearly was embarrassed by his early Christian faith in his later years and his zealous avoidance of things religious seems to have the character of the convert.

Even if the reasons behind Rogers' break with his earlier Christian faith are not known, one must acknowledge that there is a sense of completeness about it. Rogers' daughter Natalie reports of growing up with her parents: "My brother David and I grew up in a home where our parents—Carl and Helen—did not have a bible, and I never heard either of them discuss God, Jesus, or faith in an Almighty. We didn't say prayers, nor did we ever go to church" (quoted in Rogers & Cornelius-White, 2013, p vii). She found reading about her father's earlier fervency about his own Christian faith a mystery and wondered "how it could be that a man of such deep religious faith would close the door to initiating discussions with his family and colleagues about God and Jesus" (quoted in Rogers & Cornelius-White, 2013, p. viii).

If Rogers' turn from religion was complete, his turn to science seems to have retained the fervor formerly expressed religiously. As already noted, Rogers became one of the premier scientific researchers in the field of psychotherapy. He and his students spent several decades investigating what worked and did not work in therapy (e.g., Rogers, 1942, 1951, 1959; Rogers, Gendlin, Kiesler & Truax, 1967). Even things like the ephemeral nature of the therapeutic relationship were subjected to empirical research. However, despite his faith in empirical methods and his own best efforts Rogers eventually became disillusioned with what such methods could achieve and began to voice misgivings about the ability of empirical science to nurture human flourishing (Kirschenbaum & Henderson, 1989; Rogers, 1955). During the latter part of this period there is a deepening conviction that there is something valuable in humans that cannot be captured through empirical science (Kirschenbaum, 2009).

Rogers' Last Years and the Question of Religion

In this phase of Rogers' life there is a shift away from the empiricism and atheism of his previous adult years to a position more open to the transcendent. Brian Thorne, who knew Rogers during this last decade of his life, reports that Rogers' reluctance to talk about religious issues changed, at least with him. Thorne (2013) speaks of his surprise at the number of occasions where Rogers sought him out to discuss religious questions. This renewed openness to a transcendent dimension in humans is motivated by several concerns and events in Rogers' life.

During this period Rogers showed an increasing dissatisfaction with the ability of scientific approaches to fully address his ardent humanistic concerns. As far back as his mid-fifties, during the heart of his own work at empirical verification of the theoretical constructs of his own approach to therapy, Rogers (1955) had expressed misgivings about the direction that science and psychology as a science were headed. In his writings (e.g., Coulson & Rogers, 1968; Rogers, 1980) and in things like his debates with B.F. Skinner (Kirschenbaum & Henderson, 1989; Rogers & Skinner, 1956), Rogers voiced increasing discomfort with the movement toward prediction and control of behavior that seemed to undercut notions of human choice and freedom, a pillar of his humanism (cf. O'Hara, 1995). Rogers joined with others like Abraham Maslow to help foster a so-called third force in psychology that sought to preserve this more human dimension (Kirschenbaum, 2009).

Just what is the nature of this something more? Though he had long wondered whether his research methods into therapeutic exchanges could really capture the kind of deep, often spontaneous contact that seemed to take place in therapy (e.g., Coulson & Rogers, 1968; Rogers & Dymond, 1954), during the last decade or so of his life Rogers began to speak more about a transcendent quality that seemed to characterize these times when he and a client seemed especially connected emotionally (Kirschenbaum, 2009). For instance, of a particularly powerful demonstration session in 1980 he wrote in his diary, "I realize there was a spiritual quality to our relationship in that hour. We were so in tune with each other that somehow we were in tune with the universe" (quoted in Kirschenbaum, 2009, p. 478). He often characterized this in terms of a sense of "presence" that could be freeing and healing for the other (cf. Thorne, 1992). In one of his last works, he wrote "when I am closest to my inner, intuitive self, when I am somehow in touch with the unknown in me, when perhaps I am in a slightly altered state of consciousness [in the relationship], then whatever I do seems to be full of healing. Then, simply my presence is releasing and helpful to the other" (Rogers, 1980, p. 129).

Rogers' growing openness to a spiritual dimension took another form as well. Rogers became open to spiritualism and paranormal phenomena. This movement was aided by several things that happened in Rogers' life and with his colleagues. One of Rogers' long-time colleagues was from Brazil and had maintained a personal interest in the spiritualism of her native country and in a trip to Brazil with this colleague Rogers observed some native religious ceremonies that he found fascinating, though he was not convinced that there had been actual contact with another realm. However, when Helen's health began to fail, she became interested in psychic phenomena and convinced Carl to accompany her on a visit to a medium. Following Helen's death Rogers consulted with mediums again in an effort to contact her. From a concern about whether Helen's consciousness might survive beyond death, he became more personally interested in whether his own consciousness might survive beyond death (Kirschenbaum, 2009; Wood, 1998).

Kirschenbaum (2009) mentions one other possible influence on Rogers' increasing openness to things spiritual. In the years leading up to Helen's death, Rogers underwent a good bit of distress and decided to go back into therapy to address this. His therapist was a former Catholic priest who had Rogers doing meditation and breathing exercises as part of the therapy.

How then might one characterize this last period of Rogers' life in terms of spiritual journey? I have tried to chart a path from that of a teenager fervently committed to a Christian faith like his parents to a young adult who had moved to a more humanistic Christianity to a later adult who dropped the need for a Christian or religious framing for his retained humanistic values. In this last phase of his life, one sees the atheistic humanism of Rogers' later adult years giving way to a humanism more open to transcendent dimensions. Here in the last years of his life is a renewed interest in things spiritual though it had a decidedly non-Christian cast. Nevertheless, Rogers has not escaped the initial interest in things spiritual that found its first articulation in a Christian framing, but found a later framing in scientific and humanistic language (about human purpose and meaning), before returning to language that more overtly acknowledged transcendent dimensions to reality.

What are the forces that helped shape this trajectory? Rogers makes the journey from Christian evangelical to Christian humanist primarily under the influence of the China trip with its exposure to liberal Christian humanists and the dialogues about the nature of Christ's divinity. A second impetus for this move is the individuation from his family of origin. The movement from Christian humanist to a humanist without the need for Christian framing begins during his second year at Union under the influence of the Social Gospel with its influence on character development apart from specific Christian doctrines. Then, having left the ministry he sees psychology as a more effective means to bring in the "kingdom of God" (Nicholson, 1994). But minus the commitment to ministry, he sees no further need for a

Christian framing for his betterment of society and humanity and so moves to an atheistic humanism. The movement from an atheistic humanism to a returned concern with spiritual dimensions in humans is brought about in large part by the death of his wife and his need to reconnect with her; this moves him to spiritualism during the last decade of his life. This move is further connected to his disillusionment with empirical positivism.

Having traced the contours of Rogers' religious interests I turn now to the question of whether and in what ways Rogers' religious background may have influenced his work. Another comment from long-time colleague Elizabeth Sheerer is intriguing in this regard. In speaking of Rogers' development of his person-centered approach, she notes that "in the years that he was developing the theory, he just didn't want any part of formal religion or, as far as I could tell, any religion. But of course, his work is so profoundly influenced by his background in Christianity. I don't think he could have developed without that background" (Barrineau, 1990, p. 424). A later section explores these hypotheses, but first a brief review of some key ideas in Rogers' work will make that section more intelligible.

Some Key Ideas in Rogers' Work

As with the other psychologists in this book, a review of all Rogers' ideas is not possible in such short compass. Only those ideas which will illuminate the connections drawn later are noted here and even then, not every aspect of these ideas is noted. Recall that such brief comments risk oversimplifying complex ideas.

The Actualizing Tendency

One of Rogers' key ideas about the person concerns the question of what motivates humans. Rogers (1957/1961b, 1959) only identified one motivation in humans which he labeled the actualizing tendency. Rogers' description of this tendency is key to understanding several other ideas in his work. Rogers argues that all species have a directional drive toward growth that is rooted in their biology. Thus, the human organism, like all organisms, is designed to grow and to become what it is designed to be. Like flowers that seek the light even if placed in a dark basement, humans also seek to grow whatever their conditions (cf. Rogers, 1980). The only constraints to the actualizing tendency arise from the environment and of course, some conditions are more favorable for growth than others (Rogers, 1958, 1959). Rogers dubbed environments that restricted the expression of the organism as having "conditions of worth" (i.e., external expectations about who the person needed to be to be acceptable; Rogers, 1958; 1959, 1960/1961d).

Rogers (1959) also made it clear that it is only the organism as a whole that has this tendency. He was aware that parts of the system might lead to maladjustment on the part of the organism. The chief way this would manifest in humans is in his articulation of the self. For Rogers the self is only part of the organism and the influence of the various parts, such as the self-concept might distort the total organismic functioning. For instance, since one's self-concept can fluctuate from happy to sad within short periods, tendencies to actualize the self based on such fluctuating self-perceptions might be at variance with the tendency of the total organism. For Rogers, the actualizing of the total organism is not defined simply as the actualizing of the self. This differentiation between the self as a part or sub-system of the total organism is important in understanding Rogers' (1961a) oft repeated notion that the organism can be trusted. Rogers even thought such organismic harmony characteristic of the whole universe (Rogers, 1980). This harmony in the total organism (and in the larger universe) means one's organismic functioning can be trusted to show the path that is right for one's growth; one need not rely on external authorities to determine the path forward (he called this the organismic valuing process; Rogers, 1961a).

So, what is it one will move toward if this organismic valuing process is followed? Rogers spoke of this in several ways but one way he described the goal toward which one moved was the "fully functioning person" (Rogers, 1957/1961b; It is important to note that this telos of the fully functioning person is a process, not an achievement.) In one summary statement, Rogers spoke of the fully functioning person as one who had "the capacity to perceive realistically, to accept responsibility for one's own behavior. to evaluate experience in terms of the evidence coming from one's own senses . . . to accept others as unique individuals different from oneself and to prize oneself and to prize others' (Rogers, 1959, p. 207). In another place he noted that the fully functioning person was also open to the full range of experience that the organism has and not simply its pleasant experiences or those experiences that might be acceptable to others (Rogers, 1957/1961b). In attending to a full range of experiences one can not only live more fully in the present moment but also can attend to both the pulls of individuality and sociality (Rogers, 1953, 1981/1989).

This last point is often overlooked in critiques that Rogers is too individualistic (e.g., Vitz, 1977). Thus, in Rogers' emphasis on being open to the full range of one's experiences he noted of a fully functioning person that "one of his own deepest needs is for affiliation and communication with others. As he becomes more fully himself, he will become more realistically socialized" (Rogers, 1961b, p. 194). In another place he wrote "I have taken the view that man belongs to a particular species. He has species characteristics. One of those, I think, being the fact that he is incurably social; I think he has a deep need for relationships" (Rogers & Tillich, 1966/1989, p.66). Rogers' assumption of a basic harmony within one's experience (and the universe) means that for him the human who is fully experiencing will find a harmony between individual and social needs (Kirshenbaum & Henderson, 1989, p. 137). This essential social nature in the human also has implications for Rogers' theory of therapy; it is the relationship (i.e., its quality) that makes healing in therapy possible (Rogers, 1958, 1959).

Another implication of Rogers' ideas about the actualizing tendency is his oft repeated assertion that humans at their core are not inherently evil or destructive but essentially forward moving (Rogers, 1953, 1959, 1961a, b). For instance, he wrote, "one of the most revolutionary concepts to grow out of our clinical experience is the growing recognition that the innermost core of man's nature, the deepest layers of his personality, the base of his 'animal nature,' is positive in nature—is basically socialized, forward-moving, rational and realistic" (Rogers, 1953, p. 56). Although such comments left Rogers open to charges of being too optimistic (if not naïve) regarding human nature (e.g., May 1982/1989), he was clear that despite "the incredible amount of destructive, cruel, malevolent behavior in today's world—from the threats of war to the senseless violence in the streets—I do not find that this evil is inherent in human nature" (Rogers, 1989, p. 237–38).

If humans are not inherently evil, from whence does evil come for Rogers? "My experience leads me to believe that it is cultural influences which are the major factor in our evil behaviors" (Rogers, 1989, p. 238). If provided a growth-promoting environment Rogers is convinced that even those who might otherwise choose destructively would make socially constructive choices.

The Three Attitudes

This last comment about providing a growth-promoting environment takes us to probably the most well-known concept in Rogers' work, his thoughts regarding the three conditions or attitudes that make therapy possible. Rogers articulated these concepts in various ways over the course of his career (Rogers, 1942, 1951, 1959). Early on when his writings were primarily about the "non-directive" techniques of good therapy, he referred to them as conditions; later as he began to write more about the quality of the therapeutic relationship, he tended to refer to these as attitudes of the therapist

(Kirschenbaum, 2009). He saw these attitudes as deeply intertwined and used various terms to refer to these qualities. He presented them in various orders but eventually came to see a logic in the ordering of the qualities (Thorne, 1992).

Congruence/Genuineness

Although it came last in Rogers' articulations of the three attitudes, in the end he concluded that the most important of the three was what he called congruence or genuineness (Rogers, 1959; Rogers & Russell, 2002; Rogers & Sanford, 1989). This attitude pointed to several qualities of the therapist. That is, the therapist is congruent in terms of being able to express what he or she is truly experiencing. The therapist is "real" or genuine in the sense that the therapist does not fake feelings that are not being felt or experienced. For instance, the therapist does not pretend a liking that is not felt, nor engage in actions she or he is opposed to, nor agree with thoughts not believed. The therapist who is congruent or genuine will address with the client any persistent feelings that manifest in the session, even if these feelings are negative in value (it is important therapeutically to note that he speaks of persistent feelings and not initial impressions.) When congruent the therapist maintains a deep level of self-awareness (Rogers, 1958) and can bring a level of transparency to human relating often missing in day-to-day relationships. This is one way the therapist provides a growth-promoting environment for Rogers. For instance, if clients have learned to deny parts of their experience to their awareness and have learned to present a façade to others, perhaps under the guise of being tactful, by modeling congruence the therapist shows the client a different way of being in the world (Rogers, 1960/1961d).

Acceptance/Unconditional Positive Regard

The second of the three qualities Rogers called acceptance in his early writings and unconditional positive regard in his later work (Rogers, 1942, 1958; Rogers & Sanford, 1989; cf. Kirschenbaum, 2009). Rogers describes this quality in various ways, calling it a non-possessive warmth or prizing of the person. This quality accepts not only a client's positive qualities or feelings, but also fully accepts a client's negative expressions, even toward the therapist (at least at a verbal or symbolic level, though not at a behavioral level). This acceptance is free of judgments and evaluations; it accepts what the person can be without expectations of what they must be. Of course, such acceptance is not easily achieved and cannot be faked. Rogers was clear that it worked only if it were genuine and thus the therapist will either believe deep down that humans are valuable in this way or will not; if the latter is the case, the therapist will not be able to express this attitude. It is important to note that by acceptance Rogers did not mean agreement and the concurrent commitment to congruence means the therapist does not express agreement that is not felt. Rogers was clear that clients who were defensive and vulnerable needed this non-judgmental atmosphere to be able to trust and move past their need to defend themselves. If clients do not feel safe from judgment, they expend their energy trying to justify what they did or who they are; in an atmosphere where they do not have to defend themselves, they can then begin to look at aspects of their lives that were previously denied.

Understanding/Empathy

The third and final attitude is that of understanding (sometimes called empathy). By this attitude Rogers meant to convey the quality of being able to enter into another's experience of the world, to see things from their point of view (Rogers, 1958; Rogers & Sanford, 1989). Clients' actions, thoughts and feelings make sense to them given their experiential history. Understanding is an attempt to enter into their way of experiencing the world sufficiently enough to explain it back to them in ways they would recognize and agree with. Rogers (1958, 1959) saw understanding or empathy as very powerful in the healing process. He wrote that "it is one of the most potent aspects of therapy because it releases, it confirms, it brings even the most frightened client into the human race. If a person can be understood, he or she belongs" (Rogers, 1986, p. 129). Rogers (1958, 1959; Rogers & Sanford, 1989) often connected empathic understanding to the concept of being known. He saw this need or desire to be known (and accepted) for what one is as a deep longing in human beings (Rogers & Tillich, 1966/1989).

How Rogers' Religious Background Influenced His Life and Thought

Several scholars have called attention to the numerous ways that Rogers' life has influenced his work (e.g., Atwood & Stolorow, 1993; Cohen, 1997; Elms, 1994). For instance, his biographers have noted how the conditional love of his childhood drove his articulation of the need for unconditional positive regard and how the lack of intimacy in his early relationships provided the impetus for its later importance in Rogers' theory (Demorest, 2005; Kirschenbaum, 2009; Thorne, 1992). This chapter extends this kind of reflection by looking more closely at how Rogers' religious development has influenced his life and work. In this regard, it is helpful to note that this background shaped Rogers' life and work as strongly in his rebellion against it as in the things he retained and adapted from it. In the Introduction we noted that the religious backgrounds of the psychologists studied here had an impact that was both indirect (via its cultural influence) and direct. One sees the more indirect cultural influences in the adoption of a developmental perspective (i.e., life moves toward some purpose) and in the legacy of the ethical traditions of Judaism and Christianity. One can see the more direct influence of these psychologists' religious background in specific ideas as well as in the way they viewed their lives and work.

A Developmental Perspective

Although Rogers did not develop a formal system of developmental stages as did some (e.g., Freud, 1905; and Erikson, 1950/1963), one can see Rogers' adoption of a developmental perspective in his articulation of a trajectory that allows one to respond differently to conditions of worth as an adult than as a child (Rogers, 1957/1961b, 1960/1961d) as well as in his idea that humans move toward certain goals or ends. We explore what these goals are in the section on key ideas influenced by Rogers' religious background. As noted previously, thinking in terms of a developmental perspective is derived from the Jewish and Christian perspective on history as linear progression toward some goal (Kirshner, 1996).

The cultural religious background to which Rogers is heir also influenced Western thought about development by way of the Christian theologian Augustine who saw development as moving toward the redress of things gone wrong (Hathaway & Yarhouse, 2021). Rogers (1961a) was certainly aware that things go awry in the lives of his clients and that psychotherapy can be a way to address these issues. However, it is interesting to note that Rogers' primary focus was not so much on correction as it was on the promotion of an optimal, naturally unfolding development. Thus, in Rogers there is less dominance of this Augustinian influence of framing the work of therapy as that of repair than one finds in others.

Ethical Legacy of His Religious Tradition

Another way that Rogers' cultural religious background influenced him indirectly was through the legacy of the Christian ethical tradition. This legacy shows up several ways in Rogers' life and work. As heir to the ethical legacy of this religious tradition one finds a cluster of ideas in Rogers. These include discussions of good vs. evil in humans, questions of right and wrong and what one ought to do, as well as the Protestant work ethic.

Goodness vs. Badness in Humans

On the question of an innate goodness in humans, Rogers (1961a) noted that the Protestant Christian tradition had permeated culture with the concept that the human is basically sinful. Rogers knew from his own personal experience how loathsome people might feel toward themselves because of this tradition and he spent a good bit of energy arguing against it. Because Rogers' remarks on this topic reveal a more direct impact of this legacy his specific comments are noted below. That he felt the need to address such issues is indebted to and framed in terms of categories bequeathed to him by his religious tradition.

What One Ought to Do

Rogers also inherited from his Christian tradition a concern for right and wrong (though the things he thinks belong to each category changed). One sees this lingering influence in his strong feelings about doing the right thing (and about being right—see below on his pursuit of the truth). Even during times when he is not overtly religious, he still has a strong sense of what is right and what is wrong (despite disliking such attitudes in others! See Rogers, 1956). For instance, in carving out his method of client-centered approaches to therapy, he and his followers had the sense that they were right and that psychology in its Freudian and behavioral manifestations was wrong in this regard (e.g., Rogers, 1951, 1955).

Like Rogers' need to do the right thing, he also inherited a notion of doing good from his religious background. For instance, Rogers' son David says that one of the messages prevalent in the Rogers' household was an understanding that one was here on Earth to be of service (Kirschenbaum, 2009). It is of interest to note that Rogers' reflections on his desire to do good in his chosen field of therapy shows it to be a revision of earlier ideas drawn from his religious background. In choosing to switch from seminary to psychological studies Rogers gave as one of his reasons that "one could do the kind of thing I was drawn to, namely helping people to change . . . and that didn't have to be done in a church" (Rogers & Russell, 2002, p. 89).

One also notes that Rogers' religious tradition also bequeathed him a sense of ethical obligation—what one ought to do. For instance, one can see this is his comment that "scientists have an ethical responsibility to use knowledge that might help the present racial . . . situation" (Rogers & Polanyi, 1968/1989, p. 161). It is important to note that his conclusion that one is *obligated* to use scientific information for good is not a result of the empirical data that one is to use; rather, this sense of obligation to so use the data comes from elsewhere. Similarly, Browning (1987) notes that

Rogers' comments about the actualizing tendency change from discussing it as a descriptive possibility to understanding it as a moral imperative (see for instance Rogers, 1954/1961e, 1957/1961b). Browning points out that in treating the actualizing tendency as a normative principle, Rogers was not arguing from his empirical research but instead drawing upon prior assumptions from various philosophical and theological traditions.

Protestant Work Ethic

Finally, one might point to Rogers' remarks that he often felt guilty for reading books in the morning (when one was supposed to be working) even though reading books was now part of his work as a professor as an indication of the influence of the Protestant work ethic in his life (Rogers & Russell, 2002). One recalls that this ethic dealt with the reasons one felt impelled to work, e.g., for a greater good than survival (see the Introduction). The influence of this ethic is also seen in the enormous amount of time and energy devoted to his writing and teaching, including the many workshops he conducted and the great sense of worth he derived from these activities.

Certain Key Ideas

One can also see the influence of Rogers' religious background in more direct ways. For instance, this influence can be seen in his reflections on the meaning and purpose of life as well as in key ideas in his thought. On the latter, this section looks at the influence of his Christian background on his understanding of aspects of the actualizing tendency as well as his thinking about the three core attitudes or conditions of therapy. One recalls that making the kinds of connections that follow will have a tentativeness to it in that rarely can one show a one-to-one correspondence between Rogers' religious background and its influence on his thought.

The Purpose of Life

Rogers' ideas of the meaning and purpose of life clearly reflect aspects of his religious background. This is perhaps most noticeable in two essays he wrote about this. The title and the chief point of each essay is worth noting. The title of the first essay conveys its chief point: "To Be that Self which One Truly Is." This essay carried the subtitle "A Therapist's View of Personal Goals." In this essay devoted to exploring "the purpose of life," Rogers evoked several possibilities before describing the end toward which life moved as "to be that self which one truly is," as the one most appropriate for human becoming (see Rogers, 1961d, pp. 164, 166). This goal is borrowed from the Christian theologian Soren Kierkegaard. In his book *Sickness unto Death*, Kierkegaard (1849/1941) spoke about the courage needed to become a self, noting that the failure to become one's true self resulted in despair. Rogers appropriated Kierkegaard's goal of life as becoming the self one truly is as one which most resonated with him, further agreeing with Kierkegaard that such becoming takes courage. Rogers further specified his understanding of becoming the self one truly is as involving movement away from façades and pleasing others and toward more openness to experience, trust of self, and acceptance of others. Although he clearly borrows from a Christian source in his appropriation of this goal for life, we note that his appropriation contains a significant loss; he omits the context of the becoming of the self for Kierkegaard which is that it takes place "before God." Thus, he has reframed a Christian idea regarding the goal of life but minus its religious context, a tendency in Rogers elaborated on below.

The second essay we look at is titled "A Therapist's View of the Good Life"; its subtitle and chief point concerned "The Fully Functioning Person." Rogers preferred this term over the "self-actualized" person lest the latter overemphasize the self rather than the total organism. Rogers (1957/1961b) summarized the character of the fully functioning person as someone that was more open to the full range of one's experience, with a sense of freely made choices that can be trusted, thus allowing one to live more fully in the moment. That this description is influenced by Rogers' religious tradition is seen in the way this description is both framed and in the description itself. Rogers (1957/1961b) framed his essay on the fully functioning person as "a therapist's view of the good life" (p.183). Discussions of the good life, what it is humans seek to accomplish in their living, have long been traditional philosophical and theological territory (e.g., Aristotle, Plato, Augustine). Rogers would certainly have encountered discussions of the good life growing up and especially in seminary. Furthermore, his discussion in this essay of the ability to make choices about one's life is framed under "the age-old issue of 'free will'" (Rogers, 1957/1961b, p. 192), another standard theological issue (Erickson, 1998; Grudem, 1995). Rogers occasionally acknowledged that discussions of meaning and purpose are religious concerns and that such questions take his work into the areas that interest ministers and religious persons (Rogers & Tillich, 1966/1989). It is also interesting to note that the Baptist and Congregationalist Christian traditions in which Rogers grew up would have held to a view of human freedom not very different from his own description of the freedom experienced by the fully functioning person. He described the fully functioning person as one who "not only experiences, but utilizes, the most absolute freedom when he spontaneously, freely, and voluntarily chooses and wills that which is also absolutely determined" (Rogers, 1957/1961b, p. 193)!

The Actualizing Tendency

One also sees the more direct influence of Rogers' religious background in his articulation of aspects of several key ideas. For instance, there are several connections one can make between Rogers' vision of the person inexorably moved toward wholeness by the actualizing tendency and his religious background. One connection is found in his firm conviction regarding the orderliness of the actualizing tendency (and of the universe) (Rogers, 1980). Early in Rogers' life he was exposed to Bible readings regarding a universe that was ordered because it was fashioned by the plan of God (cf. Gen. 1) and in his own life as a teen Rogers affirmed God's directing his life and work (Rogers & Cornelius-White, 2013; cf. Kirschenbaum, 2009). Later, he no longer saw God as responsible for this order, but the notion of order remained in the very fabric of the universe for him. Rogers (1961c) remarked of his own temperament that he was always one to seek the order that was to be found in things and that seeking such order was what drew him to science (Rogers & Russell, 2002). Despite Rogers' move away from a conservative religious stance on this question, one can see the quest to understand the order of the universe as having strong affinities with religious yearnings (cf. Tillich, 1951; cf. Rogers & Tillich, 1966/1989).

One can also see a connection between Rogers' thoughts on the actualizing tendency and his religious background in his comments on the social nature of the human. Although Rogers' early religious background no doubt exposed him to a concept of sociality (e.g., the "family of God"), Nicholson (1994) further suggests that Rogers' exposure to the Social Gospel as a young adult with its focus on social justice and relationships (e.g., in industry and commerce, politics and war) had an impact on his understanding of humans as social creatures (cf. Rogers & Cornelius-White, 2013). Another interesting religious connection from his adult years is his reading of Martin Buber, the Jewish theologian (Kirschenbaum & Henderson, 1989; Rogers, 1961a). In Buber Rogers finds confirmation of the centrality of relationships for human flourishing. Rogers wants to argue that good therapeutic encounters are "I-Thou" encounters (a claim Buber challenges; Kirschenbaum & Henderson, 1989). In Buber's (1937/1970) work, I-Thou relationships are ones in which humans encounter each other equally as "subjects" in contrast to relationships where one person is treated as an "object" (I-it relationships). Rogers thought Buber's notion of this mutual respect for each participant's personhood helped Rogers illuminate what he was attempting in therapeutic encounters. (In drawing connections between Rogers' religious background and his articulation of the sociality of humans, one must also acknowledge there were non-religious sources for this idea as well such as social Darwinism, the idea that humans are social because sociability gives survivability to the species. Such influences do not preclude religious ones however.)

Before leaving this section, we note one more connection, puzzling because of its absence. Recall that another aspect of the actualizing tendency is its trustworthiness to guide the organism in the right direction for its growth, an aspect of the actualizing tendency that pointed to the natural goodness in humans for Rogers (1953). We note below how Rogers' articulation of this natural goodness was in large part a reaction against his early religious background. What is puzzling in trying to draw positive connections between his religious background and his key ideas is the absence of any acknowledgement of potential Christian contributions to these ideas regarding human goodness. For instance, Thorne (1992) makes the point that for one so opposed to the more fundamentalist position regarding original sin that Rogers seems unaware of other Christian traditions that are much more affirming of a goodness remaining in humans despite their fall from grace. This is particularly puzzling in light of Rogers' attendance at a seminary where such alternative Christian visions would have been in vogue at the time he was there (Nicholson, 1994). The Social Gospel especially affirmed both the goodness and self-assertion of the human (Kirschenbaum, 2009). Perhaps Rogers' failure to appeal to potential Christian resources on this issue had deep roots in his repeated exposure to his mother's opposing religious view on this point (cf. Rogers, 1967).

The Three Attitudes

One also can make several connections between Rogers' religious background and his three core attitudes. We note a few of these possibilities.

Congruence/genuineness. Rogers' description of congruence/genuineness reminds one of Rogers' commitments to honesty and pursuit of the truth (Kirschenbaum, 2009; Thorne, 1992). This drive was present in Rogers at least since his adolescence and followed him into adulthood (cf. Rogers & Cornelius-White, 2013). Both in his personal life and in his professional life Rogers tried to live out these qualities, seeking to be authentic in his relationships and his research, though he conceded he was not always able to live up to his ideal (Rogers & Russell, 2002; cf. Cohen [1997] who is especially critical of Rogers on this score). We have already noted that such ideas are enshrined in the Bible where these Jewish and Christian virtues would have been mediated to the young Rogers through the shared Scripture readings he participated in as a child and reinforced as he moved into adolescence.

Rogers' description of congruence also reminds one of his earlier religious emphasis on the existential dimensions of life (Rogers & Cornelius-White, 2013). One is to live the faith (e.g., in concern for the poor), not simply espouse beliefs. Likewise, congruence involves moving toward authentic living and away from a "false self" invoked to meet the conditions of worth imposed by others (Rogers, 1958; 1959, 1960/1961d). This push toward being true to oneself has roots in the religious experience of the late adolescent Rogers (Rogers & Cornelius-White, 2013) and continued as a key value into his adult years (Rogers, 1961c). As an adult, Rogers found further support for this focus on being true to oneself in his reading of the Christian theologian Soren Kierkegaard (1849/1941) who also argued that truth must be lived and not simply a matter of what one professed.

In concluding these comments on congruity and Rogers' religious background one notes a peculiar irony in Rogers' life. As the architect of congruence as the cornerstone of authentic living and relating, it is interesting that a critical area of incongruence in Rogers' adult life was his unwillingness to engage around issues of religion (Barrineau, 1990).

Acceptance/unconditional positive regard. In trying to connect Rogers' ideas about acceptance/unconditional positive regard to his religious background one notes that this quality in Rogers is often compared to the Christian value of love, especially the kind of love God is said to have for his creatures, called *agape*, one of several Greek words used to refer to different kinds of love (Aden, 1969; Oden, 1978, Ostberg, 1982; Roberts, 1985a, b). Rogers (1956) himself once likened this quality of the therapist to the concept of agape. Thus, there seems to be some influence from the biblical narrative on Rogers' articulation of this concept. The fact that the adolescent Rogers (Rogers & Cornelius-White, 2013) described the chief message of Jesus as that of love suggests that his association of his ideas of acceptance with agape draws from his early religious tradition. Furthermore, Rogers' exposure to the Social Gospel at Union Seminary with its emphasis on the "brotherhood of man" would have strengthened his understanding of the need for and importance of positive regard toward fellow humans.

There are other obvious similarities between the way Rogers speaks of unconditional positive regard and agape. For example, Rogers (1958, 1959; Rogers & Sanford, 1989) does seem to ask therapists to assume a kind of super-ordinate love toward the other; the kind of love that does not come naturally to humans and is only possible by some extraordinary means. Such similarities clearly evoke elements of Rogers' religious background (e.g., that the ability to care in this way comes from supernatural help) and on occasion one can see Rogers positively interacting with his religious background in his explanations of acceptance (e.g., Rogers, 1956, 1960/1961d; Rogers & Tillich, 1966/1989).

However, some have asked whether it is fair to compare Rogers' concept of unconditional positive regard with the biblical concept of agape (e.g., Roberts, 1985a, b; Vitz, 1977). Does such a comparison distort either the biblical concept or Rogers' own concept or perhaps both? For instance, Roberts (1985a) outlines similarities (e.g., in their effects) as well as differences (e.g., in their motives and execution) between agape and unconditional positive regard, concluding they should not be regarded as equivalents. But even if not equivalents, one must acknowledge the similarities.

There is one other aspect of Rogers' religious background that has influenced his ideas regarding acceptance and unconditional positive regard. This influence occurs in his expression of acceptance as an ideal that was so often not met in his own experience. Recall that Rogers' reaction to his mother's fundamentalist religiosity led him to think much of Christianity harshly judgmental (Rogers, 1953, 1961c). In articulating a non-judgmental attitude in unconditional positive regard, he saw himself opposing certain aspects of his religious background. Rogers (1967; Rogers & Russell, 2002) made it clear throughout his life that he always felt unloved in the way he needed to be loved by his parents. He spoke of their subtle pressure in making the children conform, the way his mother could wither him with her glance, his father's insensitivity to his needs and his siblings joining with his parents in teasing him quite often (Rogers, 1967). Thus, Rogers described his own childhood as suffused with "conditions of worth" and such a background makes it a likely source for his development of a theory and therapy devoid of such conditions. Furthermore, Rogers' perceptions of such conditional love coming from Christian parents certainly tainted his view of Christianity (Thorne, 1990). Rogers (1967) noted one reason he moved away from his parents' religious beliefs was that he saw some hypocrisy in the way they lived their faith, particularly toward him. He offered as an example their failure to visit him during a hospitalization as a young adult during a flare-up of his ulcer. Similarly, Rogers felt his father acted poorly in trying to "bribe" him to go to Princeton. Rogers' alternative to such "love" was to develop a theory of relating that was to be full of warmth and acceptance without pressure to conform to the expectations of others. Thus, one senses a deep yearning in Rogers for the Christian ideal expressed in agape, perhaps made more acute for his experience of its absence earlier in his life.

In concluding these comments on the similarity between Rogers' ideas of acceptance and his religious background we note that some have drawn connections between Rogers' concept of acceptance and the Christian understanding of grace, which is first and foremost a quality of God (e.g., God's unmerited favor) but is also a quality that humans (as created in the image of God) may express on occasion (e.g., being gracious; Ellens, 1982; Oden, 1978). An example of these comparisons between acceptance and grace is Oden's (1978) links between the non-judgmental quality of acceptance and God's grace (though he also notes differences between the two). One also hears a similarity between Rogers's comments about acceptance and the theologian Paul Tillich's (1948) comment that God's grace means "accept[ing] the fact that you are accepted" (p. 162), a similarity they both acknowledge in dialogue with each other (Rogers & Tillich, 1966/1989). Rogers would have been familiar with the concept of grace from his early religious exposure as well as seminary and though he does not comment on grace like he comments on agape, his acknowledgment to Tillich indicates his awareness of the similarities. Like his comments on comparisons of acceptance and agape, Roberts (1985a) points out that Rogers's concept of acceptance is absent the religious context (of sin and forgiveness) present in discussions of grace.

Understanding/empathy. There is less in the literature devoted to identifying connections between the core attitude of understanding/empathy and religious concepts than for the other two attitudes. Why this is so is not obvious since understanding/empathy is a virtue endorsed in the biblical tradition (e.g., Rom. 12:15) For instance, in reading Rogers' (1958) comments about empathic understanding (and therapy) as a process of trying to enter deeply into another's experience in order to see the world from their perspective one is struck with the similarity of this undertaking and certain descriptions of Christ who was said to fully enter into and identify with human experience (cf. Jn 1:14; Heb. 4:15). Similarly, given Rogers' (Rogers & Cornelius-White, 2013) earlier comments about Jesus' love it is puzzling that Rogers makes no explicit connections in this regard. One possibility for this lack in Rogers is that by this time he is reluctant to speak of his previous religious background and may even wish to disavow it in this area. Others may not have made such connections because the biblical virtue of understanding/empathy, like agape, is not considered identical to Rogers' ideas on these topics (cf. Goodman, 1991; Roberts, 1985b).

Thus, in asking how Rogers' concept of understanding/empathy draws from his religious background one must return to his early experiences. In this regard one notes that, like his concept of acceptance or unconditional positive regard Rogers' explanation of this idea seems driven in part by a reaction to Rogers' not feeling he was well understood in his earlier years. For example, his perception of the "unmerciful" teasing growing up must have made him long for more understanding on the part of his parents and siblings (Rogers, 1967, p. 344). He will later write of the desire in all of us to be understood in such a way that one feels deeply known and accepted for who one truly is; to be known this way was certainly something Rogers longed for (Rogers, 1961a, 1986).

In reflecting upon Rogers' comments about the importance of being known, how deeply humans yearn for this kind of experience, and how such desires might be connected to his religious experience, one might recall a passage from the Gospel of John that describes a similar quality to the relationship between Jesus as the Good Shepherd and his sheep (cf. Jn. 10: 3–6, 14). Here Jesus points to the fact that the Good Shepherd knows his sheep and calls them by name. That is, he knows them at a deep, fundamental level, for to know someone's name in ancient times was not simply to know their name; such knowing of the name conveyed a certain understanding that gave one power (Willis, 2009). If there is a deep yearning in humans to be known, then God knows us in this way according to this passage. We do not know if Rogers had such Scriptures in mind in formulating his concept of understanding since there is nothing in Rogers' publications this explicit. But like his lack of acceptance, his lack of being deeply known and accepted may also reflect his longing for the ideal expressed in Jesus' knowing his sheep (cf. his comments about knowing God and being known by God; Kirschenbaum, 2009, p. 20).

Other Ways

Rogers' religious background also influenced his life and work in other ways. One important way that it influenced him was negatively, so that one sees him rebelling against the religion of his youth in several ways. However, one also sees a more positive lingering influence in Rogers' idealism, his desire to know the truth, and his tendency to reframe religious ideas in psychological language.

In Rebellion Against Religion

Rogers' earliest religious experience left him with several negative experiences that carried over into his adult life in the form of rebellion against some of these experiences. We note some of the most significant aspects of this rebellion.

His view of human goodness. One obvious way Rogers rebelled against his early religious background was in his strong reaction against the view of human nature that was espoused by his parents. His mother's phrase that "all our righteousness is as filthy rags" left a sour taste in Rogers' mouth both because it was judgmental and because it focused on sin (Rogers, 1967). Rogers clearly rejected the Christian doctrine that speaks of the inherent evil in humans (often called original sin; see Jacobs, 2008) and quite consciously as an adult sought to offer an alternate vision of human nature (Rogers, 1961c; Thorne, 1990). One sees his reactionary attitude in his comment that

> religion, especially the Christian tradition, has permeated our culture with the concept that man is basically sinful, and only by something approaching a miracle can his sinful nature be negated.... As I look back over my years of clinical experience and research it seems to me that I have been very slow to recognize the falseness of this popular ... concept. (Rogers, 1953, pp. 56–57)

One is struck by the strength with which Rogers rejects this aspect of his Christian past. His rejection is not just intellectual but seems to have deeper roots than his claims for its absence in his clinical work (e.g., Rogers, 1953, 1981/1989). Following a critical incident in his own life Rogers began personal therapy to better understand the sense of self-loathing he felt (Cohen, 1997; Kirschenbaum, 2009; Thorne, 1990). Through this therapy Rogers said he discovered he was not as worthless and unloveable as he had been taught and no doubt felt at times. Thus, it was not just his clinical work that showed him that the doctrine of original sin was "false"; he had personal understandings of the aversive feelings it could generate. Perhaps because he felt this sense of sinfulness so keenly in his own person from his early childhood exposure, he worked hard to eradicate such ideas from his theory.

His atheism. The ultimate reaction against Rogers' religious background is his becoming an atheist. We have noted that so complete was his turn to atheism that he did not welcome conversations about religion from his students or colleagues. In place of religion Rogers developed a theory of the person that did not need external authorities like God.

His (lack of a) theory of religion. Perhaps another manifestation of Rogers' negative reaction to his religious background is that he made few explicit statements about religion, either in its psychological function or its role in culture in his published writings. In his published works comments about religion are usually made as an aside such as his remark to Tillich that he thinks religion retains no explanatory power for modern people and that he tries to reframe such issues in humanistic or scientific terms (Rogers & Tillich, 1966/1989, p. 72). One can view his brief comment that he did not believe in original sin in a similar way (Rogers, 1954/1961e). Original sin is not a topic he has taken up; it is only mentioned by way of ideas that contrast with his point about the natural goodness of humans. Of course, Rogers' (Rogers & Cornelius-White, 2013) early private correspondence is replete with references to religion but these hold little relevance for assessing his adult theory of religion. One exception is a private letter to his brother-in-law in which he conceded that religious faith might provide comfort for some during hard, puzzling times in life, but that Rogers did not need it for such (cited in Kirschenbaum, 2009, p. 480). Late in his life when he finds a new openness to the spiritual dimension, Rogers will argue that "religious experience" is the experience of a deep harmony in the universe (e.g., Rogers, 1980). He remarks that he has had such experiences, sometimes brought on by an awe of nature or by times of deep therapeutic contact (Rogers, 1980; Rogers & Russell, 2002); however, he does not go on to develop any formal theory about religion.

Positive Lingering Influences

Despite the negative ways Rogers' religious background influenced him there were also ways that his religious background exerted a positive lingering influence. We note three.

His idealism. Rogers has sometimes been criticized for being overly optimistic about human potential, as being too idealistic (e.g., May 1982/1989; we note that if one reads him carefully, he does seem to assume a basic harmony in the world that is suspect given the evidence of history. See Rogers, 1960/1961d). Where might such an optimism and idealism come from? It is interesting that several of his biographers identify Rogers' early religious faith as providing the soil for his idealism (Cohen, 1997; Kirschenbaum, 2009; Thorne, 1992). For instance, at one point his religious faith gave him a way to express his idealism through going into ministry and in formulating a faith that works against oppression and for peace. As an adult one must wonder if Rogers' (1961a; 1980) perennial optimism reflects the idealism of his youth. He sometimes wondered about the source of his inordinate optimism; perhaps it does not occur to him that its origins could lie in his religious background because by this time he found this background embarrassing, a source of pessimism, and something he did not wish to talk about (Barrineau, 1990; Rogers & Russell, 2002).

His desire to know the truth. One also sees a positive influence of Rogers' religious background in his deep desire to know the truth, no matter what the cost (Kirschenbaum, 2009; Rogers, 1961c). We have already noted how this desire involved honesty and integrity for Rogers. It was a value Rogers devoted himself to throughout his life (Thorne, 1992). He voiced this desire to know the truth in his adolescent study of Christ and he later identified it as part of the reason he came to love the scientific method: it offered a means for ferreting out the truth (Rogers, 1961c). This pursuit of the truth is clearly a biblical value (cf. Ex. 20:16; Dt. 32:4; Ps. 51:6) often associated with the Hebrew prophets (e.g., 1 Kgs. 21; Jer. 28) and affirmed in the life of Jesus (cf. Mt. 5:37; Jn. 8:32), a value that Rogers would have been exposed to early on and repeatedly. It was one retained even in his most atheistic period.

His reframing of religious ideas. Finally, we note that another positive way that Rogers' religious background influenced him was in his retention of several ideas from this background though usually reframed without their religious contexts. We have already noted Rogers' comment to Tillich that he preferred to reframe traditional religious concerns with meaning and purpose in psychological language but also acknowledged that these are religious concerns and that such questions take his work into the areas that interest ministers and religious persons (Rogers & Tillich, 1966/1989). For instance, one finds a retention of religious ideas reframed in psychological language in Rogers' continued use of the existential focus that life, if it is to be meaningful, must be lived, not something one simply has beliefs about, an idea that first appeared in his adolescent faith (Kirshenbaum, 2009). We might also note how Rogers' (1958; Rogers & Sandford, 1989) comments about the importance of congruence are interwoven with his desire to know the truth, an idea that also draws heavily from his earlier religious background.

Rogers also appropriated and reframed several ideas from the Christian theologian Soren Kierkegaard For instance, in a paper on teaching, Rogers (1957) reported that he had taken from Kierkegaard the notion that one must be tentative in one's teaching. That is, one cannot claim that what is true for the teacher is necessarily true for the students. He also noted in this paper that Kierkegaard had taught him that insight cannot be given, only discovered by the learner (cf. a similar comment in Rogers, 1955). In another paper Rogers (1960/1961d) said he found Kierkegaard's emphasis on personhood as a process and not an achievement helpful along with Kierkegaard's idea that humans are free and can choose (one might note that in one place he speaks of these appropriations as more confirmation of his own ideas than as source; see Rogers, 1961a). Of course, the most obvious reframing of an idea from Kierkegaard is his appropriation of Kierkegaard's remarks about the goal of life noted above.

There are other religious ideas that Rogers reframed and incorporated into his theory. The dialogues that Rogers had with noted theologians Martin Buber and Paul Tillich, both of whose work Rogers deeply appreciated, are interesting in this regard (Kirschenbaum & Henderson, 1989). For instance,

Rogers acknowledged that he and Tillich are both interested in what makes for the optimal person (Rogers & Tillich, 1966/1989), a reframing of the traditional religious question regarding the good life. Similarly, we noted the correspondence Rogers found between his ideas about therapeutic relationships and Buber's delineation of the "I-Thou" relational paradigm. We also noted that Rogers (1960/1961d) sought to reframe in the language of science (and later humanism) his questions about the basic nature of the human (i.e., is the human basically evil or is there something constructive and good at the heart of humanity), a perennial theological question that he debated not only with theologians but with psychologists B.F. Skinner and Rollo May (see Kirschenbaum & Henderson, 1989).

This section is also the place to comment on other aspects of Rogers' thought that seem closely aligned with various Christian concepts but for which there is no obvious connection with things he has published. For instance, when reading Rogers' comments on the trustworthiness of the organismic valuing process and his earlier comments about God's guiding his life, are these not perhaps two ways of speaking of an internal guidance system in humans, one religious, the other secular? In more explicit theological language, is Rogers' organismic valuing process a way of secularizing the concept of the *imago Dei* (the image of God in humans that draws them back to their rightful purpose)? Such parallels make one wonder if, in addition to the connections Rogers explicitly made between his religious background and his thought whether he might have borrowed other ideas without realizing it.

Concluding Comments

How then is one to assess the influence of Rogers' religious background on his work? When Rogers (Rogers & Russell, 2002) noted of his college paper on Luther that he was undoubtedly working out some authority issues, he identified a more general principle at work in his life. He is clearly working out personal issues in the development of various parts of his theory (e.g., Demorest, 2005; Thorne, 1992). For instance, his own need for love and acceptance is made a central part of his theory as is his own need to be real and congruent in his own life and experience. Thus, the development of Rogers' theory is influenced by personal as well as research and clinical interests; there are unconscious as well as conscious forces at work here. This is no less true concerning the influence of his religious background. We have tried to point out some of the more important ways this happened. For instance, one might draw a line from Rogers' influence by the Social Gospel to his later concerns with eradicating injustice and fostering peace (cf. Nicholson, 1994). Nicholson further argues that Rogers' turn toward psychology as a way to help people other than being in the ministry (Rogers, 1967) was a transformation of the ideals of the Social Gospel. Similarly, when one compares Rogers' (1961c) comments that he knows no authority greater than his own experience (see opening paragraph of this chapter), one cannot help but remember the early paper on Luther where the young Rogers sees Luther's chief point to be the rejection of external authorities like the Church or the Pope (Kirschenbaum, 2009). Clearly, this 1961 comment is not an entirely new idea and one for which Rogers had found support in his earlier religious reflections. Likewise, the confirmation that truth has an existential dimension that he finds in Kierkegaard (Rogers, 1961a) harks back to insights and experiences on his China trip (Rogers & Cornelius-White, 2013). Even Rogers' movement away from his earlier embrace of the strict positivism of empirical science owes a debt to his religious background which argues for realities beyond the observable (Fuller, 1982; Thorne, 1992). One might even wonder if his late-life returns to investigating such realities is also an unacknowledged holdover of an earlier way of thinking. Finally, we note William Coulson's (1995) novel argument that Rogers' desire to stand apart from the larger body of psychology (e.g., in being part of the third wave that challenged the hegemony of behaviorism) was mirrored in his religious upbringing. In a bit of irony, Coulson connects this need to stand apart as a psychologist to Rogers introjecting at a very deep, yet personal level his mother's admonition to "come out from among them and to be separate" (Rogers, 1967, p. 344). One could conclude from such a comment that Rogers was influenced by his religious background not only in the ways elaborated in this essay, but also in more ways than he seemed aware!

Conclusion

This chapter is primarily structured around three questions that were first voiced in the Introduction. The central question raised there and that provided the main impetus for this book concerned how the early religious development in the lives of these psychologists influenced their later work, i.e., could a lingering influence from these early religious influences be demonstrated in their work. From research on this question, two other questions arose. One came from Jung's (1958a) postulate that the religious impulse is perhaps stronger than the sexual one. Given this hypothesis one might ask what happens to this religious impulse in those who supposedly abandon it. The other question arose in connection with Homans' (1982) observation that many of the early psychologists seemed drawn to their work because of various kinds of issues with their father and asked how accurate this observation might be. The chapter on each of the psychologists reviewed here has sought to address each of these questions. We return to each question in turn to summarize the main contours of the answers offered and to offer some closing thoughts on what might be learned from this study.

Is There a Lingering Religious Influence in the Work of These Psychologists?

To the central question of whether there is a lingering religious influence in the theories of these psychologists one must give a resounding yes. Each chapter has focused on the ways this is evident. As noted in the Introduction, the nature of this influence had both general and specific dimensions. The more general influence of their religious background on their work is seen primarily in two ways: (1) the influence of the Jewish and Christian traditions in the articulation of a developmental framework for understanding the structuring of human experience (Kirschner, 1996), and (2) the shaping of ethical thought and behavior bequeathed by these religious traditions (Browning, 1987). For instance, we have seen that these psychologists reflect the influence of the Jewish and Christian traditions through their adoption of a developmental perspective. For some, such as Skinner (1948/2005, 1974) this aspect of his thought is not expounded as part of this theory but is nevertheless assumed in the background. Others, such as Freud (1905) and Erikson (1950/1963), offer elaborate developmental expansions and systems of their own. One sees the developmental perspective in Rogers (1980) in his use of more organic images with which he compares human growth (e.g., plants growing toward the sun) while in Jung (1932) the developmental perspective is seen in his articulation of the consequential shifts in development of the Self that take place during midlife.

We also noted the influence of a particular Christian way of thinking about development (indebted to Augustine) in the adoption of the idea that growth toward maturity for many of these psychologists is via the repair of something broken rather than in the nurturing of something already present (Hathaway & Yarhouse, 2021). However, we also noted some differences among them in this regard. Although all of them reflect something of the focus on repair, Erikson (1950/1963), Jung (1939), and Rogers (Rogers, 1961a) also emphasize human growth as nurturing something already native to humans. In this they offer not only a less deterministic model of human behavior than either Skinner (1971) or Freud (1905) but an approach that is less indebted to this way that growth is perceived.

The other more general influence of the Jewish and Christian traditions on the life and work of these psychologists is seen in the ethical ethos that surrounded them. In common all the psychologists reviewed here shared in the adoption from these traditions the pursuit of truth as a core value (though they differ on what that truth might be). Under the influence of this ethical ethos, they also shared certain ideas concerned with goodness vs. badness in humans and offered thoughts on whether such qualities were innate or environmentally induced. For instance, Rogers (1961c) and Erikson (1977) tended to speak more in terms of an innate goodness in humans that was thwarted by environmental conditions while Freud (1930) saw an innate incorrigibility in humans. Jung (1959) developed a perspective that saw evil and good as part of the fabric of the universe while Skinner (1971) saw neither of these as innate qualities but as products of one's environment. In common as well, all of them were influenced by the so-called Protestant work ethic which induced all of them to work hard (and brought guilt or discontent if they thought themselves less productive than they ought to be) and shaped their ideas that work formed a part of human flourishing.

We noted as well the influence of this ethical ethos on the goals toward which life might be lived. For instance, we saw how Freud's (1939) quest for the truth at all costs was reflective of the prophetic tradition in Judaism (Hoffman, 2011); that he wanted his patients to be able to accept reality (face up to the truth) was a further reflection of this influence. In Erikson (1977) we saw how the movement toward mutuality and generativity as goals of development were reflective of Christian (and Jewish) virtues connected to love of one's neighbor as oneself (Hoare, 2002). Similarly, Skinner's (1948/2005) concerns with justice and benevolence as goals in his utopian society reflected aspects of the religious environment in which he grew up (Browning, 1987). Jung's (1932) observations on good vs. evil were in interaction with the ethical tradition of his religious background and Rogers' (1957/1961b) goals of moving toward qualities of genuineness and unconditional positive regard mirrored wished-for elements reminiscent of religious ideals from his religious background.

Another aspect of the ethical ethos of these religious traditions that these psychologists shared, though with differences, was that each of them retained a distinction between right and wrong (i.e., some things were good and worth pursuing; others were not) while also reacting against the specifics of these traditions regarding what was right and wrong. One sees quite a variance in the specifics of each person's reaction. For instance, Freud (1927) thought religion in and of itself to be a wrong way to engage life while Jung (1938) thought one was disengaged from life if one did not acknowledge some sort of religious framework. Erikson (1963, 1977) made several aspects of the ethical tradition of Christianity part of his own ethical thinking (e.g., see the sections on mutuality and generativity in the Erikson chapter) while Rogers (1967) and Skinner (1976) rejected some of the more restrictive articulations of right and wrong from their very conservative upbringing (e.g., Rogers noting that there was no card playing, dancing, or movie attendance in his household or Skinner's push back against certain sexual restrictions).

The influence of this ethical ethos is also seen in the related ideas regarding a sense of what one ought to do (a sense of moral obligation) that each espoused. For instance, we noted how Erikson's (1977) goals of mutuality and generativity were not merely descriptive statements about development but became prescriptive of what humans ought to move toward (Wright,

1982). Similarly, the stewardship of Skinner's (1948/2005) utopian community toward justice and benevolence (values inculcated by these religious traditions) were presented not simply as desired goods but as something that ought to be part of the fabric of the community (Browning, 1987). Wallwork (1982) pointed to an ethic of mutual respect and reciprocity in Freud that accorded with his Jewish background. Finally, both Rogers' and Jung's emphasis on self-realization not simply as desired goals but as something one ought to move toward (Browning, 1987), reflect the influence of this shared religious ethical ethos even if in reaction to earlier restrictions that such backgrounds placed on the self.

Beyond these more general influences of the religious background of these psychologists we also noted more specific influences of their religious development on some of their key ideas. The influences tended to vary with each psychologist. For instance, Freud's (1900, 1927) own struggle with his ineffective father caused him to see all religion as ineffective (ironically one might note, because in his own system it involved a projection of one's father onto God). Rogers (1958), in reaction to his restrictive environment, offered a wished-for alternative environment in his theory of unconditional positive regard. By contrast Jung (e.g., 1952, 1961) retained much of the language of his previous upbringing though offering vastly different meanings to the terms. For Erikson (1963, 1977), several key ideas of his developmental system carry overtones of crucial religious ideas in their articulation (e.g., generativity and loving one's neighbor as oneself). In addition to the sense of justice and benevolence already noted, Skinner's (1971) retention of a sense of predictable order in the environment and of limited freedom in humans owed much to the version of Christianity to which he was exposed. Other ideas that were influenced by the early religious traditions of these psychologists are articulated in the respective chapters. There one can see more particulars of this religious influence on their life and thought.

What Happens to the Religious Impulse?

This question arose from Jung's (1958a) notion that the religious impulse is as strong as or perhaps stronger than the sexual one. It is important to note that Jung is not trying to answer the question of whether there is a religious impulse in every person (this depends in large measure on how one defines religion; see Cohn, 1962) but assumes such a drive to be present. Since we noted earlier that it was Jung's favoring of religion that contributed to his breach with Freud, we might note that Freud (1927) also acknowledged a religious impulse but saw it as derivative from the libidinal instincts. Jung

(1958a), on the other hand saw the religious impulse as more autonomous (i.e., on par with the sexual instinct, if not stronger) and therefore not derivative but a given in human nature. Jung, of course was not the first to believe the religious impulse universal (e.g., Pascal's [1670/1995] idea of a God-shaped vacuum in humans) nor was he the last (e.g., Fowler [1981] has argued that religion—called "faith" in his model and defined as meaning making—is a universal phenomenon in humans). Even among the psychologists reviewed here we also saw that Erikson (1958) argued that humans were naturally religious. Leaving aside the question of whether religion can be shown to be a universal phenomenon, we simply note a logical question that arises if Jung's claim is true: what then happens to the religious impulse in those who seem to abandon it, as several of the psychologists reviewed here seem to have done in self-identifying as atheists.

If Jung (1958a) is correct, then one would anticipate some sort of endurance in the religious impulse even among those who supposedly do not attend to it. If we look at the three psychologists who self-identified as atheists, we still see their early religious environment wielding a significant influence even if most often in a negative way. What do such strong reactions against religion suggest about the endurance of the religious impulse?

If one looks for some enduring quality of the religious impulse in Freud, one is immediately struck by how central a place religion holds in his thought. Given the amount of time and energy Freud expended in writing against religion (e.g., three major books, several essays), one could reasonably conclude that he is not entirely free of the influence of the religious impulse no matter how negative his writings against it might be; one might even suspect this as an example of the "return of the repressed" (where aspects of one's psyche that one tries to deny simply re-emerge in another form) in Freud's own life (Freud, 1915). Thus, one can see a survival of the religious impulse in Freud's life-long interest in religion and its power in people's lives. One could also argue that the religious impulse survived in Freud's (e.g., 1901) superstitious behavior and his interest in the uncanny. Perhaps more obviously, one might simply argue that rather than being diminished the religious impulse in Freud has simply been displaced (to evoke one of his own defense mechanisms) onto his interest in antiquities (his "old and dirty gods"; cited in Cooper-White, 2018, p. 2). Some (e.g., Clifford, 2008) have also noted how the religious impulse may have survived in the quasi-religious atmosphere that characterized the early psychoanalytic association that he formed.

If we inquire about the endurance of the religious impulse in Rogers, we also see that this impulse did not entirely disappear though it does seem to lessen for a good portion of his adult life as seen in his saying very little about religion in his published writings and in his never developing a theory about religion. However, there are two things about this lessening of his interest in religion that are of interest in trying to assess the endurance of the religious impulse in his life. We first recall that religion seemed to remain something of a sore spot for Rogers. As one colleague noted, it became obvious to those who worked closely with Rogers that religion was a subject to be avoided in conversation with him (Barrineau, 1990). This behavior suggests that his burial of the religious impulse has not been altogether successful and that things connected to it lie perilously close to the surface psychologically. Whether it is simply embarrassment about his early religious fervor (as he claimed—see Rogers & Russell, 2002) or something deeper is harder to say but this enduring sensitivity at least suggests some support for Jung's (1958a) claim for the strength of the religious impulse. Offering even greater support for the endurance of the religious impulse is the re-emergence of an interest in spiritual things in the last decade of Rogers' life (Kirschenbaum, 2009; cf. Rogers, 1980). Although his interest in spiritualism is a far cry from the conservative Christianity of his youth it nevertheless lends support to Jung's claim.

If one were to try to make a case for the disappearance of the religious impulse altogether, Skinner seems to be one's best example. His rejection of and lack of subsequent interest in religion that manifested in his late adolescence and early adulthood seems to have endured throughout the remainder of his life. This is not to say that Skinner is unaware of religious phenomena, only that he showed little interest in it during his adult life. However, even with Skinner there are a couple of things of interest in terms of the enduring nature of the religious impulse. First, what is of interest is that the few comments Skinner made about religion seem to be reactionary. They primarily focus on how religious beliefs and behaviors are employed in the control of behavior (Skinner, 1953, 1971). On a more personal level when Skinner (1976) spoke of the religiousness of his youth, he either poked fun at it or relegated it to something to be left behind as one grew up. His few appreciative comments about religion come in his utopian novel, *Walden Two*, and have mostly to do with how Jesus used positive reinforcement (rather than negative reinforcement or punishment) in his ministry (Skinner, 1948/2005). As with Rogers and Freud one must wonder if such a negative attitude toward religion masks the evidence of its presence lingering not far from the surface. Second, in terms of the enduring presence of the religious impulse in Skinner one is struck by his admission late in life that he remained Presbyterian in some ways (cited in Wiener, 1996, p. 177; cf. his remarks regarding his abiding guilt over his level of productivity [Skinner, 1976]; chapter 4 identifies other ways this manifest in the adult Skinner). Although Skinner finds it uncomplimentary of himself that he has not entirely rid himself of the vestiges of the religion of his youth, it is an acknowledgement that the influence of his early religion development has left an indelible imprint that he has not been able to entirely escape despite his best efforts.

In summarizing some thoughts on the endurance of the religious impulse in those who self-identified as atheists, the critical thing to note is that it seems to go underground but does not disappear altogether. It can be rejected or reacted against but continues to exert influence even in those who reject it. Often it simply manifests or reemerges in some other form.

Regarding the endurance of the religious impulse in Erikson and Jung, one sees evidence for its positive lingering impact in their life and work. Given Jung's (1957) view that the religious impulse lies at the heart of what it means to be human, one is not surprised to see his interest in the manifestation of this impulse remaining strong throughout his life. Because Jung felt so strongly about the need to attend to the religious impulse, he expended much energy on elaborating and clarifying his rather complex theory of religion. More germane to this summary is the obvious ways in which Jung continued to attend to and refine his understanding of his own religious experience as he matured. One can characterize Jung's adult journey in this area as one devoted to finding and developing a religion that would once again revitalize not only himself but those he saw as having lost or abandoned the awe and meaning that religion can provide. Erikson, like Jung, was deeply affected by the religious impulse in ways that continued to influence him throughout his life. Bound up with his search for identity, Erikson's religious interest remained a key component of his work as he interacted with the religions of his childhood and his wife (e.g., 1958, 1981). Like Jung and unlike Freud, Erikson came to view religion as a powerful positive force in human life and it was the source of much of his ethical thought. One clearly sees the influence of Erikson's religious journey reflected in the refinement of his developmental theory (e.g., in his continued elaborations of the concepts of mutuality and generativity; see for instance Erikson, 1963, 1977).

In conclusion, the answer to our question is that the religious impulse remained present in some form for all the psychologists studied here, even in those who tried to abandon it, though its level and manner of presence varied. Its endurance was most positive in Erikson and Jung. Its endurance in Freud took the form of increasing protest while in Rogers it seems to remain just below the surface for a while before re-emerging in a different form late in life. It seems most muted in Skinner though present in ways he did not value. Thus, at least for the psychologists reviewed here, Jung (1958a) is right in his assertion that the religious impulse is an especially strong one (though we have not tried to ascertain whether it is stronger than the sexual one nor have we sought to identify its origins—those are topics for another day). What we see is its endurance despite attempts to ignore or obliterate it. Jung (1957) would even suggest that one ought to embrace such deep motivations rather than flee them.

Do Father (or Family) Issues Draw One to Psychology?

This final question arose from Homans' (1982) observations about the influence of religion in the lives of several early psychologists (including several of those covered in this book) and how this was connected to their relationships with their fathers. In trying to answer such a question, the recounting of the religious development of the psychologists noted in this book has commented on the quality of the interactions between them and their parents in general while keeping the focus on the impact of these relationships on their religious development. In his remarks about the influence of fathers and religion on these early psychologists Homans describes a tension that these psychologists experienced between the religious cultures in which they had grown up and the secular cultures they encountered in their contemporary world with its turn to newer ways of understanding the inner workings of the human. Homans (1982) observes that at the center of this tension lay a "vague father" and that it was the effort to come to terms with such fathers that motivated these early psychologists to become "originative psychologist(s)," (i.e., a developer of original thinking in the emerging discipline of psychology—p. 130). That is, these psychologists were trying to develop alternate explanatory systems for human thought and action to replace the loss of the religious meaning systems that had been represented by their fathers. In abandoning such a powerful explanatory system as religion is regarding why people are the way they are and do the things they do, it is understandable that these early psychologists were drawn to the kinds of alterative explanations that could be discovered or developed in psychology. Although they might have found similar opportunities in sociology, anthropology, history, even economics, it was the new emerging discipline of psychology that provided the soil for the growth of the early psychologists Homans identified. (In this regard it is interesting to note that most of the psychologists studied here, in their search for an alternative explanatory system to religion cast themselves in the role of a prophet or evangelist for their new explanations, including (maybe especially?) those who became atheists!)

One notes that Homans' (1982) identification of conflict with their religious fathers as a motivation for the development of and turn to newer psychological theories reminds one of the oft cited observation that many who are drawn to the mental health disciplines (psychology, counseling, social work, human services) are so drawn because of their own personal and familial struggles (Elliott & Guy, 1993; Fussell & Bonney, 1990; Friedman, 1971; Goldberg, 1986; Kier & Lawson, 1999; Wheelis, 1958). Although such reasons are not the complete picture for a person's entrance into such fields, our study of the five psychologists reviewed in the pages of this book lend support to Homans' claim that interactions with their religious fathers certainly contributed to their later development as psychologists (David McClelland made a similar observation; see Cohen, 1977). This study has offered two elaborations of this influence that are worth highlighting.

First, we note that the interactions described in this study give some contour to Homans' (1982) observations regarding the "vague father" (p. 130). For the psychologists reviewed here the vague father is one perceived as weak or ineffective. For instance, we noted the palpable disappointment of the young Freud with his father as recounted in the incident with his father's hat (Freud, 1900). Similarly, Jung had what he considered an ineffective father in that Jung (1961) did not think his father believed what he preached week by week. Skinner (1976) clearly saw his father as weak and ineffective, never able to live up to the expectations that his father's mother had for him. Rogers felt his father did not really understand him and so in a sense was ineffective as well (Kirschenbaum, 2009). Similarly, since Erikson neither knew his biological father nor felt comfortable with his stepfather one cannot avoid attributing some level of ineffectiveness to his experience of being fathered (Friedman, 1999).

In observing this characterization of their fathers as weak or ineffective it is also noteworthy that these negative assessments of their fathers were often associated with adolescence, a time of both questioning and distancing from one's family of origin, especially around religious issues (Fowler, 1981; cf. Erikson, 1968a). Furthermore, if Freud (1913) is correct that one's father has much to do with one's conception of God, then it is not unreasonable to assume that the rejection of God and religion by Freud, Skinner and Rogers coupled with their attraction to psychology was simply a way to distance themselves from certain qualities in their fathers.

This brings us to the second elaboration of this study on the nature of the influence of family on one's motivation to move toward psychology. This second elaboration comes from Erikson's (1950/1963; 1977) expansion of Freud's (1913) idea that one's conceptions about God (and religion) come from one's paternal context and interactions. Erikson argued in addition that these conceptions came from one's maternal interactions as well. Hence, in this study we have pointed out some of the powerful maternal influences on the religious development of these psychologists in addition to those of their fathers. For instance, we noted how Freud's early encounter with his mother contributed to some ideas regarding the harshness of God (often Freud simply referred to the harshness of the cosmos, given his atheism; see Breger, 2000; Freud, 1900). The other mother figure in Freud's early life, his nanny, also left the young Freud with ideas regarding the harshness as well as the love of God (Vitz, 1988). Jung's (1961) mother left him with both fasciation and dread of the uncanny and mysterious, religious themes that preoccupied him throughout the remainder of his life. From Erikson's (1950/1963) own model we attribute a sufficient level of care from his mother during his formative years to foster within him a life-long positive affirmation (i.e., basic trust) of religion as contributing to one's growth and integrality (Erikson, 1982, 1984). With Skinner (1967, 1976), his mother's conservative religiousness took the form of concern with what others might think, a concern with which her son struggled for the remainder of his life. Similarly, Rogers' mother's religiousness left him with an overwhelming sense of his unworthiness, something he seems to have struggled with throughout his life (Kirschenbaum, 2009; Rogers & Russell, 2002). Thus, we noted in the various chapters how these powerful influences of mothers (and fathers) were negative or positive and often both.

In concluding our thoughts on this last question of whether father or more properly, family issues, draw one toward psychology, one can obviously see in the psychologists studied that the relationship with their religious fathers (and mothers) certainly played a role in their development and in their turn toward psychology to come to grips with the legacies this left (for good or ill). For Skinner and Rogers their interest in religion seems to have been arrested by the turn to psychology, while for Jung and Erikson psychology provided a way to further explore their religious sentiments. Psychology functioned similarly for Freud, although his conclusions about religious sentiments were decidedly more negative. In affirming that family issues played a role in the movement toward psychology for the psychologists reviewed here, one must take care not to overgeneralize such a conclusion from so small a sample (one must look to other research for answers to this question, e.g., Elliott & Guy, 1993; Fussell & Bonney, 1990).

Closing Thoughts on Lessons Learned

The first thing we might ask in concluding this study is what to make of the fact that three of these five psychologists who were instrumental in shaping their discipline became atheists. Is this an indication that psychology might be hazardous to one's spiritual health? Several have noted the tendency for those in psychology (following some of these early leaders?) to be less religious than those they serve (Delaney, Miller & Bisono, 2007; Shafranske, 1996). The question of whether psychology might be hazardous to one's spiritual health also becomes relevant to those in therapy where the research indicates that clients tend to move toward the view of spirituality that their therapist or counselor holds (Sorenson, 2004). Given that three of the five psychologists studied here were self-identified atheists one could not be blamed for wondering if psychology might indeed be hazardous to one's spiritual health (although one must be careful in generalizing from such a small sample). Even for these, however, one must question whether psychology is to blame or whether the answer lies elsewhere.

As noted in the unfolding of each psychologist's developmental history, there were other forces at work in the formation of their attitudes toward their early religious exposure. Some of these were more personal while others were more social-cultural in nature. For instance, Hoffman (2011) has pointed to various social-cultural forces present during the emergence of the new discipline of psychology that exerted tremendous pressure on the new "science" to clarify its differences from philosophy and religion even though it dealt with many of the same issues that had been the domain of these ways of viewing the world (cf. Clifford, 2008). Others have pointed to various developmental or personality factors that influenced the movement toward atheism in these men (e.g., see Rizzuto [1998] on Freud's atheism). Rogers is especially interesting in this regard. For instance, Rogers' movement toward atheism following his time in seminary is interesting because while at seminary he was exposed to ideas (e.g., the Social Gospel) and professors (e.g., Goodwin Watson) that offered possibilities for integrating religious interests with psychological ones. Rogers chose to split or separate the two and so in his turn to psychology he became an atheist and abandoned his interest in religion. Although there may have been social-cultural factors like those Hoffman identifies still at work in his case, it seems more likely that there were developmental or personality factors at work, given that much of Rogers' personal work and growth were devoted to themes of becoming a more integrated person (Rogers, 1961a; Kirschenbaum, 2009). Given that Rogers seems to have struggled with how to live an integrated life in other areas besides the religious, one could reasonably surmise that his earlier either/ or decision regarding the place of religion in his life was not caused by his movement toward psychology but is more likely the result of personality factors. Thus, one cannot conclude from the psychologists studied here that psychology is necessarily hazardous to one's spiritual health (remember Jung and Erikson), even if some of them suggest such (e.g., Freud, 1927; Skinner, 1971).

Although the beginnings of psychology with its struggle to define itself apart from religious influences has left not only a legacy of distance between the two disciplines but also a legacy of considering religion dangerous to one's health, as a general observation, this latter idea is not substantiated by the research. Of course, the picture that emerges is more complex and involves questions of what type of religion one has in mind (e.g., Koenig, 1998) as well as how one puts religion into practice (e.g., Pargament, 1997). Without doubt some uses and types of religion can be detrimental to one's health, but the overall balance of the research shows religion to be more positive than negative in terms of one's health (Koenig, Dana & Carson, 2012) and more recent research shows that those in the mental health professions are recognizing this (e.g., Delaney, et al., 2007; the American Psychological Association website now lists over 1000 resources to help practitioners in understanding and addressing the role of religion and spirituality in clinical practice). Such research reminds one once again of Jung's (1958a) claims about the strength of the religious impulse and the above comments about its durability.

What else might one take away from this study of the religious development of these psychologists? That their religious development influenced their thought is certain. But we also have seen that religious development is bound up with one's overall development; one would not expect things to be otherwise (cf. Parker, 1999). Similarly, we have seen that all the psychologists were influenced both positively and negatively by their upbringing and this is no less true of their religious upbringing. Thus, we need not be surprised to find these psychologists speaking both positively and negatively about their parents as well as about their religious development. That is, one takes away from this study the idea that religious development (or any aspect of human development) is not some sort of uninterrupted trajectory toward the positive. As with Erikson (1950/1963), although one might hope for an overbalance of the positive over the negative, one recognizes that the negative pole of development is also necessary to healthy growth (e.g., being healthy requires not only trust but also wariness in some situations). All these psychologists in their own way acknowledge that growth in humans involves a tension between positive and negative aspects. For instance, for Freud (1916, 1940) growth involves a tension between two very powerful forces or drives that pull against each other while for Jung (1928, 1939) growth must include attention not only to one's positive qualities but also to one's shadow side. Skinner (1953, 1971) recognizes a similar dynamic in his idea that one is shaped not only by positive reinforcement but also by negative reinforcement and punishment (though the first is certainly preferred). Rogers (1961a) is perhaps different with his optimistic vision of growth but even he recognizes that this is an ideal not always in accord with reality. From this study of the religious development of these psychologists, one might conclude that such tensions are not the exception in human growth (including spiritual growth) but the norm.

References

Note on citation format. It is customary to cite Freud from the Standard Edition (SE) published by Hogarth Press, London, Vols. 1–23, 1953–1964. APA citation usually follows a double citation process in the text wherein the year of original publication is followed by the date of the Hogarth volume. Because the historical context is often important to the points made in the text and because of the numerous times his work is cited, to aid readability the APA format has been modified so that within the text the original date of publication only is cited; however, page numbers in the citations are to the SE. In the reference section, the original date appears first, and the date of the Standard Edition follows later as "SE, Vol.#, inclusive page numbers, date." Similarly, it is customary to cite Jung from the Collected Works (CW) published by Princeton University Press, Princeton, NJ, Vols. 1–20, 1945–1990. Here and in the text a similar pattern to that used with Freud is adopted. Modifications in the references include extra dates where Jung has published multiple versions.

Aden, L. (1969). Rogerian therapy and optimal pastoral counseling. In W. B. Oglesby (Ed.), *The new shape of pastoral theology: Essays in honor of Seward Hiltner* (pp. 263–272). Abingdon Press.

Allport, G. W. (1978). *Waiting for the Lord: 33 meditations on God and man*. Macmillan Publishing.

American Psychiatric Association. (2013). *Diagnostic and statistical manual of mental disorders* (5th ed). doi.org/10.1176/appi.books.9780890425596.

Anzieu, D. (1986). *Freud's self-analysis*. The Hogarth Press.

Atwood, G. E. & Stolorow, R. D. (1993). *Faces in a cloud: Intersubjectivity in personality theory*. Jason Aronson.

Bair, D. (2003). *Jung: A biography*. Little, Brown & Company.

Bakan, D. (1958). *Sigmund Freud and the Jewish mystical tradition*. Free Association Books.

Barrineau, P. (1990). "Chicago revisited: An interview with Elizabeth Sheerer." *Person-Centered Review*, 5(4), 416–424.

Benner, D. G. (1998). *Care of souls: Revisioning Christian nurture and counsel*. Baker Books.

Bennett, H. V. (2008). Justice: OT. In K.D. Sakenfeld (Ed.), *The new interpreter's dictionary of the Bible*. Vol. 3 (pp. 476–477). Abingdon Press.

Berman, M. (1975). Erik Erikson: The man who invented himself. NY: *New York Times book review*, March 30.

Bernays-Heller, J. (1956). Freud's mother and father. *Commentary*, 21, 418–421.

Bjork, D. W. (1993). *B.F. Skinner: A life*. Basic Books.

Blass, R. (2001). The teaching of the Oedipus complex: On making Freud meaningful to university students by unveiling his essential ideas on the human condition. *International Journal of Psychoanalysis*, 82, 1105–1121.

Bloland, S. E. (2005). *In the shadow of fame: A memoir by the daughter of Erik H. Erikson*. Viking.

Boehlich, W. (Ed.). (1990). *The letters of Sigmund Freud to Eduard Silberstein, 1871–1881* (A.J. Pomerans, Trans.). Belknap Press of Harvard University Press.

Bollas, C. (1987). *The shadow of the object: Psychoanalysis and the unthought known*. Columbia University Press.

Bonaparte, M., Freud, A. & Kris, E. (Eds.). (1954). *Origins of psychoanalysis, letters [of Sigmund Freud] to Wilhelm Fliess, drafts and notes: 1887–1902* (F. Mosbacher & J. Strachey, Trans.). Basic Books.

Breger, L. (2000). *Freud: Darkness in the midst of vision*. John Wiley & Sons.

Browning, D. (1987). *Religious thought and the modern psychologies*. Fortress Press.

Buber, M. (1952). *Eclipse of God: Studies in the relationship between religion and philosophy*. Harper Torch Books.

Buber, M. (1970). *I and thou* (W. Kaufman, Trans.). Charles Scribner Sons. (Original work published 1937).

Bufford, R. K. (1981). *The human reflex: Behavioral psychology in biblical perspective*. Harper & Row.

Burston, D. (2007). *Erik Erikson and the American psyche: Ego, ethics and evolution*. Jason Aronson.

Capps, D. (1984). Erikson's life cycle theory: Religious dimensions. *Religious Studies Review* 10(2), 120–127.

Capps, D. (1985). Beatitudes and Erikson's life cycle theory. *Pastoral Psychology* 33(4), 226–244.

Capps, D. (2014). *Erik Erikson's verbal portraits: Luther, Gandhi, Einstein, Jesus*. Rowman & Littlefield.

Capps, D. (2015). Erik Erikson's *Young Man Luther*: A classic revisited *Pastoral Psychology* 64, 327–343.
Carlisle, C. (2019). *Philosopher of the heart: The restless life of Soren Kierkegaard*. Farrar, Straus, & Giroux.
Carter, J. D. & Narramore, B. (1979). *The integration of psychology and theology: An introduction*. Zondervan Academic.
Clarkson, C. R. (2017). Presbyterian Church (USA). In G. T. Kurian & S. C. Day (Eds.), *The essential handbook of denominations and ministries* (pp. 218–221). Baker Books.
Clifford, V. (2008). *Freud's converts*. Karnac Books.
Cohen, D. (1977). David McClelland. *Psychologists on Psychology* (pp. 20–45). Taplinger Publishing Co.
Cohen, D. (1997). *Carl Rogers: A critical biography*. Constable.
Cohn, W. (1962). Is religion universal? Problems of definition. *Journal for the Scientific Study of Religion, 2*(1), 25–35.
Coles, R. (1970). *Erik H. Erikson: The growth of his work*. Atlantic Monthly Press.
Cooper-White, P. (2018). *Old and dirty gods: Religion, antisemitism, and the origins of psychoanalysis*. Routledge.
Cosgrove, M. P. (1982). *B. F. Skinner's behaviorism: An analysis*. Zondervan.
Coulson, W. R. (1998). Presentation to the Christian Association for Psychological Studies, Eastern Regional Conference, LaDore Lodge, PA, November 6–8.
Coulson, W. R. & Rogers, C. R. (1968). *Man and the science of man*. Charles E. Merrill.
Crews, F. (1998). *Unauthorized Freud: Doubters confront a legend*. Viking.
Delaney, H. D., Miller W. R, & Bisono, A. M. (2007). Religiosity and spirituality among psychologists: A survey of clinician members of the American Psychological Association. *Professional Psychology: Research and Practice, 38*, 538–546.
Demorest, A. (2005). *Psychology's grand theorists: How personal experiences shaped professional ideas*. Psychology Press.
Dillenberger, J. (1953). *God hidden and revealed: the interpretation of Luther's deus absconditus and its significance for religious thought*. Muhlenburg Press.
Dittes, J. E. (1990). Analytical (Jungian) psychology and pastoral care. In R. J. Hunter (Ed.), *Dictionary of pastoral care and counseling* (pp. 29–35). Abingdon Press.
Edwards, J. (1957). Freedom of the will. *The works of Jonathan Edwards*, Vol. 1. P. Ramsey (Ed.). Yale University Press. (Original work published 1754).
Edwards, J. (1980). The mind. *The works of Jonathan Edwards, Vol. 6: Scientific and philosophical writings*. W. E. Anderson (Ed.). Yale University Press.
Elkind, D. (1967). Egocentrism in adolescence. *Child Development, 38*(4), 1025–1034.
Ellenberger, H. F. (1970). *The discovery of the unconscious: The history and evolution of dynamic psychiatry*. Basic Books.
Ellens, J. H. (1982). *God's grace and human health*. Abingdon Press.

Ellerhoff, S. G. (2015). Luke Skywalker's individuation. *Jung Journal: Culture & Psyche*, 9(3), 44–54.

Elliott, D. M. & Guy, J. D. (1993). Mental health professionals versus non-mental health professionals: Childhood trauma and adult functioning. *Professional Psychology: Research and Practice*, 24, 83–90.

Elms, A. C. (1994). *Uncovering lives: The uneasy alliance of biography and psychology.* Oxford University Press.

Epstein, R. (Ed.). (1980). *Notebooks: B. F. Skinner.* Prentice-Hall, Inc.

Erickson, M. (1998). *Christian theology.* Baker Academic.

Erikson, E. H. (1950/1963). *Childhood and society* (2nd ed). W. W. Norton. (Original work published 1950).

Erikson, E. H. (1956). The problem of ego identity. *Journal of American Psychoanalytic Association*, 4, 54–121.

Erikson, E. H. (1958). *Young man Luther: A study in psychoanalysis and history.* W. W. Norton.

Erikson, E. H. (1963). The Golden Rule and the cycle of life. In R. W. White (Ed.), *The study of lives* (pp. 413–428). Appleton, Century-Crofts.

Erikson, E. H. (1964). *Insight and responsibility.* W. W. Norton.

Erikson, E. H. (1968a). *Identity, youth and crisis.* W. W. Norton.

Erikson, E. H. (1968b). On the nature of psychohistorical evidence: In search of Gandhi. *Daedalus*, 97, 695–730.

Erikson, E. H. (1969) *Gandhi's truth: On the origins of militant nonviolence.* W. W. Norton.

Erikson, E. H. (1970). Autobiographic notes on the identity crisis. *Daedalus*, 99, 730–759.

Erikson, E. H. (1974). *Dimensions of a new identity: The Jefferson lectures.* W. W. Norton.

Erikson, E. H. (1975a). *Life history and the historical moment.* W. W. Norton.

Erikson, E. H. (1975b). Postscript and outlook. In E. E. Erikson *Life history and the historical moment* (pp. 98–109). W. W. Norton. (Reprinted from *Daedalus*, 99 (no pagination given), 1970).

Erikson, E. H. (1976). Reflections on Dr. Borg's life cycle. *Daedalus*, 105, 1–31.

Erikson, E. H. (1977). *Toys and reasons: Stages in the ritualization of experience.* W. W. Norton.

Erikson, E. H. (1981). Galilean sayings and the sense of "I." *The Yale Review*, April, 321–362.

Erikson, E. H. (1982). *The life cycle completed: A review.* W. W. Norton.

Erikson, E. H. (1984). Reflections on the last stage—and the first. *The Psychoanalytic Study of the Child*, 39, 155–165.

Evans, R. I. (1968). *B. F. Skinner: The man and his ideas.* E. P. Dutton & Co., Inc.

Evans, R. I. (1981). *Dialogue with B. F. Skinner.* Praeger Publications.

Feldman, B. (1992). Jung's infancy and childhood and its influence upon the development of analytical psychology. *Journal of Analytical Psychology*, 37, 255–274.

Feltham, C. (2010). *Critical thinking in counselling and psychotherapy*. Sage Publications.
Finlay, S. W. (2000). Influence of Carl Jung and William James on origins of Alcoholics Anonymous. *Review of General Psychology*, 4, 3–12.
Fitzgerald, J. J. (2019). A considerably common morality: Catholic ethics and secular principlism in dialogue. *Christian bioethics: Non-Ecumenical Studies in Medical Morality*, 25 (1), 86–127.
Flood, G. D. (1996). *An introduction to Hinduism*. Cambridge University Press.
Fowler, J. W. (1981). *Stages of faith*. Harper & Row.
Freeman, J. (1959). Face to face interview with Carl Jung. London: BBC.
Freud, E. (Ed.). (1960). *Letters of Sigmund Freud* (T. Stern & J. Stern, Trans.). Basic Books.
Freud, M. (1967). Who was Freud? In J. Fraenkel (Ed.), *The Jews of Austria: Essays on their life, history and destruction* (pp. 197–211). Vallentine, Mitchell & Co., Ltd.
Freud, S. (1895). Studies in hysteria (with J. Breuer). SE 2, 1–335, 1955.
Freud, S. (1900). The interpretation of dreams. SE 4, 1–338; 5, 339–621, 1953.
Freud, S. (1901). The psychopathology of everyday life. SE 6, 1–289, 1960.
Freud, S. (1904). Obituary for professor S. Hammerschlag. SE 9, 255–256, 1959.
Freud, S. (1905). Three essays in sexuality. SE 7, 125–245, 1953.
Freud, S. (1907a). Delusions and dreams in Jensen's *Gradiva*. SE 9, 3–95, 1959.
Freud, S. (1907b). Obsessive actions and religious practices. SE 9, 116–127, 1959.
Freud, S. (1909). Notes upon a case of obsessional neurosis. SE 10, 153–320, 1955.
Freud, S. (1910). Leonardo da Vinci and a memory of his childhood. SE 11, 59–137, 1957.
Freud, S. (1911). Formulations of the two principles of mental functioning. SE 12, 213–226, 1958.
Freud, S. (1912). A note on the unconscious in psycho-analysis. SE 12, 255–266, 1958.
Freud, S. (1913). Totem and taboo. SE 13, 1–161, 1958.
Freud, S. (1914a). On the history of the psychoanalytic movement. SE 14, 2–66, 1957.
Freud, S. (1914b). The Moses of Michelangelo. SE 13, 211–236, 1958.
Freud, S. (1915). Repression. SE 14, 141–158, 1957.
Freud, S. (1916). Introductory lectures on psychoanalysis. SE 15, 1–239, 1961; 16, 241–463, 1963.
Freud, S. (1918). From the history of an infantile neurosis. SE 17, 3–123, 1955.
Freud, S. (1919). The 'uncanny.' SE 17, 217–256, 1955.
Freud, S. (1920). Beyond the pleasure principle. SE 18, 1–64, 1955.
Freud, S. (1921a). Group psychology and the analysis of the ego. SE 18, 65–143, 1955.
Freud, S. (1921b). Psychoanalysis and telepathy. SE 18, 173–193, 1955.
Freud, S. (1922). Dreams and telepathy. SE 18, 195–220, 1955
Freud, S. (1923). The ego and the id. SE 19, 1–66, 1961.
Freud, S. (1924). The dissolution of the Oedipus complex. SE 19, 171–179, 1961.

Freud, S. (1925). An autobiographical study. *SE* 20, 3–74, 1959.
Freud, S. (1927). The future of an illusion. *SE* 21, 3–56, 1961.
Freud, S. (1930). Civilization and its discontents. *SE* 21, 59–145, 1961.
Freud, S. (1931). Female sexuality. *SE* 21, 221–243, 1961.
Freud, S. (1932a). New introductory lectures on psycho-analysis. *SE* 22, 3–182, 1964.
Freud, S. (1932b). Question of a weltanschauung. *SE* 22, 158–182, 1964.
Freud, S. (1939). Moses and monotheism: Three essays. *SE* 23, 3–137, 1964.
Freud, S. (1940). Outline of psychoanalysis. *SE* 23, 139–207, 1964.
Freud, S. (1969). Some early unpublished letters of Freud. *International Journal of Psycho-Analysis, 50*, 419–427.
Freud, S. & Pfister, O. (1963). *Psychoanalysis and faith: The letters of Sigmund Freud and Oskar Pfister*. H. Meng & E. I. Freud (Eds.), E. Mosbacher, Trans. Basic Books.
Friedman, E. H. (1971). The birthday party: An experiment in obtaining change in one's own extended family. *Family Process, 10*, 345–359.
Friedman, L. (1999). *Identity's architect: A biography of Erik H. Erikson*. Scribner.
Fromm, E. (1942). *Escape from freedom*. Farrar & Rinehart.
Fuller, R. C. (1982). Carl Rogers, religion, and the role of psychology in American culture. *Journal of Humanistic Psychology, 22*, 21–32.
Fussell, F. W. & Bonney, W. C. (1990). A comparative study of childhood experiences of psychotherapists and physicists: Implications for clinical practice. *Psychotherapy, 27*, 505–512.
Gay, P. (1987). *A godless Jew: Freud, atheism, and the making of psychoanalysis*. Yale University Press.
Gay, P. (1988). *Freud: A life for our time*. W. W. Norton & Company.
Glover, W. B. (1984). *Biblical origins of modern secular culture*. Mercer University Press.
Goldberg, C. (1986). *On being a psychotherapist: The journey of the healer*. Gardner.
Gonzalez, J. L. (1975). *A history of Christian thought, Vol. III*. Abingdon Press.
Goodman, G. (1991). Feeling our way into empathy: Carl Rogers, Heinz Kohut and Jesus. *Journal of Religion and Health, 30*, 191–205.
Graf, M. (1942). Reminiscences of Professor Sigmund Freud. *Psychoanalytic Quarterly, 11*, 465–476.
Groothuis, D. (2000). *Truth decay*. Intervarsity Press.
Grosskurth, P. (1986). *Melanie Klein: Her world and her work*. Jason Aronson.
Grudem, W. (1994). *Systematic theology: An introduction to biblical doctrine*. Zondervan.
Hannah, B. (1974). Some glimpses of the individuation process in Jung himself. *Quadrant 16* (2), 26–33.
Hannah, B. (1991). *Jung his life and work: A biographical memoir*. Shambhala.
Hathaway, W. L. & Yarhouse, M. A. (2021). *The integration of psychology & Christianity: A domain-based approach*. Intervarsity Press.
Hauerwas, S. (1997). Christian ethics in America. *Journal of Religious Ethics, 25* (3), 57–76.

Hawthorne, G. F. (1992). Prophets, prophecy. In J. B. Green, S. McKnight, & I. H. Marshall (Eds.), *Dictionary of Jesus and the Gospels* (pp. 636–642). Intervarsity Press.
Hayman, R. (1999). *A life of Jung.* W. W. Norton.
Heisig, J. W. (1976). Jung and the Imago Dei: The future of an idea. *Journal of Religion, 50* (1), 88–104.
Hemingway, L. (1990). *My brother Ernest Hemingway.* Pineapple Press.
Hempelmann, L. D. (1986). Is the Jungian approach Christian? An analysis. *Concordia Journal,* 12 (5) (September), 161–166.
Hoare, C. H. (2002). *Erikson on development in adulthood: New insights from the unpublished papers.* Oxford University Press.
Hoffer, E. (1966). *The true believer.* Harper Perennial.
Hoffman, E. (1994). *The drive for self: Alfred Adler and the founding of Individual Psychology.* Addison-Wesley Publishers.
Hoffman, M. T. (2011). *Toward mutual recognition: Relational psychoanalysis and the Christian narrative.* Routledge.
Homans, P. (1982). A personal struggle with religion: Significant fact in the lives and work of the first psychologists. *Journal of Religion, 62* (2), 128–144.
Horney, K. (1980). *The adolescent diaries of Karen Horney.* Basic Books.
Hunt, J. (2018). Psychological perspectives on the Garden of Eden and the fall in light of the work of Melanie Klein and Erich Fromm. *Pastoral Psychology, 67,* 33–41.
Hurding, R. (1985). *Tree of healing: Psychological and biblical foundations for pastoral care.* Zondervan.
Jacobs, A. (2008). *Original sin: A cultural history.* HarperCollins.
James, W. (1902). *The varieties of religious experience.* Longmans, Green & Co.
Johnson, R. (1977). Psychohistory as religious narrative: The demonic role of Hans Luther in Erikson's sage of human evolution. In R. A. Johnson (Ed.), *Psychohistory and religion: The case of Young Man Luther* (pp. 127–161). Fortress Press.
Jones, E. (1953, 1955, 1957). *The life and work of Sigmund Freud.* (Vols. 1–3). Basic Books.
Jones, E. (1959). *Free associations: Memoirs of a psycho-analyst.* Basic Books.
Jones, S. L., & Butman, R. E. (1991). *Modern psychotherapies: A comprehensive Christian appraisal.* Intervarsity Press
Jung, C. G. (1911–1912/1952). Symbols of transformation. *CW* 5, iii–495, 1956/1967.
Jung, C. G. (1916/1957). The transcendent function. *CW* 8, 57–91, 1960/1969.
Jung, C. G. (1917/1926/1943). On the psychology of the unconscious. *CW* 7, 3–119, 1953/1966.
Jung, C. G. (1919). Instinct and the unconscious. *CW* 8, 129–138, 1960/1969.
Jung, C. G. (1921). Psychological types. *CW* 6, iii–583, 1971.
Jung, C. G. (1925). Marriage as a psychological relationship. *CW* 17, 187–204, 1954.
Jung, C. G. (1927a/1931). The structure of the psyche. *CW* 8, 139–158, 1960/1969.

Jung, C. G. (1927b). Woman in Europe. *CW 10*, 113–133, 1964/1970.
Jung, C. G. (1928). The relations between the ego and the unconscious. *CW 7*, 123–305, 1953/1966.
Jung, C. G. (1929). Commentary on "The secret of the golden flower." *CW 13*, 1–56, 1967.
Jung, C. G. (1932). Psychotherapists or clergy. *CW 11*, 327–347, 1958/1969.
Jung, C. G. (1935). Analytical psychology: Its theory and practice (the Tavistock Lectures). *CW 18*, 1–182, 1954.
Jung, C. G. (1936a). The concept of the collective unconscious. *CW 9i*, 42–53, 1959/1968.
Jung, C. G. (1936b). Individual dream symbolism in relation to alchemy. *CW 12*, 39–223, 1953/1968.
Jung, C. G. (1936c). Wotan. *CW 10*, 179–193, 1964/1970.
Jung, C. G. (1937). Religious ideas in alchemy. *CW 12*, 225–523, 1953/1968.
Jung, C. G. (1938). Psychology and religion (the Terry Lectures). *CW 11*, 3–105, 1958/1969.
Jung, C. G. (1939). Conscious, unconscious, and individuation. *CW 9i*, 275–289, 1959/1968.
Jung, C. G. (1940a/1950). Concerning rebirth. *CW 9i*, 113–147, 1959/1968.
Jung, C. G. (1940b). The psychology of the child archetype. *CW 9i*, 151–178, 1959/1968.
Jung, C. G. (1942a/1948). A psychological approach to dogma of the Trinity. *CW 11*, 107–200, 1958/1969.
Jung, C. G. (1942b/1954). Transformation symbolism in the Mass. *CW 11*, 201–296, 1958/1969.
Jung, C. G. (1944). Introduction to the religious and psychological problems of alchemy. *CW 12*, 1–37, 1953/1968.
Jung, C. G. (1946). The fight with the shadow. *CW 10*, 218–226, 1964/1970.
Jung, C. G. (1947/1954). On the nature of the psyche. *CW 8*, 159–234, 1960/1969.
Jung, C. G. (1951). Aion. *CW 9ii*, iii–300, 1959/1968.
Jung, C. G. (1952). Answer to Job. *CW 11*, 355–470, 1958/1969.
Jung, C. G. (1955). Appendix: The mandala. *CW 9i*, 385–390, 1959/1968.
Jung, C. G. (1955–1956). Mysterium coniunctionis. *CW 14*, iii–647, 1963/1970.
Jung, C. G. (1957). The undiscovered self (present and future). *CW 10*, 245–305, 1964/1970.
Jung, C. G. (1958a). Flying saucers: A modern myth of things seen in the sky. *CW 10*, 307–433, 1964/1970.
Jung, C. G. (1958b). A psychological view of conscience. *CW 10*, 437–455, 1964/1970.
Jung, C. G. (1959). Good and evil in analytical psychology. *CW 10*, 456–468.,1964/1970.
Jung, C. G. (1961). *Memories, dreams and reflections*. A. Jaffe (Ed.). NY: Random House.

Kahn, M. (2002). *Basic Freud.* New York: Basic Books.
Kier, F. J. & Lawson, D. M. (1999). A comparison of family-of-origin perceptions of doctoral student psychotherapists with doctoral students in other fields: Implications for training. *The Family Journal, 7*(2), 118–124.
Kierkegaard, S. (1941). *The sickness unto death* (W. Lowrie, Trans.). Princeton University Press. (Original work published 1849).
Kierkegaard, S. (1987). *Either/or, Part II.* Kierkegaard's writings, Vol. 3 (H. V. Hong & E. H. Hong, Eds. and Trans.). Princeton University Press. (Original work published 1843).
Kirkpartrick, L. A. (2004). *Attachment, evolution, and the psychology of religion.* Guilford Press.
Kirschenbaum, H. (2009). *The life and work of Carl Rogers.* American Counseling Association.
Kirschenbaum, H. & Henderson, V. L. (Eds.). (1989). *Carl Rogers: Dialogues.* Houghton Mifflin Company.
Kirschner, S. R. (1996). *The religious and romantic origins of psychoanalysis: Individuation and integration in post-Freudian theory.* Cambridge University Press.
Klein, M. (1948). *Envy and gratitude and other works, 1946–1963.* Hogarth Press.
Klein, M. (1975). *Love, guilt, and reparation and other works 1921–1945.* Hogarth Press.
Koenig, H. G. (Ed.). (1998). *Handbook of religion and mental health.* Academic Press.
Koenig, H. G., King, D. E. & Carson, V. B. (2012). *Religion and health* (2nd ed.). Oxford University Press.
Korn, J., Davis, R. & Davis, S. (1991). Historians' and chairpersons' judgments of eminence among psychologists. *American Psychologist, 46,* 789–792.
Kradin, R. (2015). *The parting of the ways: How esoteric Judaism and Christianity influenced the psychoanalytic theories of Sigmund Freud and Carl Jung.* Academic Studies Press.
Kris, E. (1952). *Psychoanalytic explorations in art.* International Universities Press.
Kristeva, J. (2001). *Melanie Klein* (R. Guberman, Trans.). Columbia University Press. (Original work published 2000).
Krull, M. (1986). *Freud and his father* (A. J. Pomerans, Trans.). W. W. Norton & Company. (Original work published 1979).
Kuptersmid, J. (1992). The 'defense' of Sigmund Freud. *Psychotherapy: Theory, Research, Practice and Training, 29,* 297–309.
Lifton, R. (1998). Entering history: Erik Erikson's new psychological landscape. In R. S. Wallerstein & L. Goldberger (Eds.), *Ideas and identities: The life and work of Erik Erikson* (pp. 99–114). International Universities Press.
Loeffler, J. (2020). The problem of the "Judeo-Christian Tradition." *The Atlantic.* theatlantic.com/idea/archive/2020/08/the-judeo-christian-tradition-is-over/614814. Accessed 9/28/2021.
Luther, M. (1958). *Luther's Works,* Vo. 1–8 Lectures on Genesis. Concordia Press. (Original work published 1535–1545).

Maddi, S. R. (1996). *Personality theories: A comparative analysis*. Brooks/Cole Publishing Company.

Masson, J. M. (1984). *The assault on truth: Freud's suppression of the seduction theory*. Farrar, Straus & Giroux.

Masson, J. M. (1985). *The complete letters of Sigmund Freud to Wilhelm Fliess, 1887–1904* (J. M. Masson, Ed. & Trans.). Belknap Press of Harvard University Press.

May, R. (1989). The problem of evil: An open letter to Carl Rogers. In H. Kirschenbaum & V. L. Henderson, (Eds.) (pp. 239–251). (Reprinted from *Journal of Humanistic Psychology*, 22(3), 10–21, 1982).

McCabe, I. (2015). *Carl Jung and alcoholics anonymous: The twelve steps as a spiritual journey of individuation*. Karnac Books.

McClymond, M.J. (1998). *Encounters with God: An approach to the theology of Jonathan Edwards*. Oxford University Press.

McGuire, W. & Hall, R. F. C. (1977). *C. G. Jung speaking: Interviews and encounters*. Princeton University Press.

McLynn, F. (1996). *Carl Gustav Jung*. St. Martins Press.

Monte. C. F. (1999). *Beneath the mask: An introduction to theories of personality* (6th ed.). Harcourt Brace & Company.

Moseley, R. M. (1990). Analytical (Jungian) psychology and theology. In R. J. Hunter (Ed.), *Dictionary of pastoral care and counseling* (pp. 35–38). Abingdon Press.

Myers, I. B. & McCaulley, M. H. (1985). *Manual: A guide to the development and use of the Myers-Briggs type indicator*. Consulting Psychologists Press.

Neher, A. (2007). Ethics. In F. Skolnik & M. Berenbaum (Eds.), *Encyclopaedia Judaica*, Vol. 6, 531–537.

Nicholson, I. (1994). From the kingdom of God to the beloved community, 1920–1930: Psychology and the social gospel in the work of Goodwin Watson and Carl Rogers. *Journal of Psychology and Theology*, 22, 196–206.

Niebuhr, R. (1941). *Nature and destiny of man*, Vol. 1. Scribners.

Niebuhr, R. (1943). *Nature and destiny of man*, Vol. 2. Scribners.

Noll, R. (1994). *The Jung cult: Origins of a charismatic movement*. Princeton University Press.

Oden, T. C. (1978). *Kerygma and counseling*. Harper & Row.

O'Hara, M. (1995). Carl Rogers: Scientist and mystic. *Journal of Humanistic Psychology*, 35 (4), 40–53.

Olson, R. E. (2002). *The mosaic of Christian belief*. Intervarsity Press.

Ortberg, J. C. (1982). Accepting our acceptance: Some implications of a Rogerian approach to the nature of grace. *Journal of Psychology and Christianity*, 1, 45–50.

Palmer, M. (1997). *Freud and Jung on religion*. Routledge.

Pargament, K. I. (1997). *The psychology of religion and coping: Theory, research, practice*. Guilford Press.

Parker, S. (1999). Hearing God's Spirit: Impacts of developmental history on adult religious experience. *Journal of Psychology and Christianity*, 18, 153–163.

Partridge, S. (2014). The hidden neglect and sexual abuse of infant Sigmund Freud. *Attachment: New Directions in Psychotherapy and Relational Psychoanalysis*, 8, 139–150.

Pascal, B. (1995). *Pensées* (A. J. Krailsheimer, Trans.). Penguin Classics, Rev. Ed. (Original work published 1670).

Payne, L. & Perotta, K. (1988). The unconscious confusions of Christian Jungianism Part 2. *Pastoral Renewal 12* (10) (May), 3–6.

Peri, T. (2010). A Freudian and a Kleinian reading of the midrash on the Garden of Eden. In L. Aron & L. Henik (Eds.), *Answering a question with a question: Contemporary psychoanalysis and Jewish thought* (pp. 155–185). Academic Studies Press.

Perkins, P. (2007). Gnosticism. In K. D. Sakenfeld (Ed.), *The new interpreter's dictionary of the Bible*, Vol. 2 (pp. 581–584). Abingdon Press.

Perkins, P. (2008). Justice: NT. In K. D. Sakenfeld (Ed.), *The new interpreter's dictionary of the Bible*. Vol. 3 (pp. 475–476). Abingdon Press.

Perry, C. (1991). *Listen to the voice within: Jungian approaches to pastoral care*. SPCK.

Pfrimmer, Theo. (1982). *Freud: Lecteur de la Bible*. Universities of Paris Press.

Phillips, A. (2014). *Becoming Freud: The making of a psychoanalyst*. Yale University Press.

Piaget, J. (1970). Piaget's theory. In P. Mussen (Ed.), *Carmichael's manual of child psychology* (3rd ed.), Vol. 1 (pp. 703–732). John Wiley & Sons.

Rainey, R.M. (1975). *Freud as student of religion: Perspectives on the background and development of his thought*. The American Academy of Religion.

Rauschenbusch, W. (1917). *A theology for the social gospel*. Macmillan Company.

Ricoeur, P. (1977). *Freud and philosophy: An essay on interpretation*. Yale University Press.

Rieff, P. (1966). *Triumph of the therapeutic*. Harper & Row.

Rieff, P. (1979). *Freud: The mind of the moralist*. University of Chicago Press.

Rizzuto, A-M. (1998). *Why did Freud reject God? A psychodynamic interpretation*. Yale University Press.

Roazen, P. (1975). *Freud and his followers*. Random House.

Roazen, P. (1976). *Erik Erikson: Power and limits of a vision*. Free Press.

Robert, M. (1977). *From Oedipus to Moses: Freud's Jewish identity*. Routledge & Kegan Paul.

Roberts, R. C. (1985a). Carl Rogers and the Christian virtues. *Journal of Psychology and Theology*, 13, 263–273.

Roberts, R. C. (1985b). Carl Rogers' quiet revolution: Therapy for the saints—does "empathy" equal Christian love. *Christianity Today*, 29 (no. 16, N 18), 25–28.

Roberts, R. C. (1993). *Taking the word to heart: Self and other in an age of therapies*. Eerdmans.

Rogers, C. R. (1942). *Counseling and psychotherapy: Newer concepts in practice*. Houghton Mifflin.

Rogers, C. R. (1951). *Client-centered therapy: Its current practice, implications, and theory*. Houghton Mifflin.

Rogers, C. R. (1953). Some directions and end points in therapy. In O. H. Mowrer (Ed.), *Psychotherapy: Theory and research* (pp. 44–68). Ronald Press.

Rogers, C. R. (1955). Persons or science? A philosophical question. *American Psychologist, 10,* 267–278.

Rogers, C. R. (1956). Review of Reinhold Niebuhr's "The self and the dramas of history." *Chicago Theological Seminary Register, 46,* 13–14.

Rogers, C. R. (1957). Personal thoughts on teaching and learning. *Merrill-Palmer Quarterly, 3,* 241–243.

Rogers, C. R. (1958). Characteristics of a helping relationship. *Personnel and Guidance Journal, 37,* 6–16.

Rogers, C. R. (1959). A theory of therapy, personality, and interpersonal relationships, as developed in the client-centered framework. In S. Koch (Ed.) *Psychology: A study of a science, study 1,* Vol. 3: Formulations of the persona and the social context (pp. 184–256). McGraw-Hill.

Rogers, C. R. (1961a). *On becoming a person.* Houghton Mifflin Company.

Rogers, C. R. (1961b). The therapist's view of the good life: The fully functioning person. In C. R. Rogers, *On becoming a person* (pp. 183–196). Houghton Mifflin Co. (Original work published 1957).

Rogers, C. R. (1961c). This is me. In C. R. Rogers *On becoming a person* (pp. 3–27). Houghton Mifflin Company.

Rogers, C. R. (1961d). "To be that self one truly is": A therapist's view of personal goals. In C. R. Rogers, *On becoming a person* (pp. 163–182). Houghton Mifflin Co. (Original work published 1960).

Rogers, C. R. (1961e). What it means to become a person. In C. R. Rogers, *On becoming a person* (pp. 107–124). Houghton Mifflin Co. (Original work published 1954).

Rogers, C. R. (1967). Carl R. Rogers. In E. Boring & G. Lindzey (Eds.), *History of psychology in autobiography,* Vol. 5 (pp. 341–384). Meredith Publishing Company.

Rogers, C. R. (1980). *A way of being.* Houghton Mifflin.

Rogers, C. R. (1986). Rogers, Kohut, and Erickson: A personal perspective on some similarities and differences. *Person-Centered Review, 1* (2), 125–140.

Rogers, C. R. (1989). Notes on Rollo May. In H. Kirschenbaum & V. L. Henderson (Eds.), *Carl Rogers: Dialogues* (pp. 237–39). (Original work published 1981).

Rogers, C. & Cornelius-White, J. H. D. (2013). *Carl Rogers: The China diary.* PCCS Books.

Rogers, C. R. & Dymond, R. (Eds.) (1954). *Psychotherapy and personality change.* University of Chicago Press.

Rogers, C. R. & Polanyi, M. (1989). Dialogue. In H. Kirschenbaum & V. L. Henderson (Eds.), *Carl Rogers: Dialogues* (pp. 155–175). (Original work published 1968.)

Rogers, C. R. & Russell, D. E. (2002). *Carl Rogers: The quiet revolutionary: An oral history.* Penmarin Books.

Rogers, C. R. & Sanford, R. C. (1989). Client-centered psychotherapy. In H. I. Kaplan & B. J. Sadock (Eds.), *Comprehensive textbook of psychiatry* (5th ed.) Vol. 1–2 (pp. 1482–1501). Williams & Wilkins.
Rogers, C. R. & Skinner, B. F. (1956). Some issues concerning the control of human behavior: A symposium. *Science, 124*, 1057–1066.
Rogers, C. R. & P. Tillich. (1989). Dialogue, Parts 1 & 2. In H. Kirschenbaum & V.L. Henderson (Eds.), *Carl Rogers: Dialogues* (pp. 66–78). (Original work published 1966).
Rogers, C. R., Gendlin. E. T., Kiesler, D. J. & Truax, C. B. (Eds.) (1967). *The therapeutic relationship and its impact: A study of psychotherapy with schizophrenics*. The University of Wisconsin Press.
Rollins, W. G. (1983). *Jung and the Bible*. John Knox Press.
Roudinesco, E. (2016). *Freud in his times and ours* (C. Porter, Trans.). Harvard University Press. (Original work published 2014).
Ruitenbeek, H. M. (Ed.). (1973). *Freud as we knew him*. Wayne State University Press.
Ryback, D. (1983). Jedi and Jungian forces. *Psychological Perspectives, 14*, 238–244.
Sall, M. (1975). *Faith, psychology and Christian maturity*. Zondervan.
Sanford, J. A. (1989). *Dreams: God's forgotten language*. Harper Collins.
Scarborough, E. & Rutherford, A. (2018). Women in the American Psychological Association. In W. E. Pickren & A. Rutherford (Eds.), *125 years of the American Psychological Association* (pp. 321–357). American Psychological Association.
Schall, D. J. (2001). *By the sweat of your brow: Reflections on work and the workplace in classic Jewish thought*. Yeshiva University Press.
Schwarzschild, S. S. (2007). Justice. In F. Skolnik & M. Berenbaum (Eds.), *Encyclopaedia Judaica*, Vol. 11, 578–579.
Scott, I. W. (2009). Truth. In K. D. Sakenfeld (Ed.), *The new interpreter's dictionary of the Bible*. Vol. 5 (pp. 681–686). Abingdon Press.
Seilhamer, F. H. (1977). *Prophets and prophecy*. Fortress Press.
Shafranske, E. P. (1996). Religious beliefs, affiliations, and practices of clinical psychologists. In E. P. Shafranske (Ed.), *Religion and the clinical practice of psychology* (pp. 149–162). American Psychological Association.
Shea, D. B. (1974). B.F. Skinner: The Puritan within. *The Virginia Quarterly Review*, Summer, 416–437.
Siegel, P. F. (1996). The meaning of behaviorism for B. F. Skinner. *Psychoanalytic Psychology, 13*(3), 343–365.
Skinner, B. F. (1952). A case history in scientific method. *American Psychologist, 11*, 221–233.
Skinner, B. F. (1953). *Science and human behavior*. Macmillan Co.
Skinner, B. F. (1957). *Verbal behavior*. Appleton-Century Crofts.
Skinner, B. F. (1967). B. F. Skinner. In E.G. Boring & G. Lindzey (Eds.). *A history of psychology in autobiography*, Vol. 5 (pp. 385–413). Appleton-Century Crofts.
Skinner, B. F. (1971). *Beyond freedom and dignity*. Alfred A. Knopf.

Skinner, B. F. (1974). *About behaviorism*. Alfred A. Knopf.
Skinner, B. F. (1976). *Particulars of my life*. Alfred A. Knopf.
Skinner, B. F. (1979). *The shaping of a behaviorist: Part two of an autobiography*. Alfred A. Knopf.
Skinner, B. F. (2005). *Walden two*. Hackett Publishing. (Original work published 1948).
Slife, B. D. (2012). Religious implications of Western personality theory. *Pastoral Psychology, 61*, 797–808.
Sorenson, R. L. (2004). *Minding spirituality*. The Analytic Press.
St. Clair, M. (1994). *Human relationships and the experience of God: Object relations and religion*. Paulist Press.
Stein, M. (1995). Introduction. In M. Stein (Ed.), *Jung on evil* (pp. 1–24). Princeton University Press.
Stekel, W. (1950). *Autobiography of Wilhelm Stekel*. Liveright.
Stevenson, R. L. (1886). *Strange case of Dr. Jekyll and Mr. Hyde*. Longmans, Green & Co.
Storr, A. (1983). Introduction. In A. Storr (Ed.), *The essential Jung* (pp. 13–27). MJF Books.
Tacey, D. (2001). *Jung and the new age*. Routledge.
Thorne, B. (1990). Carl Rogers and the doctrine of original sin. *Person-Centered Review, 5*, 394–405.
Thorne, B. (1992). *Carl Rogers. Key figures in counseling and psychotherapy series*. Sage Publications.
Thorne, B. (2013). Comments located on the flyleaf of C. Rogers & J. H. D. Cornelius-White (Eds.). *Carl Rogers: The China diary*. PCCS Books. (no pagination).
Tillich, P. (1948). *The shaking of the foundations*. Charles Scribner's Sons.
Tillich, P. (1951). *Systematic theology*, Vol. 1. University of Chicago Press.
Toates, F. (2009). *Burrhus F. Skinner: The shaping of behavior*. Palgrave Macmillan.
Ulanov, A. B., & Dueck, A. (2008). *The living God and our living psyche: What Christians can learn from Carl Jung*. Eerdmans.
Vitz, P. C. (1977). *Psychology as religion: The cult of self-worship*. Eerdmans Publishing.
Vitz, P. C. (1988). *Sigmund Freud's Christian unconscious*. The Guilford Press.
Wallace, E. R. (1983a). Freud and religion: A history and reappraisal. *The Psychoanalytic Study of Society, 10*, 113–166.
Wallace, E. R. (1983b). Reflection on the relationship between psychoanalysis and Christianity. *Pastoral Psychology, 31*, 215–243.
Wallwork, E. (1982). Thou shalt love thy neighbor as thyself: The Freudian critique. *Journal of Religious Ethics, 10*, 264–319.
Wallwork, E. (1991). *Psychoanalysis and ethics*. Yale University Press.
Watts, R. E. (1998). The remarkable parallel between Rogers's core conditions and Adler's social interest. *Journal of Individual Psychology, 54*(1), 4–9.
Weber, M. (1958). *The Protestant ethic and the spirit of capitalism* (Talcott Parsons, Trans.). Charles Scribner's Sons. (Original work published 1904).

Wehr, G. (1987). *Jung: A biography*. Shambhala.
Welchman, K. (2000). *Erik Erikson: His life, work and significance*. Open University Press.
Wheeler, B. G. (2006). Who needs the church? In R. H. Bullock (Ed.), *Presbyterians being reformed: Reflections of what the church needs today* (pp. 121–128). Geneva Press.
Wheelis, A. (1958). *The quest for identity*. W. W. Norton.
Whitebook, J. (2017). *Sigmund Freud: An intellectual biography*. Cambridge University Press.
Wiener, D. N. (1996). *B. F. Skinner: Benign anarchist*. Allyn & Bacon.
Williams, D. R. (1981). Horses, pigeons, and the therapy of conversion: A psychological reading of Jonathan Edwards' theology. *Harvard Theological Review*, 74(4), 337–352.
Willis, T. M. (2009). Names, naming. In K. D. Sakenfeld (Ed), *The new interpreter's dictionary of the Bible*, Vol. 4 (pp. 217–219). Abingdon Press.
Winnicott, D. W. (1948). Reparation in respect of mother's organized defence against depression. In D. W. Winnicott, *Collected papers: Through paediatrics to psycho-analysis* (pp. 91–96). Basic Books, 1958.
Winnicott, D. W. (1960a). Effects of psychosis on family life. In D. W. Winnicott, *The family and individual development* (pp. 61–68). Tavistock, 1965.
Winnicott, D. W. (1960b). Ego distortions in terms of true and false self. In D. W. Winnicott, *The maturational processes and the facilitating environment* (pp. 140–152). International Universities Press, 1965.
Winnicott, D. W. (1964). Review of memories, dreams, reflections. In C. Winnicott, R. Shepherd & M. Davis (Eds.), *Psychoanalytic explorations* (pp. 482–492). Harvard University Press.
Winnicott, D. W. (1971). *Playing and reality*. Routledge.
Woefel, J. W. (1977). Listening to B. F. Skinner. *Christian Century*, Nov. 30, 1112–1116.
Wood, J. K. (1998). Carl Rogers and transpersonal psychology. *The Person-Centered Journal*, 5, 3–14.
Wright, J. E. (1982). *Erikson: Identity and religion*. Seabury Press.
Wright, R., Jones, P, & Strawn, B. D. (2014). Tradition-based integration. In E. D. Bland & B. D. Strawn (Eds.), *Christianity and psychoanalysis: A new conversation* (pp. 37–54). InterVarsity Press.
Zock, H. (2004). *A psychology of ultimate concern: Erik H. Erikson's contribution to the psychology of religion* (2nd enlarged ed). Rodopi.

Index

Abraham, xv, 9, 29
Abrahamsen, Karla, 74, 75–76, 82;
  family of, 74, 75, 76
acceptance, 153–54, 158, 161–64,
  168. See also unconditional positive
  regard
active imagination, 55
actualizing tendency, 150–52, 157,
  159, 160
Adler, Alfred, xii, 63, 71
adolescence, xx, 13, 47, 73, 89, 100,
  102, 112–13; egocentrism, 112;
  questioning, 9–10, 113, 140, 142,
  179. See also identity crisis
aesthetic stage of life, 101
agape, xx, 131, 161–63
agent, 124. See also autonomy; freedom;
  volition
Age of Aquarius, 42
Albert. See "little Albert"
alchemists/alchemy, 56–57, 67
Alcoholics Anonymous, 41
Allport, Gordon, xii
altered states, 139, 148
Amenhotep, 34

American Psychological Association
  (APA), xxi, 182, 185
anima/animus, 44, 61–62, 64, 66, 70, 92
animal/animalistic, 20, 22, 30, 108–9,
  122–23, 126, 152
antiquities, 17–18, 26, 34, 175
anti-Semitism, xxii n1, 12, 13, 15, 19,
  26, 34, 58, 83, 84
Apostle Paul. See St. Paul
Aquinas, 10
archetypes, 41, 59, 60–62, 64, 65, 66,
  70. See also anima; self, archetype;
  shadow
Aristotle, xvi, 158
assimilated/assimilation, xxi, 2. See also
  upward mobility
Assumption of Mary. See Mary
atheism/atheist, 175, 177, 178, 181.
  See also, Freud, Sigmund, atheism;
  Rogers, Carl, atheism; Skinner, B.F.,
  atheism
attitudes: in personality, 62–63, 64, 67;
  therapeutic, 152–54, 157, 160–64.
  See also acceptance; congruence;
  empathy; extravert; introvert

attunement, 92. *See also* mutuality; relationships
Augustine, xvi, 25, 29, 64, 72, 90, 120, 155, 158, 172
Austin Riggs Center, 83, 85, 87, 102, 105
Austria, 6, 8, 11, 27, 34, 80
automatic writing, 54
autonomy, xvii, 8, 26, 175; vs. shame and doubt, 89. *See also* agent; freedom; volition
aversion, 11, 34, 146, 147

bad/badness, 21, 36, 107, 113, 131; vs. good/goodness, xvi, 25, 26–27, 62, 91, 121, 156, 172. *See also* evil
Bakan, David, 29, 30
baptism, 41, 86, 110
Baptist, 114, 137, 158
bar mitzvah, 77
Basel, 43
basic trust, 89, 92, 95, 180; vs. mistrust, 88
Beatitudes, 87
behavior: conditioning of, 117, 127; consequences of, 118, 124, 125, 131; control of, 109, 122, 124, 125, 127, 130–32; emitted, 117, 125; engineering of, 127–28, 131; observations of, 107, 118, 123; prediction of, 107, 122, 124, 148, 174; theory of, 107, 113, 116–18, 124, 128–29, 132, 135, 156, 169. *See also* contingencies; reinforcement
behaviorism. *See* behavior, theory of
"being", 85
belief, 14, 31, 84, 116, 137, 142, 146; loss of, 31, 113, 114, 116; origin of, 31–32, 97–98; systems of (e.g., Jewish beliefs), xv–xvi, 2, 8, 11, 12, 33, 34, 48, 55, 64, 95, 113, 115, 124, 130, 131, 143, 145, 146, 161, 162,

167, 176. *See also* faith; religion; spirituality
believe, 17, 19, 37–38, 49, 56, 141–43, 147, 165; vs. knowing, 49, 67, 70
believer, 10, 18, 80, 82, 83, 84, 99, 113, 115
believing, 13–14, 19; foundations for, 38, 97–99
beloved, 4, 61
Benedictine monastery, 116
benevolence, 38, 73, 99, 105, 112, 133, 173, 174
Bentham, Jeremy, 132
Beowulf, 60
Bernays, Martha. *See* Freud, Martha
Beyond Freedom and Dignity, 112, 124
Bible, xv, 3, 5, 6, 7, 8, 9, 87, 111, 129, 135, 137, 138, 141, 143, 147, 159, 160; Philippson, 3, 4, 6, 18. *See also* Scripture
Bleuler, Eugen, 52
Bloland, Sue (Erikson), 75
Bollas, Christopher, 20
Bollingen, 58
boogey-man. *See* archetypes
Brazil, 149
Breger, Louis, 4
Bretano, Franz, 10–11, 13, 15, 29
Breuer, Josef, 11
Browning, Don, 18, 25, 65, 92, 99, 121, 127, 156–57
Brucke, Ernst, 12
Buber, Martin, 159, 167–68
Buddha/Buddhism, 57, 70
Burgholzli Psychiatric Hospital, 50–52

Calvin, John, xviii–xix, 42, 72, 108, 122, 123, 125
Calvinism, xviii, 115, 125, 126
capital, xviii–xix; moral, xix–xx
Capps, Don, 78, 87, 94
care of souls. *See* souls, cure of

caritas, 92–93, 101. *See also* love command
catechism, 48, 49
cathedral, destruction of. *See* Jung, Carl, his dreams
Catholic/Catholicism, xiii, xxii n1, 5–6, 34, 43, 71, 149. *See also* Christianity
cavern, dream of. *See* Jung, Carl, his dreams
Charcot, Jean, ix, 11, 28
Chicago, Illinois, 136–37
Childhood and Society, 82–83, 88, 95, 98, 103
China, 140–44, 149, 169
Chinese religions, 56
Christ, xv, 11, 13, 57, 65, 70, 71, 77, 82, 111, 140, 141, 142, 143, 149, 163, 167. *See also* Jesus
"Christian apprentice". *See* Erikson, Erik, "Christian apprentice"
Christian ethics, xvii–xx, 25, 64, 85, 97, 172–73; comparison with Jewish ethics, xiii, xv, xvi, xvii, xix–xx, 24, 25, 27; legacy of, xiii, xvi–xvii, xviii–xx, 24, 25, 27, 36, 63–64, 90, 91, 93, 113, 120, 121, 127–28, 155–55, 158, 161, 165, 172–74. *See also* Jewish ethics; Protestant work ethic; truth, pursuit of
Christian identity. *See* Erikson, Erik, "Christian apprentice"
Christianity: differing theologies in, xiii, xvi, 15, 26, 39n1, 71, 72, 144, 145, 160; existential dimensions, 75, 82, 85, 103, 104, 142–43, 167, 169; Reformed, xiii, 15, 42, 48, 65, 122. *See also* Baptist; Calvinism; Catholic; Christian ethics; Congregational; Episcopal; Presbyterian; Protestant
Civilization and its Discontents, 33
clairvoyance, 16, 44

cognition, 123–24
collective unconscious, 51, 55, 56, 57, 58, 59, 60, 61, 64, 66, 69, 70, 71. *See also* unconscious
Columbia University, 145–46
"common unhappiness", 28
communion, 86. *See also* Lord's Supper
compulsions, 31
conditioning. *See* behavior, conditioning of
conditions: environmental, 124, 130, 150, 172; therapeutic, 152, 157; of worth, 151, 155, 161, 162. *See also* environment; attitudes, therapeutic
confirmation (religious), 43, 48, 77
Confucius, 86
Congregational (church), 115, 136, 137, 158
congruence, 153, 154, 160–61, 167. *See also* genuineness
conjoining opposites, 57, 61
consciousness, 29, 31, 47, 50, 69, 94, 126, 148; beyond death, 149
consequences. *See* behavior, consequences of
contingencies/contingent, 119–20, 123, 130–31; of reinforcement, 119, 120; of survival, 119, 121
control of behavior. *See* behavior, control of
conversion, xii n1, 43, 80, 81, 147
Cooper-White, Pamela, 12, 34
cosmos, 131, 180
Coulson, William, 169
counseling, xvi, xix, 136, 179; pastoral, 42; as profession/field of study, x, xi, xii, 73, 135, 136. *See also* psychotherapy; therapy
"creation, fall, redemption", xv
creative, 21, 54, 61, 89, 93, 95, 96. *See also* generative
crises. *See* psychosocial crises

culpability, 119. *See also* responsibility
cura animarum. *See* soul, cure of

Darwin/Darwinism, 112, 160
defense mechanisms, 20–21, 30, 34, 39, 175. *See also* projection
denial. *See* defense mechanisms
Denmark, 75, 76, 82
despair, 89, 158
determinism, 124, 126, 132, 172; biological, 132, 172; environmental, 118–19, 120, 121, 123, 124, 125, 128. *See also* drives
devil, 17, 30. *See also* Satan
development: concept of, xv–xvi, xviii, xx, 24–25, 63–64, 90, 120, 155, 172; Erikson's stages of, xvi, 63, 73, 77, 83, 84, 87, 88–90, 91, 92–94, 95, 96, 100, 101, 102, 173; Freud's stages of, xvi, 1, 22–24, 25, 30; Kierkegaard's stages of life, 101; positive vs. negative in, 6, 7, 38, 49–50, 84, 89, 91, 100, 108, 166, 180, 182–83; processes of, xiv, 13, 24, 37, 38, 39, 41, 43, 47, 48, 74, 115, 119, 134, 140, 162, 168, 178, 179, 180, 181, 182
Dickens, Charles, 139
displacement. *See* defense mechanisms
dominant functions. *See* personality functions
dominant orientation, 63
doppelganger, 16
"doubting Thomas", 141
dreams, 6, 18, 20, 22, 24, 28–29, 35, 38, 44, 45, 46, 47, 50, 54, 59, 60, 66, 67, 68; interpretation of, 3, 4, 22, 29–30, 35
drives, 20–22, 23, 25, 26, 28, 30, 31, 32, 33, 36, 37, 39, 94, 95, 150, 174, 183. *See also* instincts
Dr. Jekyll, 61
dualism, 56–57

duality in self, 46–47, 51, 66, 71
Dumas, Alexander, 139

Edwards, Jonathan, 115, 125–26
ego, 20, 21, 25, 28, 37, 62, 69, 88; strengths/virtues, 89–90, 91–94, 101
egocentrism, 112
Egyptian gods, 3
elect, xviii–xix, 108, 137
Ellenberger, Henri, 28–29, 54
Emerson, Henry W., 139
emitted behavior. *See* behavior, emitted
empathy, 154, 163. *See also* understanding
empirical, 19, 123, 136, 146, 147, 148, 150, 156–57, 169
empiricism, 147
enlightenment, 55, 56, 57; The Enlightenment, 12, 26, 29, 146
environment/environmental, 2, 31, 34, 87, 88, 98, 107, 108, 110, 111, 116, 117, 118–19, 120, 122, 123, 124, 125, 126, 127–28, 131, 134, 137–38, 139, 172–73, 174; constraints, 20, 108, 109, 113, 124, 150, 174; growth-promoting, 121, 152, 153; social, 20, 118–19, 123; threatening, 124, 125
Episcopal, 80, 82, 86, 114
Erikson, Erik, xi, xiv, xvi, 63, 73–105, 114, 172, 173, 174, 175, 177, 179–80, 182; adolescence, 77–79, 80, 82, 103; adult years, 76, 78, 79–88, 99; artistic interests, 77–78; attitude toward religion, 86, 97; attraction to Christianity, 77, 78, 81–83, 102–3; career choice, 77, 78, 79; as child analyst, 79; childhood, 73, 74–77, 79, 81, 85, 87, 103; "Christian apprentice", 81–86, 87; developmental perspective, 88–90; ethical interest, 84, 91–94, 96, 99, 173, 177; existential perspective, 99,

104; father, biological, 73–76, 79, 105; focus on religious characters, 102–4; goals of development, 91–94; on good life, 91–94; on good vs. bad in humans, 91; impact on culture, xi–xii, 73; influence of his religious development, 87, 90–104, 105, 172–74, 177; Jewish identity, 73, 74, 77, 79, 80, 81, 82, 83, 86–88, 105; key ideas, 88–90, 91–99; on moral obligation, 91, 96, 100; morals and ethics (distinction between), 100–101; moratorium, 77–78, 79; mother, relationship with, 74–76, 77, 78, 80, 82, 83, 105; move from "is" to "ought", 101–2; on possibility of belief, 97–99; "resignation" from Temple, 77; stepfather, relationship with, 76–77, 79, 80, 98, 179; stepson identity, 74, 81, 87; theory of religion, 94–99; training analysis, 79; wandering artist, 77–78; woodcuts, 78; work ethic, 91; writing of *Young Man Luther*, 83–85, 86. *See also* development, Erikson's stages of; generative; identity crisis; mutuality
Erikson, Joan (Serson), 80, 82, 86, 94
Erikson, Kai, 103
Erikson, Sue. *See* Bloland, Sue
eros, 20
ethics/ethical, xvi, xviii–xix, 2, 8, 9, 15, 16, 25–26, 27, 29, 34, 39, 65, 84, 91–94, 96, 99–102, 124, 127, 130, 131, 145, 156; egoism, 25; stage of life, 101; vs. morals/morality, 95, 100. *See also* Christian ethics; Jewish ethics; Protestant work ethic; truth, pursuit of
evil, 25, 41, 56–57, 64, 72, 91, 97, 112, 152, 155, 165, 168, 172, 173. *See also* bad/badness
evolution, 99, 118, 123, 124

existential/existentialism, 63, 75, 85, 99, 104, 142, 143, 161, 167, 169. *See also* Christianity, existential dimensions
experience/experiencing. *See* Rogers, Carl, experience
exploitation, 100, 142
extravert/extraversion, 57, 62–63, 71

faith, 49, 80, 83, 97, 101, 102, 104, 111, 112, 175; adolescent, character of, 112–13, 139–40, 142, 167; as believing, 3, 49, 80, 82, 97, 98, 110, 112, 113, 136, 137, 140, 141, 145, 147, 166, 175; as existential, 82, 136, 142, 143, 161, 162; loss of, 115, 136, 146–47; psychological origins of, 98–99; as a religious framework (e.g., Christian faith), 4–5, 36, 49, 52, 68, 70, 80, 82, 84, 85, 86, 88, 92, 93, 98, 103, 104, 112, 113, 136, 137, 138, 140, 141, 143, 144, 145, 146, 147, 149, 166. *See also* belief; religion; spirituality
false self. *See* self, false
fate, 32, 33, 34, 38, 56
father: ineffective/weak, 6, 32, 43, 49, 174, 179; issues, xi, 171, 178–80; vague, 178, 179
father complex. *See* Oedipus complex
Faust, 17
feeling function. *See* personality functions
feeling(s): denial of by Skinner, 118, 123, 124; religious, 7, 14, 18, 77, 83; in transference, 35. *See also* Rogers, Carl, feelings
Ferenczi, Sandor, 17
Feuerbach, Ludwig, 12
Fleiss, Wilhelm, 18, 39n2
Fluss, Emil, 8
"the force", 41
Fowler, James, 175

Frazier, 127, 131. *See also* Walden Two
free association, 22
freedom, 23, 28, 122, 123–27, 128, 148, 158, 174. *See also* agent; autonomy; volition
free will, 126–27, 158
Freud, Amalie, 4–5
Freud, Anna, 79–80, 82, 86
Freud, Jacob, 2–4, 5, 6
Freud, Martha (Bernays), 8, 10–11, 13, 16
Freud, Sigmund, vii, ix, xi, xii, xiii, xiv, xvi, xvii, xix, 1–39, 43, 52–54, 58, 59, 63, 69, 71, 79–80, 83, 86, 88, 90, 94, 95, 96, 97, 98, 100, 132, 147, 155, 172, 173, 174, 175, 176, 177, 179, 180, 181, 183; adolescence, 7–10, 13, 32; adult years, 10–19; and anti-Semitism, 12, 13, 15, 19, 26, 34; atheism, 1, 10, 11, 12–14, 15, 16, 26, 37–38, 180–81; attitude toward religion, 12, 13, 37–38, 176; childhood, 1, 2–7, 8, 19, 24, 37–38, 39n1; and Christianity, 2, 3, 6, 10, 13, 15, 17, 24, 25, 26, 27, 29, 35, 36, 37, 39n1; developmental perspective, 22–25; his dreams, 3–6, 18, 22, 24, 28, 38; on essence of Judaism, 11, 13, 15, 34, 38; father, relationship with, 3–4, 6, 12–13, 17–18, 30, 32, 39n2, 174, 179; and father's hat, 3, 6, 12, 32, 179; on good life, 25, 28; on good vs. bad in humans, 26–27; greed for knowing, 35–36; impact on culture, xi–xii, 1; influence of his religious development, 8, 9, 24–37, 172–74; Jewish identity, 2, 6, 8, 9, 12, 15–16, 18–19; and Jung, 17, 42, 52–54, 58, 59, 63, 69, 71; key ideas, 19–24, 27–35; on moral obligation, 25, 26; mother, relationship with, 4–5, 6, 37–38, 180; nanny, relationship with, 5–6, 17, 38, 39n2; personal ethics, 25–26; on providence, 8–9, 32; pursuit of the truth, xix, 28, 30, 35–36, 173; reframing religious ideas, 36–37; and religious observances, 9, 11, 12, 13; schooling, 7–12; self-analysis, 18, 28, 39n2; superstitions, 12, 13, 16, 29, 31; theory of religion, 11, 30–35, 94–95, 97; on why people believe, 18, 31–32; work ethic, 27. *See also* defense mechanisms; development, Freud's stages of; drives; ego; id; models of the mind; Oedipus complex; superego
Freudianism, 135
Freudian slip, 22
Freiburg, 2
Friedman, Lawrence, 75, 80, 86, 105
Frost, Robert, 114
fully functioning person, 151, 158
functions. *See* personality functions
Future of an Illusion, 32–33

Galilee, 104
Gandhi, 78, 85, 86, 93, 100, 102–3
Gay, Peter, 4, 12, 16, 35
generative/generativity, 89, 93–94, 100, 101, 102, 173, 174, 177. *See also* productive
Genesis, xvi, xviii, 9, 28
Gentile, 73, 76–77, 79, 105
genuineness, 153, 160, 173. *See also* congruence
Germany, 74, 77, 83
Gettysburg Address, 78
Glen Ellyn, Illinois, 136, 137
Gnosticism, 55–56, 67
goals, xiii, xvii, xviii, 24, 25, 28, 57, 62, 63, 64, 65, 79, 90, 91, 102, 151, 155, 157–58, 167, 173, 174. *See also* meaning; purpose; telos
God, xv, xvi, xviii–xix, 1, 5–6, 9, 10, 13, 14, 28, 34, 38, 47, 48, 49, 55, 57,

58, 60, 68, 71, 72, 94, 97, 98, 108, 111, 113, 123, 125, 126, 128, 131, 135, 137, 139–40, 143m 146, 147, 158, 159, 161, 163, 164, 165, 168, 175; as archetype, 60; as collective unconscious, 56, 58, 59, 69, 70; dark side of, 48, 49, 55, 56–57, 65, 68, 70, 72; experiential encounter with, 48–49, 67, 68, 72; favor of, xix, 107, 113, 122; feminine in, 70–71; gods, 3, 17–18, 33, 37, 46, 175; hidden, 29, 46, 72; "the loving God", 5–6, 17; and maternal matrix, 97–98, 105, 180; as projection, 1, 6, 29, 31–32, 69, 94, 97, 99, 174, 179–80; proofs for existence of, 10–11, 116; providence of, 8–9, 32, 72, 127; psychological origins of, 1, 30–31; as quaternity, 70; reality of, 69–70, 99; sovereignty of, 125, 127; as trinity, 57, 70. *See also* Holy Spirit; Trinity
Golden Rule, 93–94
good life (vision of), xiii, xvi, xviii, 25, 28, 64, 91–94, 121, 122, 127–28, 158, 168
good/goodness, 8–9, 38, 98, 99, 121, 145, 160, 164–65; innate, 91, 121, 156, 160, 166, 172. *See also* bad/badness vs. good/goodness
Gospel(s), 77, 82, 86, 94, 111, 142, 144, 164. *See also* Social Gospel
grace, xvii, xix–xx, 42, 47, 48, 49, 57, 72, 95, 131, 145, 160, 163
Graves, Mary, 111, 113–14, 125, 129
guilt, 24, 31, 32, 33, 36, 89, 95, 103, 111, 115, 122, 157, 173, 176
Gymnasium, 7, 8, 9, 10

Hamilton College, 114, 115, 116
Hammerschlag, Samuel, 7–8, 26
harmony, 14, 101, 151–52, 166
Harvard University, 81, 85, 114, 116
Hasidic Judaism. *See* Judaism, Hasidic

hell, 5, 6, 7, 17, 128, 129, 130, 131
Helmholtz, Hermann, 12
Hercules, 60
hero. *See* archetypes
Hinduism, 57, 65, 86
history, as linear, xv, 24, 63, 90, 120, 155
Hitler, Adolf, 19, 34, 85
Hoare, Carol, 92, 94, 97
Hoffman, Marie, xii, 19, 181
Holbein, Hans, 11
holistic view of human, 101
Holy Spirit (Ghost), 70, 77
Homans, Peter, 171, 178–79
Homberger, Theodor, 74, 76, 82, 88
homo religious, 96, 103
hope, 89, 92, 95–96, 97, 99, 101
Horney, Karen, xii, xxn1
Hugo, Victor, 139
human as social/relational, 151–52, 159–60
human freedom. *See* freedom
humanism, 140, 146, 148, 149, 165, 168; atheistic, 136, 149, 150; Christian, 136, 144, 145, 146, 149
Humphrey, George, 139
hysteria, ix
hysterical misery, 28

I Ching, 56
id, 20, 25, 36, 37, 88
idealizing, 61
idea of God. *See* God, psychological origins of
identity, 8, 9, 54, 74, 76–77, 78, 79, 80, 83, 88, 96, 104–5, 114, 116, 128, 142, 177; development, 75; formation, 76, 77, 83, 89, 94, 96, 102, 104–5, 114; religious, 12, 37, 74, 75, 76, 78, 80, 81, 86, 103, 114–16; stepson, 74, 81, 87. *See also* Erikson, Erik, "Christian apprentice",

Jewish identity; Freud, Sigmund, Jewish identity; identity crisis
identity crisis, 73, 89, 102, 105, 114
ideology, 33, 96, 100, 116
imitation of Christ, 65
individualistic, 151
individuation, 62, 64, 65, 142, 149. See also self-realization
Indonesia, 142
industry vs. inferiority, 89
initiative vs. guilt, 89
innate goodness. See good/goodness
inner/interior: life, 44, 45, 61, 67, 95, 119, 133–34, 148, 178; motives, 114, 119, 133–34, 134n1, 152, 178
instincts, 19, 20, 21, 28, 34, 37, 39n1, 61, 174–75. See also drives
institutional religion. See religion, institutional/organized
integrality, 101, 180
integrity vs. despair, 89, 101
Interpretation of Dreams, 15–16
introvert, 45, 46, 47, 50, 57, 62–63, 67, 71
intuition. See personality functions
Irenaeus, 16, 72
"is" to "ought" (from), 92–93, 101. See also ought

Japan, 142
Jefferson, Thomas, 94, 102, 104
Jesus, xvi, 13, 44, 45–46; Lord Jesus, 45–46, 49. See also Christ
Jewish ethics, 8, 12, 24, 25–26, 27, 35; comparison to Christian ethics, xiii, xv, xvi, xvii, xx, 24, 25, 27; legacy of, xiii, xvi–xx, 24, 25–27, 28, 35–36, 90, 91, 127, 155, 172–74. See also Christian ethics; truth, pursuit of
Jewish identity. See Erikson, Erik, Jewish identity; Freud, Sigmund, Jewish identity
Jews for Jesus, 87

Jones, Ernest, 11, 17
Joseph (husband of Mary), 77
Joseph (son of Jacob, dream interpreter), 29
Judaism, 2, 8, 9, 11, 15, 26, 27, 35, 37, 80, 87, 173; ceremonies/rituals, xxii n1, 2, 5, 9, 11, 76, 77; essence of/uniqueness, 11, 13, 15, 34, 38; Hasidic, 2; as life-affirming, 11, 12, 26–27; mystical tradition in, 29; Orthodox, 2, 4–5; Reform, 2, 76. See also Jewish ethics; truth, pursuit of
Judeo-Christian tradition, xv
Jung, Carl, vii, ix, xi, xii, xiii, xiv, 17, 41–72, 77, 80, 113, 171, 172, 173, 174–75, 176, 177–78, 179, 180, 182, 183; adolescence, 41, 47–50; adult years, 46, 48, 50–58; ambivalence, 46, 49, 68; and anti-Semitism, 58; attitude toward religion, 57, 68, 69; childhood, 41, 42–47, 48, 49, 53, 58, 67, 68; confirmation, 43, 48, 77; developmental perspective, 63–64, 172; his dreams, 44, 45–46, 47, 50, 54, 59, 60, 66, 67, 68; father, relationship with, 42–43, 45, 47, 48, 49, 52, 68, 72, 179; and Freud, 17, 42, 52–54, 58, 59, 63, 69, 71; on good life, 64; on good vs. bad in humans, 64–65; impact on culture, xi–xii, 41–42, 62, 71–72; influence of his religious development, 63–71, 172–74; his introversion, 45, 46, 47, 49, 50, 51, 58, 67; on moral obligation, 64–65; mother, relationship with, 43, 44–45, 46, 47, 50, 51, 66, 67, 71, 180; and occult/uncanny, 44–45, 46, 50–51, 53, 67, 71, 180; as prophetic figure (sense of being), 68; psychosis/creative illness, 54–55, 71; and purpose, 42, 54, 57, 68, 77; revitalizing Christian doctrines, 42, 48, 53, 56, 57, 65, 68,

69, 70–71, 177; theory of religion, 68–71; tower of solitude, 58; work ethic, 64, 66. *See also* alchemy; archetypes; collective unconscious; personality functions; personality types
Jung, Emilie, 43–44
Jung, Paul, 42–43
just world, xvi, 128
justice, xvii, xix–xx, 26, 27, 35, 127–28, 144, 145, 159, 173, 174

Kabbalistic. *See* Judaism, mystical tradition in
Kierkegaard, Soren, 75, 77, 78, 82, 85, 86, 100–101, 102, 103, 158, 161, 167, 169
kingdom of God/heaven, 135, 143, 144, 149
Kirschner, Susan, xv–xvi, 24, 63, 120
Klein, Melanie, xii, xxi–xxii n1
Korea, 142

labor movement, 142. *See also* workers
Leonardo da Vinci, 31, 32
Les Miserables, 139
libidinal drives. *See* drives
life cycle stages. *See* development, Erikson's stages of
Lifton, Bob, 87
linearity of history. *See* history, as linear
"little Albert", 117
Lord Jesus. *See* Jesus
Lord's Prayer, 78, 82
Lord's Supper, 71. *See also* communion
lost watch. *See* Skinner, B.F., lost watch
love, xvi–xvii, xx, 4, 5, 6, 26, 44, 46, 72, 89, 92, 101, 109, 131, 138, 140, 143, 144, 154, 161, 162, 163, 168, 180; God's, xvi, 131, 140, 161, 180; of neighbor, xvii, 27, 39n1, 92, 93, 161, 173; and work, 27, 28. *See also* caritas; love command

love command, 27, 39n1
Luther, Martin, 71, 72, 78, 83–85, 86, 93, 95, 100, 102, 104, 143, 168, 169

Madonna, 11. *See also* Mary
mandala(s), 62, 70
Mary, 71, 77–78; Assumption of, 71. *See also* Madonna
Maslow, Abraham, 148
materialism, 10, 16, 50
McClelland, David, 179
meaning, xvii, xviii, 29, 33, 54, 91, 92, 104, 145, 149, 157, 158, 167, 175, 177, 178. *See also* goals, purpose
meditation, 149
medium(s), 50–51, 149
Memories, Dreams and Reflections, 55
mentalist, 118
Michelangelo, 15
midlife, 62, 63, 89, 93, 96, 100, 101, 102, 104, 172
Mishna, 27
Mithraic religion, 52
models of the mind, 19, 20; structural, 21, 36–37; topographical, 21
monastery. *See* Benedictine monastery
Monte, Christopher, 109
moral(s), xvi, xviii, xx, 25–26, 61, 64, 78, 91, 100; capital, xix–xx; obligation, xvii, 25, 65, 121, 157, 173; vs. ethics, 96, 100
moratorium. *See* Erikson, Erik, moratorium
Moses, xv, 7, 8, 15, 34, 36
Moses and Monotheism, 34
mother archetype. *See* archetypes
motivation/motives, xxii n1, 15, 20, 21, 28, 31, 33, 34, 118, 133–34, 134n1, 148, 150, 162, 178–79
Mr. Hyde, 61
mutuality, 89, 92–93, 95, 98, 101–2, 173, 177. *See also* attunement; relationships

Myers-Briggs Type Indicator, 62
Mysterium Coniunctionis, 57
mystical/mysticism, 29, 46, 53, 54, 67, 112, 113, 116, 143
mythology, 51, 52, 56, 59, 60, 66, 69

natural selection, 118. *See also* survival
Nazi(s), 19, 58
negative reinforcement. *See* reinforcement, negative
neglect of women in psychology, xxi n1
neuroses/neurosis, 23-24, 31, 53, 95, 98, 147
New Age religion, 42
New York City, 85, 144
Nicholson, Ian, 159, 169
Niebuhr, Reinhold, 85, 92, 103
Niebuhr, Ursala, 85, 103
no. 1 personality, 44, 46, 51, 57
no. 2 personality, 44, 46, 51, 57, 67
non-dominant functions. *See* personality functions
non-judgmental, xx, 154, 162–63
non-possessive warmth. *See* acceptance; unconditional positive regard
non-rational functions. *See* personality functions
North Dakota, 139
numinous, 60, 66, 69, 96, 97–98

Oak Park, Illinois, 136, 137
obsessions, 15, 31
occult, 16–17, 45, 50, 53, 71. *See also* mediums; paranormal; seances; uncanny
Oden, Thomas, 163
Oedipus complex, 3, 4, 23–24, 30, 31, 32
omnipotent control, 23
ontogenetic origins of religion, 97, 99
openness to experience. *See* Rogers, Carl, experience

operant conditioning. *See* behavior, conditioning of
oppression, 166; political/social, 34, 142
order, 23, 50, 89, 107, 108, 113, 122–23, 126, 133, 153, 159, 174
original sin, 37, 91, 160, 165. *See also* sin/sinful
origin of idea of God. *See* God, psychological origins of
organism/organismic, 117–18, 124, 150–51, 158, 160
organismic valuing process, 151, 168
organized religion. *See* religion, institutional/organized
Orthodox Judaism. *See* Judaism, Orthodox
"ought", xiii, xvi, 25, 64–65, 91, 119, 121, 122, 140, 155, 156, 173–74, 178. *See also* "is" to "ought"
out of body experience. *See* altered states
overbalance (of positive vs. negative), 84, 89, 92, 182

paranormal, 53, 54, 148. *See also* psychic phenomena; telepathy; uncanny
pastoral counseling. *See* counseling, pastoral
patterns of reinforcement. *See* reinforcement, patterns of
Paul. *See* St. Paul
Pavlov, Ivan, 117
Pentateuch, 111
persona, 62, 72
personality functions, 57, 62, 63, 64, 67
personality types, 57, 62–63, 66, 67, 71. *See also* extravert; introvert
Pfister, Oskar, 15, 19, 33, 34
Philemon, 54
Philippson Bible. *See* Bible, Philippson
Phillips, Adam, 19, 35
Plato, xvii, 158

pleasure principle, 28
Poe, Edgar Allan, 139
positive reinforcement. *See* reinforcement, positive
positivism/positivist, 12, 150, 159
prayer, 45, 137, 147. *See also* Lord's Prayer
preconscious, 20
predestination, xviii, 127
prediction of behavior. *See* behavior, prediction of
Preiswerk, Helen, 50
Presbyterian, 108, 110, 111, 112, 113, 123, 125, 127, 132, 133, 176 *See also* Calvin; Calvinism
presence, xvi, 1, 7, 43, 98, 109, 148, 176; of Christ/Jesus, 71, 94; of evil, 57, 72; God's, 48
Princeton Theological Seminary, 144, 162
privatio boni, 56
prizing. *See* acceptance; unconditional positive regard
productive/productivity, 89, 93, 102, 122, 133, 173, 176. *See also* generative
projection, 15, 21, 30, 31, 32, 61–62, 69–70, 97, 99, 174
prophet/prophetic, xx, 30, 34, 36, 68, 128, 135, 167, 173, 178
pro-social behavior, 131
prosperity, xix, 122
Protestant, xviii–xix, 42–43, 71, 78, 132, 156; Reformation, xviii, 83–84, 143. *See also* Christianity; Protestant work ethic
Protestant work ethic, xviii–xix, 27, 66, 108, 110, 114, 122, 133, 137, 155, 157, 173
pseudo-species, 93
psychic phenomena, 50, 56, 149. *See also* paranormal; telepathy

psychoanalysis, 15, 18, 21, 25, 28, 34, 35, 36, 53; goals of, 25, 28
psychoanalytic meetings, 18, 39n1, 175
psychology: as hazardous to religious/spiritual health, 181–82; motivations to study, xi, 178–80; "originative" psychologist, 178; and pressures to distinguish from religion, 181, 182; as profession/field of study, x–xii, xv–xvi, xxi n1, 1, 56, 64, 73, 107, 116, 120, 128, 135, 136, 144, 148, 149, 169, 178, 179, 180, 181; and religion, x, xvi–xix, 1, 15, 31–32, 38, 56, 57, 68–70, 92, 121, 164, 167; theories of, xi xiv, xxi, 19–24, 57, 59–63, 75, 88–90, 102, 117–19, 121, 129, 146, 147, 150–54, 156
psychosexual stages. *See* development, Freud's stages of
psychosocial crises, 89, 90, 91, 93
psychosocial processes, 89
psychosocial stages. *See* development, Erikson's stages of
psychotherapy, 136, 147, 155. *See also* counseling; therapy
Pueblos, 56
punishment, 110, 118, 125, 130, 131, 176, 183; and negative reinforcement, difference from, 118
purpose, xvi, xvii, xviii, xix, xx, 18, 24, 33, 54, 57, 62, 63, 64, 66, 68, 69, 77, 89, 90, 91, 120, 141, 149, 155, 157–58, 167, 168. *See also* goals; meaning; telos
pursuit of truth. *See* truth, pursuit of

radical behaviorism, 118, 124
Raphael, 11
rational functions. *See* personality functions
rationalism, 12, 26 146
rationalization. *See* defense mechanisms
Rat Man, 31

reality principle, 28
redemption, xv–xvi, 139
reductionism, 98
Reformed Christianity. *See* Christianity, Reformed
Reform Judaism. *See* Judaism, Reform
reinforcement/reinforcers, 108, 117–18, 119, 126–28, 130, 132, 137; negative, 108, 118, 121, 129, 176, 183; patterns of, 108, 117–18, 122, 124; positive, 108, 118, 121, 129, 131, 176, 183; schedules of, 108, 118. *See also* behavior, conditioning of; contingencies; punishment
relationship(s): as healing, xix, 35, 148, 152, 159; oedipal, 3, 4, 23; in therapy, 35, 147, 148, 152, 153, 168; unconscious dimensions of, 21, 23, 28, 61–62, 63. *See also* attunement; mutuality
religion: as adaptive, 95–96, 98; authority of, 32, 130, 143, 169; as compensation, 32, 140; existential dimensions of, 63, 75, 82, 85, 99, 103, 104, 142, 143, 161, 167, 169; as formative, x, xiv, 41; as harmful, 182; as illusion, 33, 79, 80, 82, 86, 94, 147; as infantile, 69, 96; institutional/organized, 42, 45, 48, 49, 52, 58, 67, 68, 82, 97, 143; loss of interest in, xi, 174–78; as natural, 69, 96; as noetic, 53; as obsessional neurosis, 31, 53, 95, 98, 147; prohibitions of, 139; psychological origins of, 1, 11, 14, 31–33, 37, 97–98; rituals in/of, 9, 13, 31, 33, 42–43, 48, 52, 56, 77, 82, 95–96, 130, 137, 138; role in society, xv, xvi, 36, 37, 67, 83–84, 86, 94, 95–97, 102, 130, 182; social dimensions of, 130, 140, 144, 159; symbols of, 52–53, 55–57, 70; as universal, 31, 51, 175. *See also* belief; Christianity; faith; Judaism; psychology, and religion; Social Gospel; spirituality
religious identity. *See* identity, religious
religious impulse, ix, xi, 58, 171, 174–78, 182. *See also* spirituality
responsibility, 26, 41, 119, 151, 156. *See also* culpability
return of the repressed, 175
Rieff, Phillip, 26, 29
righteousness, 137, 165
Rizzuto, Ana-Maria, 8, 17–18
Roberts, Robert, 162, 163
Rogers, Carl, xi, xiv, 52, 109, 135–169, 172, 173, 174, 175–76, 177, 179, 180, 181–82, 183; adolescence, 136, 138–43, 160, 161, 167; adult years, 135, 136, 137, 138, 143–50, 159, 160, 161, 162, 164, 165, 175; agriculture major, 139, 140, 143; atheism, 136, 146–47, 149–50, 165, 167, 181; attitude toward religion, 176; childhood, 135, 136–38, 139, 154–55, 161, 162, 165; China trip, 141–43, 149, 169; developmental perspective, 155, 172; experience/experiencing, 135, 151, 152, 153, 154, 158; family worship, 137–38; father, relationship with, 136, 138, 162, 179; on feelings, 136, 153, 154, 156, 165; on good life, 158, 168; on good vs. bad in humans, 156, 160, 164–65, 166; idealism, 164; impact on culture, xi–xii, 135–36; influence of his religious development, 142, 143, 145, 149, 150, 154–69, 172–74; integration/integrity, 142, 166, 181; his isolation, 138, 139; key ideas, 150–53, 157–64; ministry work, 143, 144–45, 149–50, 166, 169; on moral obligation, 140, 156–57; mother, relationship with, 137, 138, 145, 160, 162, 165, 169, 180; optimism,

152, 166, 183; on purpose of life, 157–59; reading, 138, 139, 157, 159, 161; reframing religious ideas, 146, 158, 165, 167–68; seminary training, 141, 144–45, 156, 158, 160, 161, 163, 181; and Skinner, 148, 168; socially conscious Christianity, 141, 142; and spiritualism, 136, 148–49; ulcers, 138, 162; work ethic, 137, 157. *See also* actualizing tendency; attitudes, therapeutic; fully functioning person; humanism; organismic valuing process
Rogers, David, 147, 156
Rogers, Helen, 144, 147, 149
Rogers, Julia, 137
Rogers, Natalie, 52, 147
Rogers, Walter, 136, 137
Rolland, Romain, 14

Sabbath, 3, 11, 27
salvation, xv–xvi, 55
Satan, 45, 56, 70, 128. *See also* devil
schedules of reinforcement. *See* reinforcement, schedules of
Schleiermacher, Friedrich, 43
Science and Behavior, 130
Scripture, xv, 29, 161, 164. *See also* Bible
seances, 44, 45, 50–51, 66. *See also* occult, uncanny
seduction theory, 23
self, 20, 21, 47, 51, 56, 58, 74, 96, 101, 126, 151, 157–58, 174; actualization, 158; awareness, 50, 54, 94, 96, 104, 151, 153; concept, 151; control, 37, 117, 132; deception, 129; false, 75, 161; preservation, 20, 126; true, 158. *See also* self (archetype); self-realization
self (archetype), 57, 62, 64, 67, 70, 72, 172
self-realization, 65, 69, 70, 174

sensing/sensory function. *See* personality functions
Serson, Joan. *See* Erikson, Joan
"Seven Sermons to the Dead", 54
sex/sexuality, ix, xi, 6, 18, 20, 21, 23, 25, 31, 32, 33, 35–36, 53, 95, 111, 113, 115, 129, 130, 171, 173, 174, 175 178
shadow, 41, 58, 60–61, 64, 65, 66, 70, 72, 183
shaman, 55
Sheerer, Elizabeth, 146, 150
Shiva, 65
Sickness unto Death 158
Signorelli, 17
Silberstein, Eduard 8, 9, 10
sin/sinful, xiii, 30, 91, 95, 97, 103, 129–30, 156, 163, 165. *See also* original sin
Skinner, B. F., xi, xiv, xx, 107–34, 148, 168, 172, 173, 174, 176–77, 179, 180, 182, 183; adolescence, 111–14, 176; adult years, 113, 114–17, 123, 132; atheism, 114–115, 116; attitude toward religion, 176; celebration, lack of, 128, 129; childhood, 108–11, 114, 116, 117, 130, 132; compensation, theory of, 112–13; "dark year", 114, 116, 122; developmental perspective, 120; on equality/justice, 127–28, 133, 173; escape, theme of, 108, 109, 113–14, 117, 132–34, 177; father, relationship with, 109–10, 114, 179; on freedom. 123–27, 128; on good life, 121, 122, 127–28; on good vs. bad in humans, 121; impact on culture, xi–xii, 107–8; influence of his religious development, 110–11, 113–14, 115, 117, 120–32, 172–74; on interiority, 119, 133–34; key ideas, 117–19, 127–28; lost watch, 107, 112–13; on moral obligation,

121; mother, relationship with, 109, 110, 132, 180; as prophetic figure (sense of), 128–29; and Rogers, xx, 148, 168; sexual awakening and religion, 111, 113, 115, 129, 130, 173; theory of religion, 130–32; work ethic, 122, 133. *See also* behavior; contingencies; reinforcement
Skinner, Grace, 109
Skinner, William, 109
Skinner box, 108
Skywalker, Luke, 41, 60
Social Gospel, 144, 149, 159, 160, 161, 168–69, 181
social dimensions of human. *See* human as social
Song of Solomon, 43
soul(s), xvi, 17, 45, 61, 72, 141; cure of (*cura animarum*), 18, 72
sovereignty. *See* God, sovereignty
spirit, 2, 8, 92, 99. *See also* Holy Spirit
spiritual, x, 13, 16, 27, 38, 45, 55, 56, 58, 60, 66, 69, 92, 100, 101, 104, 146, 148–49, 150, 166, 176, 181, 182, 183; enlightenment, 55, 56; substitutes, 16–19. *See also* religion; religious impulse
spiritualism, 50–51, 67, 136, 148–49, 150, 176
spirituality, x, xvi, 41–42, 43–44, 45, 51, 53–54, 57, 66, 71, 72, 97, 181, 182. *See also* religion; religious impulse; spiritual
spontaneous behavior. *See* behavior, emitted
Squires, William, 115, 126
stages of development. *See* development, Erikson, stages of; Freud, stages of; processes of
stages of lifecycle. *See* development, Erikson's stages of
Star Wars, 41
stepson identity. *See* identity, stepson

St. Francis, 143
stimulus-response, 117
St. Jerome, 129
Stockbridge, Massachusetts, 85
St. Paul, 129, 130, 133
structural model of mind. *See* models of the mind, structural
sublimate. *See* defense mechanisms
Sunday school, 110–11, 115, 125
superego, 20, 21, 25, 36, 88, 100
Superman, 60
supernatural, 12, 44, 51, 53, 96, 123, 130, 131, 162
superstitions, 12–13, 16, 29, 31, 44, 175
survival, xviii, 20, 66, 91, 119, 124, 125, 126, 157, 175; contingencies of, 119, 121
Swiss Reformed. *See* Christianity, Reformed
Switzerland, 42, 44

Talmud, 3, 27, 29, 35, 87, 93
telepathy, 16, 54
telos, 64, 151
Ten Commandments, xvi
Temple (Reform), 76, 77
thanotos, 20
therapeutic attitudes. *See* attitudes, therapeutic
therapy, xvi, xix, xx, 25, 60, 64, 104, 136, 147, 148, 149, 152, 154, 155, 156, 157, 162, 163, 165, 182. *See also* counseling, psychotherapy
thinking function. *See* personality functions
third wave/force in psychology, 135, 148, 169
Thorndike, E.L., 117
Thorne, Brian, 148, 160
Thornton, John, 86
Tillich, Paul, 85, 92, 103, 104, 146, 163, 165, 167–68
Titian, 11, 13

Index 215

topographical model of mind. See models of the mind, topographical
Torah, xvi–xvii, 7, 27, 86
Totem and Taboo, 1, 32
transcendent, 60, 94, 148, 149; function, 57
transitional object, 18
transparency, 153
trickster. See archetypes
Trinity, 48, 49, 57, 70. See also God, as trinity
truth, xvii, 18, 36, 82, 112, 141–42, 147, 161, 169, 172, 173; pursuit of, xvii, xix–xx, 28, 30, 35–36, 142, 156, 160, 164, 166–67, 172, 173; telling, xvi, 36, 128
Twain, Mark, 139

ulcers. See Rogers, Carl, ulcers
uncanny, 17, 44–44, 46, 51, 67, 175, 180. See also medium; paranormal; seances
unconditional positive regard, xx, 153–54, 161–63, 173, 174. See also acceptance
unconscious, 19–22, 23, 24, 28, 29, 30, 31, 53, 54, 57, 59, 61–63, 63, 70, 78, 168. See also collective unconscious
understanding (in Rogers), 154, 163–64. See also empathy
underworld, 17
Union Theological Seminary, 85 144–45, 146, 149, 161
unitive view of humans. See holistic view of human
University of Wisconsin, 139
upward mobility, 76. See also assimilated

Vader (Darth), 41

Valjean, Jean, 139
Vienna, 3, 5, 7, 8, 10, 12, 27, 34, 53, 79
Vietnam war. See war, Vietnam
volition, 123–24. See also agent; autonomy; freedom

Walden Two, xx, 122, 127, 128, 131, 133, 176. See also Frazier
Wallwork, Ernest 25, 39n1, 174
war, 142, 143, 152, 159; Vietnam, 88, 100; WWI, 26. 72; WWII, 58, 72, 83, 88
watch (lost). See Skinner, B.F., lost watch
Watson, John B., 117
Watson, Goodwin, 144, 181
Weber, Max, xvii–xix, 122
Welchman, Kit, 75
West/Western civilization, xii, xv–xvii, xix, xxii n1, 25, 26, 36, 55, 56, 57, 60, 64, 65, 67, 68, 84, 90, 100, 103, 120, 122, 127, 155
Wiener, Daniel, 132
Williams, David, 125–26
Winnicott, D.W., 28, 75
wise one. See archetypes
Wolf Man, 15
workers (striking), 93. See also laborers
Wycliffe, John, 143

yetzer, 30
Yoda, 41
Young Man Luther (YML), 83–85, 86, 95, 98, 103
Young Men's Christian Association (YMCA), 136, 139, 140, 141

Zwingli, Ulrich, 71

About the Author

Stephen E. Parker is professor emeritus in the School of Psychology and Counseling, Regent University, Virginia Beach. He is the author of *Winnicott and Religion*, an exploration of the impact of D. W. Winnicott's early Wesleyan Methodist background on his life and work, published by Jason Aronson. He earned a PhD in theology and personality studies from Emory University, is a licensed professional counselor in the Commonwealth of Virginia, and has an interest in the intersection of religion/spirituality and clinical practice.

www.ingramcontent.com/pod-product-compliance
Lightning Source LLC
Chambersburg PA
CBHW020117010526
44115CB00008B/860